CRAFTING SOLUTIONS FOR TROUBLED BUSINESSES

*A Disciplined Approach to Diagnosing and
Confronting Management Challenges*

CRAFTING SOLUTIONS FOR TROUBLED BUSINESSES

A Disciplined Approach to Diagnosing and Confronting Management Challenges

STEPHEN J. HOPKINS

AND

S. DOUGLAS HOPKINS

Beard Books
Washington, D.C.

Preface

CRAFTING SOLUTIONS FOR
TROUBLED BUSINESSES

The book you have in your hands is filled with opinions.

For more than a quarter century, the authors have provided advice, insight, guidance and management to a varied universe of financially "troubled" businesses. We have personally either managed or played a key role in more than 150 consulting assignments in a wide range of industries. This book attempts to distill what we've learned into actionable advice and observations that we hope will be useful to our readers.

This is not an academic presentation. It is neither scientific nor theoretical in its approach. While we have relied heavily on real, factual, personal experiences – which we cite liberally – everything that follows has been filtered through our eyes and memories as long-term practitioners in what is euphemistically described as the Turnaround Management Industry.

Turnaround Management, Crisis Management, or Restructuring Advisory Consulting, however it is described, encompasses three distinct – and sometimes conflicting – tasks:

1. Crisis Management – a focus on business stabilization
2. Viability Assessment – the diagnosis of turnaround potential
3. Operational and/or Financial Restructuring – the implementation of operational or strategic changes and the negotiation and resolution of conflicting interests and agendas

In most conversation and discussion, practitioners in our field seem to focus upon Tasks 1 or 3, the mechanics of crisis management or implementing change, and to give little direct attention to the evaluation process and diagnosis. Yet it is precisely this often-neglected diagnosis process upon which real value-added services and successful outcomes are built. Over the years we have found that viable solutions are most effectively crafted as the result of careful, disciplined and factual analysis and evaluation.

The genesis of this book was a recurring conversation with a number of our long-term friends at senior lending institutions. In these talks, we jointly bemoaned the lack of institutional memory regarding the cycles of boom and bust, and the difficulties of trying to maintain credit vigilance during boom periods when many of their firms' younger associates had no experience with "problems" and fairly narrow experience overall, often limited to a single market segment. This led to several invitations to address gatherings of lending and workout officers where we were challenged to share some of the wisdom and experience they had helped pay us to acquire over the years. Rather than simply relying on anecdotes and war stories, over time we commenced some disciplined analysis to see if our general impressions and opinions could be supported with facts. While our initial pass at this was prepared very quickly and informally, we found the process to be an extremely interesting intellectual exercise that revealed recurring themes and patterns of cause and effect. As a result, we found ourselves periodically drawn back to the issues and questions that arose from the data.

This book arose from the ruminations stimulated by the above exercise and our work over the years to detail and codify what is necessary for an adequate diagnosis of a troubled company's problems.

The core of this book is our views, advice, and recommendations about how to conduct an objective factual diagnosis and evaluation of a "troubled business" – what to look for, how to respond, and why we believe such a diagnosis is a critical component of maximizing the value of a business operating under financial stress.

The book has five distinct segments:

I. **Conceptual Approach and Key Issues**
    Sets forth the framework of our approach and discusses our view of key issues that arise in every turnaround or troubled company situation.

II. **Managing the Crisis**
    Discusses the challenges and pitfalls that arise near the zone of insolvency and how critical liquidity issues and conflicting agendas of opposing parties can threaten to derail the pursuit of maximum value.

III. **The Diagnosis Process**
    Presents the specific diagnostic process actions necessary to obtain a full understanding of a financially troubled business, including its history and trends, competitive situation, internal resources, strengths and weaknesses.

IV. Alternatives and Action Plans

Steps to take related to determining strategy, evaluating risks and rewards, obtaining consensus, cooperation and support, and ensuring that the right management and resources are in place

V. Lessons Learned in 100 Completed Assignments

A distillation of more than 50 years of the authors' experiences with financially troubled businesses. Patterns and perspectives we have found illuminating and instructive.

Throughout the book, we offer brief case histories from our "Authors' Casebook" to illustrate our points. A few use readily available public information and are cited by name, but most of the material is from project files and personal recollections. Unless previously available publicly, we do not identify these companies or individuals in order to protect client confidentiality.

At the end of Chapters 6, 9, 10, and 11, we offer assessment checklists that cover categories of risk related to the subject matter of the chapter. These are intended to help readers recognize patterns that translate into potential major risk areas. Our experience teaches us that the greater the number and areas of such patterns of risk, the lower the probability of a turnaround. Always bear in mind that these are not intended to provide quantitative benchmarks triggering decision choices, but rather a simple discipline of forcing oneself to ask each question and think about its relevance as an aid in eliminating blind spots.

In the text, we refer frequently to sources and authors we have found useful in turnaround management consulting. We would like to acknowledge specifically the great and influential work of the late Peter Drucker, who died in 2005 at age 95 and who, over the years, made such major contributions to business literature with his many insights into how businesses work and what is important. We are also grateful for the wisdom and clarity of a much less well-known business consultant, Ichak Adizes, who clearly understood and wrote in depth about the management of businesses. We enjoy, and employ, the terminology of Adizes, particularly his characterization of companies at different stages in their lifecycles. Finally, like so many others, we have found Warren Buffett's extensive discussions in the Berkshire Hathaway annual reports and various reported interviews an enormous help in differentiating between good and bad businesses.

This book was created with several audiences in mind:

- Current or potential practitioners of turnaround management.
- Lenders faced with requests to supply additional funding or to waive loan agreement covenant defaults.

- Private equity firms asked to supply additional funding to a struggling portfolio company.
- Boards of directors that are attempting to understand the reasons why a business is failing to meet expectations.
- Potential acquirers of a troubled business.
- CEO coaches, a rapidly expanding field, who come from a human relations background and need more background on operations and what "financially troubled" means.
- Managers of publicly held conglomerates with a portfolio of unrelated standalone businesses, one or more of which is not performing up to expectations.

Chief executive officers of troubled businesses may also find this book to be highly useful, but we are not writing with them in mind. Rather, we reach out to the independent outsiders – be they lender, private equity sponsor, or business acquirer.

Authors' Background

Steve Hopkins started his career with 18 years of financial management at General Electric. After surviving GE's difficult but highly rewarding training programs, including three years on the rigorous Corporate Audit Staff, he served in a number of financial management positions. Among them were two years as credit manager of GE's electronic components division. At that time, GE was aggressively growing market share by providing extended terms and other financing assistance to its distributors, many of which ended up in severe financial difficulties. A major portion of the job was, with the help of highly skilled staff members, taking hands-on control of these distributors both to prevent credit losses and to maintain the valuable distribution channels in place. This experience and later extensive work in strategic planning led Steve to leave the stability, financial resources and bureaucracy of GE for the opportunity and excitement of the turnaround world, where, he acknowledges, "I found more than I bargained for."

Little did he understand at that time the difficulties of turning around businesses where the market had changed, and the management and organization structure were not aligned with or capable of focusing on new opportunities. As chief financial officer of West Chemical Products, Inc., an 80-year-old chemical company, Steve quickly learned that making payroll and managing a barrage of creditors' calls is a lot different without the resources of GE behind you.

As with many practitioners of turnaround management consulting, Steve entered the field as a result of his hands-on experience with a Chapter 11 bankruptcy filing. With the assistance of Bill Nightingale of Nightingale & Associates, West Chemical emerged from Chapter 11 bankruptcy proceedings with 100% payment in full to all creditors. Steve subsequently joined Nightingale as a principal, staying for 23 years and serving as president from 1994 to 2000. Over the course of his consulting career, Steve has provided interim management services for a series of companies in the computer, construction, toy, financial services, and electronics industries. In either an advisory role or as an interim manager, he has been involved in such major bankruptcy cases as Evans Products, Fairfield Communities, Cuisinarts, and Doskocil.

Doug Hopkins began working with Bill Nightingale in 1978 as a result of his part-time association with cost-accounting projects at West Chemical. He continued as a part-time, special projects resource for approximately 10 years while pursuing a career in the creative and entertainment arts. He obtained a master's degree from the Peter Stark Motion Picture Producing Program at University of Southern California film school and spent several years in Hollywood developing film and television projects. After joining Nightingale full-time in the late 1980s, Doug became a principal in 1994 and has both provided advisory services and held interim management positions (including CEO, CFO, COO, and CRO) in troubled companies across a diverse spectrum of industries including international shipping, manufacturing, domestic trucking and transportation, automotive parts supply, video conferencing, consumer products, general and specialty retail, and sports trading cards.

In March 2004, Steve and Doug Hopkins established Kestrel Consulting, LLC, where they continue to operate as advisors and interim managers to troubled companies.

Both of us wish to express our appreciation to and respect for Bill Nightingale, founder of Nightingale & Associates, Inc., for his inspiration and guidance over many years of working together in difficult, stress-filled but rewarding situations. Steve also particularly wishes to thank Don Rome, now retired from Robinson & Cole, for his early encouragement to write book chapters for the Business Workouts Manual, and later, to expand our joint knowledge into a full length book. Josh Mills was a delight to work with in the editing process, providing helpful insight into both structure and content. We appreciate early assistance from Eric Hrombla in developing certain case study data and from Chip Weismiller, Gene Reilly, and Michael Hopkins for their comments and early editing of certain chapters. Mitch Perkiel of Troutman Sanders LLP was generous and supportive in ensuring that our comments on bankruptcy issues are free from gross inaccuracies.

We dedicate this book to our wives, Colleen and Angela, who put up with a great deal of family turmoil, loneliness, and assumption of what normally would be joint family responsibilities as we chased the goal of helping companies through the troubled company jungle.

CONTENTS

Preface .... *v-x*

Part I – Bad Management or Bad Business? 1
Introduction 1
Chapter 1: The Authors' Perspective:
    Our Experiences and Biases 3
Chapter 2: Business Viability:
    The Ignored Threshold Question 13
Chapter 3: Understanding the Nature of Business Problems:
    Identifying Patterns of Risk and Opportunity 26
Chapter 4: The Challenge of Management:
    Knowledge, Understanding, Insight, and Leadership 39

Part II – Managing the Crisis 59
Introduction 59
Chapter 5: First Do No Harm:
    Legal, Operational, and Political Pitfalls 61
Chapter 6: Liquidity First:
    Try Not to Bounce the Payroll Checks 71
Chapter 7: Who Wants What? and Why?
    Identifying Conflicting Agendas and Objectives 84

Part III – The Diagnosis Process 101
Introduction 101
Chapter 8: Conducting Management Interviews:
    The Quickest Source for Identifying Problems and Solutions 103
Chapter 9: Understanding Operations Improvement Potential:
    Where and Why Are You Losing Money? 117
Chapter 10: Evaluating the Competitive Environment:
    Business Cycle and Competitive Issues 138
Chapter 11: Reviewing Management and Organization Structure:
    Do Management Strengths and Business Processes
    Match Business Needs? 155

Part IV – Alternatives and Action Plans 171

    Introduction 171

    Chapter 12: Developing and Evaluating Alternatives:
            Establishing Realistic Options 173

    Chapter 13: Reaching Consensus:
            Negotiating Support for Realignment of
            Risk and Reward 191

    Chapter 14: Selecting the Right Management:
            Different Horses for Different Courses 200

    Chapter 15: Maximizing Value From Asset Sales:
            The Parts May Be Worth More Than the Whole 214

Part V – Lessons Learned 225

    Introduction 225

    Chapter 16: Training Undisciplined Racehorses 227

    Chapter 17: Lightening the Load of Overburdened Workhorses 240

    Chapter 18: Rehabilitating Aging Mules 251

Part VI – Conclusions and Advice 263

    Appendix A: Better Management Through Control of Cash 271

    Appendix B: List of Exhibits 287

    Bibliography 289

    Index 292

Part I

BAD MANAGEMENT OR
BAD BUSINESS?

INTRODUCTION

Credit executives and business writers often loosely opine that 80 percent or so of business failures are due to "bad management." Why the business is failing doesn't matter: These guys (*i.e.*, existing management) are in charge. It happened on their watch. Get rid of them. In our opinion, not only is this view wrong, it is counterproductive and damaging. It hinders the ability to address the real business problems that exist.

In contrast to assuming that management is to blame, three key issues guide our approach and form the foundation upon which our opinions, advice, and recommendations have been constructed. In Part I of this book, we examine these three issues, before taking up in subsequent parts of the book the nuts-and-bolts of crisis management and troubled business evaluations and diagnoses.

These three key issues are:

Business Viability: What constitutes a viable business and why a rapid but comprehensive reassessment of fundamental issues of viability and direction should precede any reactive responses to pressures of the day.

The Nature of Problems: What defines the key categories of problems, based on our two and a half decades of experience with dozens of troubled companies, and how these definitions are critical both to formulating remediation actions and to assessing risk.

The Challenge of Management: What role management plays in business success or failure, the tasks and processes that constitute good management, and the pitfalls and flaws that constitute bad management.

Each of these issues is applicable to understanding and evaluating the underlying risk and opportunity in any troubled company situation.

Chapter 1

THE AUTHORS' PERSPECTIVE:
Our Experiences and Biases

A typical project for turnaround management consultants like us starts with a telephone call to our offices: an anxious voice describes a financial crisis. Either loan agreement covenant defaults are about to trigger a severe penalty or "We can't meet Friday's payroll" or some other liquidity crisis looms. How the problem is described to us and what solution the caller assumes is necessary tends to vary significantly, depending on the relationship of the caller to the problem:

Lenders: Angry about the surprise they have received, lenders usually attack the credibility of management. To their minds, the solution is some good, healthy cost-cutting and maybe a change of management.

Equity Sponsors: Angry at both management, which got them into the mess, and lenders that don't understand the situation and don't want to work with them after years of a profitable relationship, the equity sponsors believe the solution is additional credit and time to change management.

Management: Saying they've been dealt a really bad hand but nonetheless have everything under control, management just wants everyone to get off their back and give them some support (*i.e.*, time and money), and a rosy future will be assured. Management's solution is for creditors to restructure the debt to reduce debt service.

Our assignment, if we choose to accept it (and as often as possible we do), is to help these universally dissatisfied and often contentious parties to jointly come to grips with their problems.

The Financially Troubled Business

"Troubled Businesses," as they exist in our experience, are businesses under financial stress. This usually means they are overleveraged and unable to meet debt service commitments. They recognized this overleverage when they failed to meet cash flow expectations. Such shortfalls may result either from operational deterioration or failure to achieve expected growth rates. When the company originally incurred its outstanding debt, the company wasn't viewed as overleveraged – highly leveraged; yes, but overleveraged; no. Overleveraged is a hindsight assessment buttressed by new facts and revised expectations.

In the broader sense, many other companies are troubled but have not yet been forced to admit it. They have not run out of cash or the ability to raise it…yet. They have not become, or been allowed to become, overleveraged…yet. While operational difficulties occur routinely in companies that are not financially constrained, management are often able to dig themselves out of whatever hole they may find themselves in, provided they have resources and time to act. In contrast, an overleveraged company is unlikely to be able to raise funds that might allow it time to respond to adverse circumstances in an orderly fashion. The resulting liquidity crisis may finally focus everyone's attention. But lenders are likely to be reluctant to offer "new money" to an existing management (that, in the lenders' minds, have at best sat idly by as the situation went from bad to worse) in order to relieve the time constraints of a real financial crisis. Should the management announce that they have decided to suspend debt service in order to fund a comprehensive strategic review, the lenders are unlikely to applaud.

In this often acrimonious crisis situation, problem diagnosis is essential and must be completed promptly. Crisis management is required because it is very late in the game, after effective solutions to operational problems have been avoided or postponed too long. Existing management have failed to take corrective action in the face of disappointing results; asset values have been allowed to dissipate, and credibility has been lost with lenders, shareholders and most other parties with a stake in the continued existence of the enterprise.

Diagnosing Turnaround Potential

We have seen many books that address the turnaround process for both underperforming and financially troubled companies. Heavy emphasis is usually placed both on bringing in new, "better" management and on the mechanics of achieving business change. Our focus falls one step earlier in the process. We stress the need for a structured approach to diagnosing problems and identifying the key issues related to understanding the potential of a troubled business before making decisions. This approach creates a logical framework for understanding situations at individual troubled firms and for devising solutions to enhance value that will inevitably depend on the highly specific problems, market position and resources at each company.

It should be obvious that it's difficult to fix something if you don't know precisely what is broken and how it came to be that way. So the first objective of the turnaround consultant should be to comprehend the origins of the troubled company's circumstances, and thus to identify the real causes of the financial crisis. Only at that point is it possible to formulate a plan to fix the problems.

Unfortunately, in the real world, there is no "pause button" to hit while you conduct your analyses, and it is essential to draw on experience in establishing priorities and making decisions as to which fires to fight first.

The Turnaround Process

A simple outline of the business turnaround process looks like this:

1. Crisis management
2. Problem diagnosis
3. Stabilization and recovery
4. Profitable continuing growth

Two common errors that we have seen over the years are companies that either "Stay the Wrong Course" or "Leap to the Wrong Solution." Both of these errors typically stem from diagnostic failure – either ignoring changing conditions or seeking to impose the solution most familiar or attractive, whether it fits the situation or not.

Yes, it is helpful to draw on experience to recognize patterns, but it is wrong to assume that what worked yesterday will work tomorrow. Yet people, naturally enough, assume just that. If a change of top management worked before (and, as before, lenders have lost confidence in existing management), then management must go. New management, with no emotional investment in the business or its individual business units, are likely to be more dispassionate and better able to make decisions about changes to operations.

Yet consider the other side of the coin: a purge of management deprives a company of much valuable information about the firm and its operations. What impact will such a change in management have on remaining employees? It may be a welcome relief – or it may severely damage morale.

Approaching a newly troubled company with preconceived notions of what is needed to fix it, then instituting (consciously or not) a prefabricated action plan may seem to others a decisive action. But such steps may impede real progress toward a successful resolution of the problem. Imposing a prefabricated plan tends to short-circuit the process of careful analysis and diagnosis and results in several potential problems:

- The focus is often on solving the problems of a bad business, rather than building on strengths and opportunities.
- Asset values will continue to be dissipated if misdirected efforts fail to reduce operating losses.
- Investments of "new money" in programs with little chance of long-term success will be wasted, compounding losses from operations
- Diversion of effort to meaningless change, rather than finding effective solutions to actual problems, will postpone any possible turnaround.

The classic "ready, fire, aim" approach of a hard-charging restructuring officer may be partially necessary in the true liquidity crisis. But whenever possible, aiming – that is, problem diagnosis – should receive its proper priority in the sequence.

In simple terms, the available options for dealing with a troubled company situation are:

1. Attempting an operational turnaround
2. Negotiating a financial restructuring to eliminate or reduce excess leverage
3. Selling the business as a continuing entity
4. Liquidating working capital and selling residual assets.

These options can best be evaluated after information is gathered in a thorough, structured, business analysis. The goal is to develop a plan to make the total pie bigger and to worry about splitting it up later. Understand what Jim Collins, in *Good to Great*[1], calls the "brutal facts" of the situation, obtain consensual agreement of parties at interest and initiate corrective action as quickly as possible in order to create maximum value. Whether this maximum value is created by engineering a true business turnaround or by operational improvements that enhance value to a strategic buyer is not of primary importance. Many people might disagree, but in our opinion, justifying survival of the firm should not be a key objective. As we said above, identifying maximum business value *potential* is the primary objective of the process. Although clearly not an irrelevant consideration to the parties directly involved, the question of which of the various stakeholders realizes the greatest benefit is a largely independent question best evaluated after assess-

---

[1] Jim Collins. *Good to Great: Why Some Companies Make the Leap…and Others Don't* (New York: HarperCollins, 2001).

ing the costs, risks and opportunities associated with pursuing the perceived maximum value potential.

It would be naïve to suggest that the various, disparate interests of the competing stakeholders don't have a massive influence upon what options may actually be possible. Having acknowledged that, we still believe that the first place to start is with a broad-based factual diagnosis and evaluation of the company's situation, an assessment that assembles the facts in an orderly manner and identifies both the reasonable options and the required resources, risks and potential rewards associated with them. The resulting clearly defined diagnosis of turnaround potential of the business then becomes the basis for evaluating alternative plans and priorities, identifying points of common interest, negotiating support and cooperation and, hopefully, enhancing value for all the participants. Acknowledging that competing stakeholders may insist on discarding some "reasonable options" does not undermine the value of the process.

The Value of Experience

In developing the material for this book, we looked back to review and examine 100 of the largest and more recent projects on which we have worked, analyzing the situations and outcomes in a variety of ways. In general, this experience base comprises mature companies with extensive operations history and significant debt repayment or collateral coverage financial issues. In every case, one of the authors had a significant role and could evaluate the situation from the inside. With a few exceptions in which the businesses were separately operating subsidiaries, our experience has been with standalone businesses with full management staff, boards of directors and independent relationships with financial institutions. Ownership included a mixture of public shareholders, private equity firms and individual entrepreneurs or families.

Despite the broad range of these cases, their selection should not be considered a representative sample of financially troubled companies for the total economy. In particular, there are relatively few large companies in the sample. Most of these fall in a range of $50 million to $500 million of revenue. Nevertheless, we believe the patterns of cause and effect clearly discernable within this experience base are illuminating and the lessons extracted transferable not only to other financially distressed situations but to underperforming companies throughout this middle-market segment. While specific observations extracted from these 100 projects will be discussed in more detail in Chapters 16, 17 and 18, an overview description of the experience base may be useful to put the views and commentary that follow in perspective.

The projects evaluated span a broad range of industries, including manufacturing (49), services (21), retail and wholesale distribution (15), and 15 others. At each company, we attempted to identify the primary cause of its trouble, and while we acknowledge that it is sometimes difficult to isolate a single cause or set of causes, we concluded that at 46 companies the key problems were external, such as competitive pressure, and at 54 companies the problems were internal.

Among the 46 with external problems, relatively few problems were technology related and all were outside the direct control of management's ability to change the environment in which they were operating. The key issue, then, was how management reacted to the new conditions in the marketplace. Of these 46, we found 15 had a weak competitive position in the market, 14 were in markets that had undergone permanent changes and 17 were involved in temporary changes in the demand cycle. Several of them were actually improving competitive position despite cyclically losing profitability.

Of the 54 situations dominated by internal problems, 21 involved inadequate management, administrative or project controls; 14 involved inattentive or inefficient management, 9 resulted from failed or faltering rollups and 10 from other acquisition problems. Certainly, to some extent all these internal problems can be considered as management weaknesses, but to label them so is an oversimplification and not constructive to either proper diagnosis or corrective action. In many cases, management strategy was rational and the advance analysis reasonable based on facts known at the time. In general in these 54 cases, management either accepted what, in hindsight at least, turned out to be excessive risk compared with potential reward or failed to provide the experienced human resources required to solve specific problems or manage change. In only three cases did the distressed situations arise from what we believed to be knowingly duplicitous actions, self-dealing or other fraud.

In the chart below, we summarize how the problems at these 100 companies were resolved, approximately two years after completion of our project work.

For these purposes, we assumed that a turnaround occurred when profitability returned to something approaching historical trend levels. In many cases, the financially restructured business effected significant cost reduction and stopped operating losses, but that alone did not mean an operational turnaround because there was little change in prospects for long-term future success. The category of financial restructurings represents those businesses that could not be classified as operational turnarounds and did not result in a sale or liquidation. Business sales were defined as when the core business continued in operation for the buyer. Liquidations represented sale or liquidation of business assets at the best available prices without regard to continuation of a definable core business.

EXHIBIT 1-1
AUTHORS' 100 PROJECT SAMPLE
PROBLEM CAUSES AND OUTCOMES

	TOTAL	Operational Turnarounds	Financial Restructurings	Business Sales	Liquida-tions
EXTERNAL PROBLEMS					
Weak Competitive Position	15	5	3	3	4
Permanent Market Shift	14	1	5	3	5
Business Cycle Issues	17	5	6	4	2
Total External Problems	46	11	14	10	11
INTERNAL PROBLEMS					
Project or Growth Management Control	21	11	3	5	2
Acquisition Plan Shortfalls	19	7	3	5	4
Unqualified/Inattentive Management	14	2	1	6	5
Total Internal Problems	54	20	7	16	11
Total	100	31	21	26	22

Of the 31 turnarounds achieved, 20 involved companies with internal problems – a finding that shaped our conceptual understanding of the turnaround process. For several reasons, internal problems are easier to correct than external ones:

- Often the solution lies in stopping unproductive or loss-generating activities that have been continued largely for emotional rather than economic reasons. In these cases, a major operational improvement results simply by returning to the historical core business trend line.
- External third-party resources can be brought to bear on internal problems with a relatively high probability of effecting a "fix" when proper management is applied. This does not necessarily mean at the top management level but rather the functional management with expertise to fix what is wrong.

- In acquisitions cases, shortfalls force recognition that unrealistic expectations, both financial and execution-related, were involved in setting objectives. With more reasonable objectives, more time to execute the original strategy and a debt restructuring, many problems go away.

Of the 31 turnarounds, 13 continued as standalone entities. The others were subsequently sold, generally to strategic buyers. Without this infusion of outside equity capital or other funding, they would likely have been unable to realize full future potential.

Among the 21 financially restructured standalone survivors, we viewed 10 as likely too weak for long-term survival and 11 as sound businesses whose principal problem was excessive leverage resulting from unreasonable expectations, rather than operational difficulties. The "weak survivors" generally hung on during an industry downturn by means of a debt restructuring, but they were unlikely, in the long term, to return to successful growth. An exit strategy for lenders and owners should be in place, but often is not. In some cases, such a strategy, either stated or unstated, is a long-term liquidation by milking declining market share as volume declines. In all of these situations, major cost reductions were achieved, but cost reduction alone does not represent a true turnaround and rarely guarantees long-term survival. However, this debt restructuring approach may result in the greatest long-term recovery of value from assets employed.

As the table shows, 48 businesses ended up with an exit strategy of liquidation or business sale without a turnaround. We applied the category of business sale when/if the majority of the value-added functions and customer relationships continued to exist and were transferred as a going concern, even if certain product lines were liquidated or the corporate operations were absorbed into the buyers' existing structure. We believe these sales and liquidations represented rational decisions regarding the best options to maximize the value of the business. In a relatively few cases an exit strategy for a viable business was forced when that may not have been the best route to maximizing proceeds. These situations were usually triggered by extended and irreconcilable conflicts between the company's management and its lenders.

Business sales were almost exclusively made to strategic buyers and were often a reasonably successful exit for all parties, considering the circumstances and options. The business continued in operation with creditors and other stakeholders having an acceptable resolution without prolonged uncertainty.

Liquidations were more often an unsatisfactory result, but even in these cases, specific product lines could often be sold with continuing business relationships, enhancing proceeds. The liquidations most often became necessary when the company's basic business model didn't work for such reasons as a permanent market shift or a long-term deterioration in the business that precluded a financial restructuring or sale.

Chapter Summary

We define troubled businesses as those that are overleveraged with excessive debt and a failure to meet covenants of loan agreements. The fact that a company is overleveraged is one factor in a series of risk profiles that affect the timing and seriousness of financial problems, but it is usually unrelated to the base cause of a deteriorating operational situation.

We compiled and evaluated a database of 100 troubled company situations we had worked on, and we found that in 46 cases the root cause was external and in 54 cases it was internal. The former involved competitive environment factors outside the direct control of management, and the critical issue was management's ability to react to these changes. The internal problems usually occurred where management made incorrect strategic decisions, failed to properly execute the actions required to capitalize on an opportunity or allowed long-term deterioration of the business. Acceptance of excessive risk or failure to provide adequate human resources were common reasons why internal problems developed. In general, internal problems were easier to resolve than external ones.

A Look Ahead

The balance of this book is devoted to identifying and resolving the problems of troubled businesses. Among the topics we take up are:

Disciplined factual assessment, a key to good decision-making and effective restructuring negotiations.

Management's role as a cause of business declines, which we believe is much less pivotal than is commonly believed.

Viability, a threshold question that is all too often ignored and avoided by the parties of direct interest.

The underlying nature of troubled business problems, specifically how businesses at different stages of their corporate lifecycle are susceptible to, and affected by, different internal and external business challenges. We identified three readily discernible categories of troubled businesses, which we define as follows:

- *Undisciplined Racehorses* – growing, dynamic, but immature businesses susceptible to internal problems;

- *Overburdened Workhorses* – mature, profitable businesses that have become overleveraged due to unduly optimistic or aggressive financial strategies;
- *Aging Mules* – businesses in decline, often too stubborn or inflexible to recognize the need for change.

In short, what follows hereafter is our attempt to set forth, describe, and discuss a **practical step-by-step diagnosis process** for evaluating and crafting solutions for troubled businesses.

Chapter 2

BUSINESS VIABILITY
The Ignored Threshold Question

The issue of fundamental business viability is typically the most important, and, often, the most neglected, diagnosis task. The management and owners of troubled businesses are usually so emotionally or financially committed to the situation that they are blinded to the fact that this threshold question must be addressed.

Management have been charged with operating the business. They accepted the challenge and embraced it. They are proud and confident of their abilities. Every day before they come to the office they put on their "game faces" because they believe that "a leader leads with optimism!" So should the business falter, they will redouble their efforts. They will seek out alternative strategies. They will redefine success. They will bemoan their fate and seek someone else to blame. They will take solace in the fact that their market is a disaster and no one can make any money in their industry, concluding that all they have to do is be the last man standing….and then they can reap their rewards.

But what management will *not willingly accept* is the fact that opportunity has passed them by and "their" company may be worth more as a consolidation target, or even in outright liquidation, than as a standalone operating entity.

The owners may have the same perspective as management. They may *be* management, or they may have stood shoulder to shoulder with management, active participants in planning and strategy. They may believe, like management, that the company's challenges were all external, that they have responded in the best ways possible, and even, perhaps, that the company is on the verge of turning the corner.

Alternatively, the owners may be furious with management. They may believe they had everything right but picked the wrong team to execute their plan. But whatever the owners believe, their financial and emotional inclinations are similar to those of management: a mix of ego, pride and financial pain that often blends into denial.

"There's got to be value here."

"Why else would those other bidders have made us pay so much to acquire the company?"

"What about that offer we turned down 18 months ago? – that proves there's value here."

And, "we're supposed to buy low and sell high; we can't get out now while the business is depressed."

Patience may be a virtue. But persistence in traveling the wrong path inevitably leads to diminution of value. The threshold questions of viability essentially present the first critical path choice:

- Is there a reasonable potential opportunity and an acceptable risk/reward profile to justify attempting either a business turnaround or survival through a financial restructuring?
- Or, should assets be deployed to other more productive uses as quickly as possible by the sale of the business or an asset liquidation?

If management are predisposed toward a blind spot on the issue of viability, why shouldn't the board or the shareholders move quickly to hire new permanent management? Because new management invariably view their charge as a challenge to turn the business around – *and pursuing a turnaround may not be a viable course of action.* At only a third of the situations we have worked on did the company achieve a true operational turnaround. In 48 of the situations in our 100-project sample, the businesses ended up being sold or liquidated without an operational turnaround. Although some within this group were viable, they did not have the financial resources to continue as standalone entities.

Definition of Viability

To be viable, a business must have customers that value its products or services and an economic/financial model that yields the cash flow for continued long-term existence. Peter Drucker used the term *theory of the business* in some of his writing about what we are discussing as a viable business model.

This *does not* mean that a company must grow or increase its share in a mature market. It *does* mean that a company must have either positive cash flow from operations, or, if cash flow is negative due to increases in working capital assets, the required asset increases must have real future value adequate to justify their financing costs, whether through debt or equity. Businesses in declining markets, the proverbial buggy-whip manufacturers, can remain viable for many years, while businesses with a good position in rapidly growing markets may not be viable. These latter might include fad or fashion product businesses where the required next big hit is not yet in development or speculative startup and venture companies with negative cash flow that, as yet, have no real theory of the business.

The competitive environment will be discussed in depth in Chapter 10, but let us note here the general types of businesses unlikely to be viable:

- Developmental businesses burning through cash from equity sources without meeting original expectations regarding product introductions. Potential rewards are viewed by venture capitalists as worth the risk involved, but a significant portion of such businesses prove to be unsuccessful speculations.
- Technology laggards that missed the latest product cycle. Most of the original midrange computer manufacturers, like Wang, Data General and MAI, fell into this category: highly profitable for extended periods, they could not adapt to the rapidly changing market environment.
- Businesses whose cost structures are not competitive, whether because of poor manufacturing practices, high material costs, or lack of leverage on marketing and distribution costs. Many smaller retailers found they couldn't compete with the efficiencies of Home Depot or Wal-Mart.
- Businesses in a market that has totally changed, such as the long-haul bus lines that lost their customers to the airlines.

Lack of viability does not mean immediate failure, but it does mean lack of ability to generate cash by means other than working capital liquidation. In some cases, businesses may be able to adapt and address their problems, but until appropriate action is taken or a clear path to a fix is defined, the business cannot be considered as viable.

Alternatively, if the problem is internal and can be corrected with resources that are either available or can be obtained, a business generally should be considered as viable. While it may face challenges regarding the anticipated risks and costs of implementing corrective actions, the business is likely to remain viable *if* customers value its products or services and are willing to pay more for them than the cost of production, delivery and return on capital invested.

Solvable Business Challenges

Let us look at some business problems that financially troubled companies are most likely to solve, remaining viable entities. Some may be viable as a standalone; others may need to be acquired by a strategic buyer in order to be provided adequate future liquidity.

Unrealistic Expectations for Profit Growth

Management convinced themselves that circumstances provided an opportunity for rapid growth and took on what proved to be excessive debt in order to finance higher levels of capital expenditures, working capital and increases in fixed operating overhead.

> **AUTHORS' CASEBOOK: Protecting the Viable Core**
>
> As a result of operating problems while integrating a series of costly acquisitions, a publicly held manufacturer of auto parts incurred large operating losses and defaulted on approximately $100 million in bank debt. The lack of financial stability led many customers to consider moving contracts to other suppliers.
>
> A plan was developed in cooperation with existing management to:
> - Divest unprofitable subsidiaries;
> - Consolidate the company's multiple plant locations;
> - Introduce new products for customers of the core business;
> - Change the organizational structure.
>
> While the company's current valuation was clearly far short of its secured debt load, its prospective five-year operating projections, assuming reduced debt service requirements, showed a baseline performance level that significantly exceeded current sale or liquidation proceeds and offered tremendous upside potential.
>
> **Critical Challenge:** The plan required the secured lenders to convert a substantial portion of their existing loan to equity and to advance nearly $10 million in additional funds to finance the stabilization of trade payables and operational restructuring.
>
> Presented with a well-documented stabilization plan and evidence of the even less palatable prospects from liquidation, the secured lenders deferred and subordinated a third of their debt in return for preferred warrants, and provided a short-term bridge loan to fund the transition. Customer relationships were stabilized by reducing financial risks and operating performance improved dramatically as the plan was implemented. Three years later, the business was sold to a strategic buyer at a highly attractive price. The secured lenders were paid in full, with interest, and holders of both debt and equity shared in a substantial distribution.

Cyclical Downturn Issues

Most business plans, whether for debt-financing purposes or general internal planning, assume a continuation of recent trends. If good investment opportunities exist, even the best, most realistic, management often find it extremely distasteful to prepare adequately for and to maintain sufficient financial reserves to manage through a cyclical downturn. This has been particularly true, in our experience, where cyclical businesses were acquired by private equity firms that did not fully understand the cyclicality involved and were not prepared to take the long view in leveraging the company. Such businesses may have great strengths and sometimes even pick up market share in a recession, but have debt service requirements that are impossible to meet in the existing economic environment. In hindsight, these businesses are clearly identifiable as overleveraged. Fortunately, they are usually viable and survive if debt service requirements are reduced through a financial restructuring.

AUTHORS' CASEBOOK: The Mask of Cyclicality

A fabricator of industrial tempered glass experienced major declines in revenues and earnings because of industry overcapacity during a period of dramatically reduced commercial construction. Its debt was in default, a liquidity crisis existed and a forced liquidation was being contemplated.

On behalf of creditors, a team evaluated market conditions, the company's competitive situation and operations at each of the company's 12 plants. It was concluded that:

- Despite the decline in operating earnings, the business was gaining market share and responding favorably to management initiatives.
- In response to the downturn, management were restructuring both their manufacturing processes and union labor agreements to implement highly flexible labor practices.
- The business had clear long-term viability as an industry leader, if cost reduction and operational restructuring actions planned or already under way were completed.
- A debt restructuring with a limited advance of new funds by secured creditors was the best course of action for maximum recoveries.

Critical Challenge: Recovery hinged on the company's credibility and its communications skills. By communicating the situation clearly to its workforce, the company obtained support for changing labor management practices to improve long-term viability. Communications with lenders made clear that the fundamental drivers of the business were trending favorably despite the reduced cash flow.

A consensual restructuring of outstanding debt was achieved, additional working capital advances were provided and, as market conditions improved, the business became highly profitable, meeting all debt service requirements and retiring debt well ahead of schedule.

Project/Acquisition Integration Delays

To some extent, these situations are similar to cyclical business. Management have been overoptimistic in their assumptions about completing bold new capital investment or marketing projects or integrating major acquisitions. In the worst case, this optimism and inability to execute growth and investment plans may kill the company. But in many cases, a company with such problems can be restored to its former health.

Authors' Casebook: Overcoming a Failed Project

An agriculture products company was incurring large operating losses and facing a liquidity crisis because of quality problems at a new state-of-the-art plant at a remote location. Process technology being installed had been used previously only in Japan. Due to the death of the company's founder and CEO, management had recently been assumed by a family member with no previous involvement with the business.

Working cooperatively with the new CEO, a turnaround plan was developed that involved:

- Installing immediately an interim CFO (co-author Steve Hopkins) and a VP for operations with extensive factory management and process control experience;
- Improving quality and production control and reporting systems at the satellite plant;
- Renegotiating the company's union contract to reduce wages by 15%;
- Increasing labor productivity with better work-flow;
- Reducing raw material costs through major changes in purchasing procedures.

Critical Challenge: Providing required functional and management expertise to solve the extraordinary problems of a difficult plant startup. Manufacturing personnel in the company, although highly experienced with the well-proven processes used at the other company plants, were not equipped to solve the problem. However, they would not admit their deficiencies and bring in outside expertise.

With the support of his new interim functional management team, the CEO implemented the turnaround plan. Cash flow was stabilized immediately, and the company was able to report a profit from operations within six months. As operations stabilized, permanent vice presidents of finance and operations were hired and the business returned to historical levels of profitability.

Management and Organization Problems

Some very solid, viable businesses in stable competitive environments can become troubled quite quickly as a result of serious management or organization issues. Such problems include loss of valuable employees who left to set up competing businesses, factory management issues or major labor relations problems.

AUTHORS' CASEBOOK: Training New Family Management

A growing personal-care products company with highly respected brands developed severe financial difficulties due to manufacturing-related operational disruptions. The longtime CEO, overwhelmed by the situation, resigned abruptly and was replaced by another family member who had neither the general management background nor the financial expertise to deal with the many operational and financial restructuring issues that existed.

Under the direction of co-author Steve Hopkins, an interim management team was retained to assist the new CEO by assuming the roles of CFO/COO, VP-Operations and Controller. Daily staff meetings with the CEO provided guidance in resolving problems. Actions taken included:

- Installing new cash-flow measurement and control systems;
- Bringing production scheduling under control to provide satisfactory service to customers;
- Revising purchasing procedures to reduce costs and improve availability of long lead-time components;
- Significantly reducing investment in receivables and inventory;
- Restructuring operations of subsidiaries in Brazil and Jamaica.

Critical Challenge: Developing an organization. One of the most common errors in vibrant family businesses is the failure to build an organization to support increasing functional demands of growth, often driven by an unwillingness to acknowledge limitations of existing family members and long-time employees. In this case, the situation could have been made worse by inserting an outside replacement CEO who did not understand the culture of the company.

Despite her lack of operating experience, the new CEO, who had worked in the company for many years, had a receptive and open attitude, promptly acknowledged the need for outside support and assistance and acted aggressively to implement required change. A major turnaround in profitability was achieved by external sourcing of specific functional skills and expertise. New second-level management were recruited and all interim managers exited the situation within 15 months. Shortly thereafter, the company was sold at an attractive price to a large European multinational consumer products company. The new CEO survived her trial by fire, gaining invaluable experience during the turnaround, and continued managing the business for the buyer.

Non-Viable Businesses

Non-viable businesses most often find themselves thus classified because of the external competitive environment. These have become bad businesses that cannot be righted by the best of managements. The importance of the viability assessment is that non-viable businesses should be identified quickly, so that further evaluation can focus on the best exit strategy to maximize value, rather than how to effect a turnaround. That's not to say there are no exceptions to this gloomy assessment, but in the vast majority of such situations, we turn to the wisdom of Kenny Rogers, who sang (in "The Gambler"), "You've got to know when to hold 'em, know when to fold 'em...." Exiting may be a defeat for management that don't want to give up, but assets should be allocated to productive uses, not, harsh as it sounds, to support losers. Among the external competition problems we find are these:

Permanent Market Change

In recent years, many U.S. industries have become globalization sourcing victims. The competitive environment for several industries became more difficult after the 1997 Asian currency crisis, which significantly reduced import prices, a trend that has continued as more plants move to or are opened in China. Manufacturing of toys, shoes and consumer electronics moved offshore in the 1970s and 1980s. The textile industry has been hit hard since then, and other industries including steel, autos and auto parts, and electronic equipment have also lost significant ground in the U.S. Despite continual management optimism and, in some cases government assistance, situations are very rare in which failing U.S. companies have effected a turnaround of domestic manufacturing operations to the point of full competitiveness. There is no reason to think these trends will not continue and accelerate. In some cases, these permanent changes in a market come with stunning swiftness (see Chapter 16, heating product with safety concerns, and Chapter 10, the fad for sports trading cards.)

AUTHORS' CASEBOOK: A Strategy Whose Time Had Passed

A designer and importer of low-end sound equipment manufactured in East Asia for distribution in the U.S. was jointly owned by a major investment bank and a Hong Kong-based manufacturer of consumer electronics products. After the company's operating performance declined precipitously, reflecting competitive pressures from manufacturers of brand-name equipment such as Sony, Pioneer and Aiwa, secured lenders refused to provide additional advances without an equity infusion by the owners.

Evaluation of the situation disclosed that:

- Product quality was not competitive with competitors' similarly priced products;
- Lower-cost, better-known brand names from Asian manufacturers were increasing their U.S. market penetration;
- Volume was too low to justify required product redesigns;
- Selling, general and administrative costs were too high for near-term profitability.

Critical Challenge: The company's market niche had been usurped. The company's early success had come as a promotional price-point product, wrapping stripped-down technical performance in distinctive packages and under-pricing products from higher-quality brand-name manufacturers. But as technical quality and manufacturing cost efficiencies improved, the established brand names moved down market and the niche market for promotional brands was being squeezed out.

After recommending that no new equity be supplied by the owners, co-author Doug Hopkins assumed the position of CEO. He immediately restructured the sales force and reduced administrative overhead by 50% in order to generate positive cash flow. The company's trademarks, product design rights and operating assets were then sold to a European consumer electronics manufacturer for integration into its U.S. operations.

Weak Competitive Position

General Electric is well known for a strategy that Jack Welch articulated as CEO of exiting most business in which they were not No.1 or No. 2. The real world may not always be quite so clear as to make this an easy decision, but the point behind this strategy is clear: if a company is in a weak competitive position and is not a market leader, its prospects are likely to be dim. This is particularly true in low-profit industries selling commodity products. While exceptions exist for niche markets or unique strategies, these are difficult to sustain and not the basis for building a growth business. The Boston Consulting Group coined the term "cash trap" to define situations in which deteriorating market conditions or increasing competition make it impossible to obtain a return from new investments in a business. The cash-trap term is often applied to capital equipment investments but also fits globalization-sourcing victims as well.

AUTHORS' CASEBOOK: The Big Box Looms

A well-established nationwide retailer with more than 600 small stores selling home furnishings was in a liquidity crisis despite its attractive reported EBITDA. Understanding and managing the situation had become extremely complex because of a weak financial reporting system and inventory control difficulties encountered during a changeover of computer systems.

Investigation of the situation focused primarily on these projects:

- Evaluating individual store operations, which disclosed that operating results were unsatisfactory at more than a third of the stores and that the most profitable stores were suffering rapid profit erosion as "Big Boxes" opened in what had historically been company strongholds;
- Analyzing financial reporting and clearly defining reasons for long-term negative operating cash flow despite excellent EBITDA. This showed that financial reporting clarity was being obscured by a combination of "non-recurring" charges, capitalizing of major software and store improvement expenses, and the accounting for debt restructurings;
- Developing improved inventory measurements and controls, which detailed major obsolescence and out-of-stock conditions;
- Installing improved cash-flow management and forecasting systems that disclosed a need for significant continuing additional cash infusions to rebalance inventory, improve store maintenance and close unprofitable stores;
- Reviewing management and organizational capabilities and staffing, which found serious weaknesses existed throughout the organization, from the top down to the store level. Excessive focus on cost reduction rather than merchandising was hurting employee morale and causing rapid loss of personnel to competitors.

Critical Challenge: Facing the brutal facts of the situation. Management had no vision for the future that would make the company competitive against the new, lower-cost, better-capitalized Big Box chains like Home Depot and Lowe's. Aggressive accounting and destructive cost-reduction actions were being used to hide the rapid deterioration of operations and to avoid facing the inevitable write-downs required for a substantive restructuring of the business.

The only hope for survival was to downsize the business to a profitable core to preserve basic viability and generate positive cash flow from the assets employed. The company filed for Chapter 11 protection so it could terminate leases on unprofitable stores. However, because the company's competitive position had deteriorated rapidly and severely, no new investment was warranted. New funding was restricted by both equity and creditors, and an eventual asset liquidation resulted in major losses to all creditors.

Technology Laggards

In today's world, technology leadership is the driving force in many industries, not just those identified as "high tech." A key to Wal-Mart's success was its early and aggressive use of computer and communication technology to drive down distribution and warehousing costs. Once a company falls seriously behind the technology curve either in product development or cost reduction, it is very difficult to catch up and earn a reasonable return on investment.

AUTHORS' CASEBOOK: Preserving a Technology Company's Value

A well-known midrange computer manufacturer operated seven European subsidiaries, which profitably sold computer hardware and country-specific application software solutions. Hardware and software maintenance services were provided to a large installed base. The largest of these businesses was a leading supplier of hospital market software solutions. Despite being profitable, the businesses had a large negative working capital position because of cash withdrawals by the parent company to fund its U.S. losses. Hardware manufacturing had been discontinued as a result of falling profit margins. Secured creditors had obtained control of the businesses through a consensual foreclosure action.

Evaluation of the situation disclosed the following:

- Falling prices and profits on computer hardware in European markets lagged by two years the U.S. downward trend that had already driven several midrange computer manufacturers out of business.
- Profits of the business resulted entirely from hardware maintenance. These revenues and related profits were eroding rapidly as lower-cost, more reliable, hardware was installed.
- Software verticals that in earlier years had provided the base for profitable hardware sales were now a "loss leader." As they had become unprofitable on a standalone basis, they were not being updated to include emerging technology.
- Outstanding European debt and large potential deferred tax liabilities exceeded the company's equity value.

Critical Challenge: Engineering an orderly exit, because the business was clearly not viable as a standalone entity. The task was to find a way to preserve core business value while effecting a sale of the going business in a way that would minimize exit liabilities and provide maximum recovery proceeds to the secured creditors, following their consensual foreclosure.

Co-author Steve Hopkins was appointed CEO and, through existing country management, took aggressive action to stabilize operations and prepare the business for sale. The steps included:

- Significantly reducing operating expenses, despite the difficulties involved in personnel reductions in most European countries;
- Selling subsidiaries in England and Switzerland;
- Selling or liquidating several unprofitable software verticals;
- Accelerating development of new hospital market software;
- Negotiating highly favorable settlements of tax liabilities.

The residual business was then sold to a Netherlands-based company serving similar markets.

Failed Industry Rollups

Let us presume that among the many, many industry rollups attempted, some have been both appropriate and successful. We must say, however, that with the nature of our practice, we haven't seen them. On the contrary, in our universe, "rollup" is often used as a loose synonym for debacle. Failed industry rollups tend to have concentrated share in specific niches. Management by a local owner is more effective than a remote bureaucracy attempting to standardize local decisions. We will discuss this category of problems more fully in Chapter 16, but let us note here that extracting value from a failed services rollup is very difficult, because low earnings and lack of management do not justify a strategic sale. Buybacks by the former owners occur, almost by definition, at low prices because such owners usually control the customer base and have all the leverage in the sale negotiations.

AUTHORS' CASEBOOK: Recovering From Acquisition Failure

A publisher of business telephone directories borrowed heavily to finance rollup acquisitions of competitors in its market area. Poor integration of the acquisitions led to large operating losses and a liquidity crisis. Rather than generating cost-reduction synergies, the complexities of integrating a series of small local businesses increased costs and caused a serious loss of control over the ability to collect large numbers of small receivables. The resulting liquidity crisis then disrupted the printing schedule for the company's numerous publications.

Critical Challenge: Getting the printing schedules back on track while cleaning up the receivable situation in preparation for a sale. Asset values and an ability to demonstrate earnings power were both contingent upon receivable collections, and the business was clearly not viable as it was being operated.

New interim management stabilized operations by using a staff of temporary employees to collect receivables while securing vendor support to bring printing back on schedule. Realistic five-year business plans were developed after the viability and cash-flow potential of three separately identifiable business segments were analyzed. These plans served as the basis for a sale memorandum outlining each segment's potential to generate significant cash flow. In three separate transactions, all of the company's operations were sold to strategic buyers.

Chapter Summary

The first critical decision point when assessing a troubled company is a determination of its fundamental viability. If a business cannot reasonably justify its standalone operations through either an operational turnaround or a financial restructuring, then energy and resources should promptly be redirected toward developing an exit strategy that will maximize proceeds to stakeholders. Viable and non-viable businesses can best be analyzed by categorizing their particular problems. Once a company is determined to be viable and the issues it must address are identified, it can:

- Develop the information and realistic projections necessary to support the financial and operational restructuring needed for the business to move forward;
- Clearly understand where it is making and losing money in order to improve profitability significantly through operational restructuring;
- Only secondarily, focus on the strategy and tactics necessary for a change in direction to improve growth.

If a financially troubled company is not viable long-term as a standalone entity – and in our experience there is something approaching a 50 percent likelihood that it is not – installing new management to attempt a turnaround is a waste of time and resources. If a reasonable rationale for its long-term viability cannot be supported, focus and attention should promptly shift to developing an exit strategy that maximizes current value. This typically involves a business sale or asset liquidation of the entire enterprise, but in rare cases some sort of residual core or high-growth potential niche product may remain as a standalone entity.

A significant number of companies do not fall immediately into any of the various viable or non-viable categories. These may include a few potential turnaround candidates, but a large portion of them will not have the potential for surviving as standalone entities even though there may be a substantial core business earnings capacity or a growing niche business segment that is not being properly supported.

The key to success in these situations is to identify the operational restructuring actions that will provide an opportunity to continue the core or turn the "diamond in the rough" segments and product lines into viable businesses. Analyses and actions required to diagnose these situations will be developed in later chapters.

Chapter 3

UNDERSTANDING THE NATURE
OF BUSINESS PROBLEMS
Identifying Patterns of Risk and Opportunity

The fundamental tasks required to effect a business turnaround are fairly straight-forward:

1. Diagnose the problem;
2. Develop a realistic plan of corrective action;
3. Marshal the support and resources required to pursue the new goals;
4. Execute the plan

Sounds simple. And in *some* ways it is simple. But not in most ways. Diagnosing the problem is often very difficult, with numerous essential background facts either unknown or in dispute. Conventional wisdom is often wrong. The risks inherent in the corrective plan are numerous and often require new investment. The apparent risks are typically intimidating, the hidden risks invariably even more dangerous. Credibility is usually weak. The parties required to provide support and resources are almost universally disappointed. Dissatisfied with recent performance, too often they make their highest priority a search for the guilty. Unsatisfactory past results distort perceptions required to develop an objective understanding of risk/reward ratios of the various alternatives. Adversarial battle lines are drawn that may make a consensual objective solution elusive, if not impossible.

As we noted in the Preface, many, if not most, business books focus primarily on the fourth step, execution, setting forth their lessons and insights as to how to achieve goals once direction has been set. The focus of this book is Steps 1, 2 and 3, how to identify and set course upon the optimal path. In order to craft a solution for a troubled company, one must first assess and understand the alternative possibilities and their associated implementation risks. We believe those who can do that effectively will find execution often becomes the easy part.

The Diagnosis

In any financially troubled company, different parties always have conflicting agendas (as we will discuss more fully in Chapter 7). Our perspective is that the primary objective should be to identify and then obtain the maximum achievable value of the business enterprise. Enterprise value may be measured by various methods, including EBITDA multiple, price/earnings multiple and discounted cash flow. Some variation of these should provide a guide to a realistic current market value, if the business were to be sold as an ongoing entity.

For many troubled businesses, the going-concern valuation is less than the value obtainable by a breakup sale or liquidation of assets. In such cases, little justification can be found for the business to survive as an ongoing entity – unless the prospect of near-term improvement is good. Management and employees, of course, are likely to have different views on this point.

The diagnosis and evaluation task is to understand the range and basis of current valuations, to identify reasonable alternatives available to maximize and extract value and to provide credible assessments of their associated risks and rewards, with the objective of facilitating informed decisions. The decision-making process often revolves around negotiating the assumption or transfer of perceived risks and rewards (an issue we discuss in Chapter 12). But the first task, upon which that decision-making process will rely, is to identify and understand the fundamental nature of the company's problems, so that potential corrective actions can be properly evaluated, along with their associated risks and rewards.

The Nature of Problems

Some things are easy to accomplish, some things harder, and to make informed decisions, the nature of the challenges and the level of difficulty in resolving them must be considered. In particular, the level of risk in different approaches must be assessed. It is very difficult to find support for high-risk options in a troubled situation, particularly if the potential risks and rewards flow to different parties. An approach with "home run" potential but only 1 chance in 20 of success is probably not viable – unless it is backed by new money and provides reliable downside protection for risk-averse constituents.

In evaluating risk, our experience has taught us that the single most important question about business problems is whether they are internal or the result of external forces. As we noted in Chapter 1, we have found in our own work that a distressed company is twice as likely to achieve an operational turnaround if its problems are primarily internal rather than external.

Internal problems have a high probability of being fixable, particularly if they are not worsened by external market forces or a liquidity crisis. Specific, narrow, self-inflicted wounds are generally reversible. The more controllable the proximate causes of the decline, the more likely they can be corrected, particularly if addressed in a timely manner.

External problems are much harder to fix, because many of them are beyond the company's control, regardless of its resolve, leadership and resources. The company is usually either starting from a position well behind the leaders or facing cyclical conditions in which the existing business model is no longer profitable or cannot meet debt service requirements.

Both external and internal problems, if allowed to linger, can too easily become insurmountable. Interestingly, we have found a strong correlation between corporate lifecycles and the nature of the problems that are encountered. Internal problems tend to be most heavily concentrated in the earlier, growing stages of a business organization's lifecycle. During later stages, external competitive problems are more likely to develop. Let us look at each in turn.

Internal Problems

During rapid business growth, aggressive actions by an entrepreneurial founder without appropriate administrative controls and processes in place tend to result in excessive risk. In many cases, the founder's ego is the driving strategic force within the business. Often, these entrepreneurial founders have achieved highly successful results over an extended period of years through such risk-taking. These historical good results, which arguably may have benefited as much from good luck as good judgment, lead to even more entrepreneurial overconfidence and greater risk-taking in an attempt to extend unsustainable growth rates in a rapidly maturing business. The result can be an indiscriminate focus on expansion and volume growth, leading to failed acquisitions or poorly implemented major expansion projects and, ultimately, to a disaster that shifts the company into the financially troubled category. In a public company, this process is aided and abetted by the interests of both the investment community and management in an ever-increasing share price. The acceptance of unreasonable risk involving acquisitions and growth projects is the largest general category of problem in the early stages of the company's lifecycle.

A second category of internal problems is the general lack of administrative controls as a business grows rapidly, leading to a failure to understand the profitability model or to control working capital. In these cases, companies engage in profitless growth in pursuit of volume; this may not result in outright losses but can consume excessive working capital. That, in turn, leads to loss of management control over inventories and receivables and requires excessive borrowing. Such issues can be readily identified by looking at where the company is making and losing its money, both in terms of profitability and return on investment.

AUTHORS' CASEBOOK: Out-of-Control Growth

Worlds of Wonder introduced innovative high-tech toys and games in the mid-1980s and recorded almost $100 million in sales in its first year and more than $300 million in Year 2. Its plan anticipated more than $700 million the following year, but that was totally unrealistic from an execution standpoint. New toy designs were completed late, East Asian manufacturing and packaging fell behind schedule, and many shipments were received by retailers too late for the Christmas season. The company filed Chapter 11 four days before Christmas and terminated 70% of its employees.

This combination of super-aggressive growth plans, high costs and unrealistic expectations for execution of difficult projects proved lethal. The East Asian suppliers were owed more than $60 million for product previously shipped and held approximately $25 million of finished goods and in-process inventories. The firm's founder-CEO resigned shortly after the Chapter 11 filing to allow creditors to begin addressing an exit strategy.

Critical Challenge: Obtaining going-concern value from a highly distressed entity. Circumstances appeared to dictate a liquidation of the business with the bulk of tangible values residing in overstocked seasonal inventories. However, unless a going concern could be maintained, pricing on distressed inventories would be deeply discounted and receivable balances would be difficult to collect from retailers. The major uncertainties were the potential "dumping" of product held by overseas suppliers, which would compete with company inventories, and the sources of supply for newly developed products.

The new CEO, co-author Steve Hopkins, took several major steps:

1. Raising cash by a massive task force focus on receivables, to clean up disputes and discrepancies. This resulted in collections from pre-petition accounts receivable of almost $40 million, approximately four times the senior lenders' original estimates of $8 million to $10 million.
2. Carefully coordinated liquidation sales of excess inventories with foreign manufacturers holding finished-product inventories participating on pari-passu basis.
3. Arrangements in Hong Kong and South Korea for the purchase of other active inventories held by overseas suppliers, in order to provide suppliers some participation in expected Christmas sales.
4. Arranging for competitively priced, timely delivery of new products for the following Christmas.

The company successfully operated through the following Christmas season without suffering margin deterioration from competitive dumping of overseas product or failure to have adequate supplies of new product. A Plan of Reorganization involving the sale of the business to an investor group was then structured and implemented.

External Problems

With the exception of cyclical industry issues, external problems most often occur in mature businesses in the declining phases of their lifecycle. Businesses begin to decline as a result of external market-environment pressures combined with a lack of the aggressive management actions required to cope with the situation. In such situations, successful turnarounds typically involve cutting operations back to the historical core business if there is a viable, ongoing, profit margin stream, while dramatically reducing overhead. This means careful review of where the business is making and losing money.

AUTHORS' CASEBOOK: Refocusing a Retail Chain

A Midwestern retailer with 150 stores and annual sales in the $350 million range was taken private during the mid-80's in a highly leveraged management buyout. Subsequently, Wal-Mart aggressively expanded into the company's traditional markets, and within a few years almost a third of the company's stores were incurring losses. The company as a whole began reporting large losses, a cash squeeze ensued and the company's secured creditors refused to advance additional credit on its working capital lines.

Working with management, outside consultants, including co-author Doug Hopkins, looked at numerous aspects of all individual stores and markets, as well as at corporate merchandising and administrative functions. The conclusion was that the business was a very low-cost operation but that its merchandising strategies were outdated and one-third of its stores were under untenable competitive pressure from Wal-Mart.

Critical Challenges: Protecting the profitable core. Rather than focusing resources on fighting the losing battles, renewed viability required using the strengths of the company's core business – low costs and capable management – and improving its performance in smaller rural markets to discourage additional competitive encroachment.

In order to reject leases on surplus real estate, the company filed Chapter 11 bankruptcy. Operations were restructured geographically to concentrate only on smaller stores in rural markets. Management implemented new merchandising strategies and programs; updated store appearance and layouts; accelerated utilization of POS inventory information; and implemented numerous other changes and improvements at both the store and corporate level. The company successfully emerged from bankruptcy as a profitable, stable business, and most of its outstanding debt was subsequently retired from the proceeds of a successful initial public offering.

Organization Lifecycles

In diagnosing and understanding the problems of troubled businesses, keep in mind the balance between measurable financial trends and intangible problems that cannot be readily discerned from charts, graphs and trend lines. Financial statements tell only a portion of the story.

Intangible problems are those things that may be affecting reported results but are not specifically identifiable in the numbers. In many cases the intangible problems represent the underlying causes of operational distress and financial decline. Examples include changes in the competitive environment resulting in a lower-margin sales mix or quality problems leading to higher manufacturing costs.

We have found organizational categorizations to be a useful tool for identifying likely problems and their solutions. In *Corporate Lifecycles*[2], Dr. Ichak Adizes used the terminology shown in Exhibit 3.1 to identify lifecycles of businesses and other organizations. His work discusses extensively the characteristics of each phase of the lifecycle and the type of management required at different times in the lifecycle of an organization.

EXHIBIT 3-1
ORGANIZATIONAL LIFECYCLES

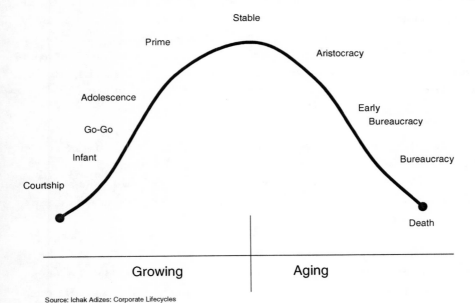

Source: Ichak Adizes: Corporate Lifecycles

At different points in their lifecycles, businesses face different challenges and problems. Some are easily addressed; some can prove insurmountable. Understanding where the business is in its lifecycle can provide many insights into both its challenges and problems, as well as the opportunities and likelihood of achieving a successful turnaround. Among the categories identified by Adizes on the chart above, we find the following to be of particular interest in understanding troubled company issues and problems:

---

[2] *Ichak Adizes,* Corporate Lifecycles: How and Why Corporations Grow and Die and What to Do About It *(Englewood Cliffs, N.J.: Prentice-Hall, 1988).*

Growth

Go-Go: Operations are flourishing and growth is rapid, but administrative controls over the entrepreneurial management are inadequate. In this stage, a company can go seriously off track with poor factory processes, customer service, inadequate working capital controls or new high-risk investments. These are the classic, very fixable internal problems of troubled companies.

Adolescence: Major organizational conflicts develop within a successful, growing business as administrative controls are installed to manage the business properly. Power struggles arising from the implementation of these controls leads to management friction and high turnover, and tensions are heightened as the founder-CEO tries to get rid of potential successors he sees as threats. Over the objections of more experienced professional managers, the successful entrepreneur often expands into low-margin products or makes unsuccessful acquisitions in unrelated businesses in a quest to maintain high revenue growth rates.

Maturity

Between Adolescence and the clear aging of Early Bureaucracy, Adizes identifies three organizational phases of maturity: Prime, Stable and Aristocracy:

Prime: A mature, profitable business is working well, with an appropriate balance between its entrepreneurial growth spirit and necessary, but not excessive, administrative controls.

Stable: The business continues to be profitable but is beginning to lose creativity and the ability to innovate.

Aristocracy: The business is cash-rich with an overbalanced focus on internal controls and procedures as it begins to lose touch with its customers and the external environment.

Mature companies, in these middle lifecycle phases, should not, at least in theory, be financially troubled. These businesses should be generating excellent profits and have a strong balance sheet. While significant troubles may be beginning to develop in the Aristocracy stage due to lack of attention to the external environment, such problems are evident only to the most astute external observer.

Aging

Early Bureaucracy: A mature business begins to decline, generally because of its failure to adapt to changes in the external competitive environment and the departure of the aggressive young managers who want to drive growth. Financial resources are eroded by deteriorating operating results. This stage is followed by descent, which may take many years, into full bureaucracy and ultimately corporate death.

Authors' Categorization of Troubled Companies

As we reviewed and evaluated our experience base, examining it in the context of both the internal and external challenges and the Adizes lifecycle categories, we found that the troubled company assignments with which we had been involved began to fall quite neatly into three distinct and identifiable groups, with clear patterns related both to the nature of the problems and the most likely solutions. We believe these categories provide a very useful framework for understanding problems and diagnosing turnaround potential at financially troubled businesses.

Undisciplined Racehorses: These are dynamic, growing businesses that have suffered reverses and become financially troubled. As we noted above, these reverses are most often internal operating problems or strategic failures. Either excessive risk has been assumed in order to ensure continued rapid growth, adequate resources have not been put in place to manage sales growth or new expensive projects, or strategic changes have diverted the company from its core strengths. On rarer occasions, these dynamic, growing businesses can be beset by external market factors, most likely in the form of an unexpected, permanent market change.

Overburdened Workhorses: These are stable businesses in the maturity phases of their lifecycles that are generating positive cash flow, the type of companies with product lines that Peter Drucker, in *Managing for Results*[3], called "Today's Breadwinners." While, for the reasons outlined previously, these businesses should not be financially troubled, they may have become overleveraged financially as a result of either unrealistic profit growth expectations or cyclical downturns that reduced debt service capacity. In addition, despite better controls, these businesses can be susceptible to the some of the same types of internally inflicted wounds, particularly acquisition integration difficulties, as the Undisciplined Racehorses. Unrealistic growth expectations of companies in this category frequently result in excessive acquisition financing.

Aging Mules: These businesses are on the downward slope of their lifecycle. Growth has either slowed significantly or stopped. Operations have become bureaucratic, customer focus is lost and competitive strengths are deteriorating. However, management stubbornly persist in their unsuccessful strategies. Most such businesses are suffering from external problems such as loss of competitive position to more aggressive, lower-cost competitors. Often they are finally pushed over the edge into financial trouble by down-trend business cycles or commodity raw material price increases. Because most problems of the Aging Mules are external, turnarounds are more difficult and less likely than for the Undisciplined

---

[3] Peter Drucker, *Managing for Results: Economic Tasks and Risk-Taking Decisions* (New York: Harper & Row, 1964).

Racehorse business with internal problems. If internal issues are a problem for companies in this category, they will generally be in the form of strategic errors after management recognize the onset of stagnation and tries to branch out and reinvent their business model. In this category, even self-inflicted wounds are difficult to recover from, because the misguided attempt depletes resources and the core business is, by definition, itself in decline.

Exhibit 3-2 shows the Adizes lifecycle chart with the authors' categorizations of troubled companies superimposed.

EXHIBIT 3-2
AUTHORS' CATEGORIZATIONS OF TROUBLED BUSINESSES

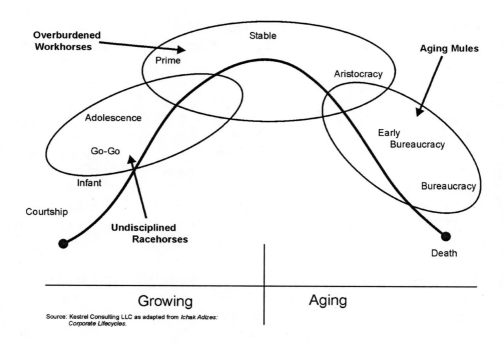

Source: Kestrel Consulting LLC as adapted from *Ichak Adizes: Corporate Lifecycles.*

Exhibit 3-3 provides a summary of the split between external and internal problems of our project sample among the three lifecycle categories discussed above.

EXHIBIT 3-3

TYPE OF PROBLEMS BY LIFECYCLE CATEGORY

Type of Problem	Undisciplined Racehorses	Overburdened Workhorses	Aging Mules	Total
External	5	17	24	46
Internal	31	19	4	54
Total	36	36	28	100

A basic tenet of our work, developed over many years, is that business diagnosis involves understanding the basic problems rather than focusing on symptoms. Fixing symptoms may reduce losses but without providing a reasonable chance of ever generating profits. Achieving the best results from management efforts to force change requires careful attention to setting the correct priorities, and these priorities are likely to vary greatly depending on the problem category. In later chapters (16, 17 and 18), we will examine more closely our work with companies in these different categories.

Timing of the Problem Diagnosis

Very often, the first question asked of a prospective consultant is, "How long will the diagnosis take?" The usual response is, "How long do you have?" The answers to these two questions will not always conveniently coincide.

Accuracy and completeness of information obtained will depend heavily on how much time is available, what resources are applied and the complexity of the business situation. The goal, remember, is not exhaustive due diligence but rather to determine the information needed for a quick overview evaluation of alternative scenarios. For a first pass on an expedited basis, 10 days may be enough to get a handle on a company's problems. In no case should the problem diagnosis extend beyond 45 to 60 days.

In assuming that the initial evaluation and fact-finding process must be completed in 45 to 60 days, we make the assumption that the company has no more than 90 days to come to a decision and begin action on saving itself. If the management at a troubled company believe that they have more than 90 days to address their challenges, the company has not yet come to see itself in crisis. In fact, the time available to correct problems is often much shorter.

AUTHORS' CASEBOOK: Manufacturing Business Meltdown

An overleveraged multi-plant manufacturer of molded-plastic housewares products and disposable plastic bags began to experience serious operating losses as a result of price increases for resin, the raw material it used for its products. These price increases could not be passed on to customers. A liquidity crisis developed, management lost credibility, and working capital lenders stopped all advances to the company. Lacking funding for payroll, manufacturing operations at the company's five plants were abruptly shut down.

Critical Challenge: The impasse between the senior lenders and the equity, which triggered the precipitous shutdown of the business, had already answered the viability question, and the goal had become, by default, maximizing value from a liquidation.

On a Wednesday, co-author Steve Hopkins was retained by the company's secured lenders to develop a plan of action. Starting the following day and working with company management through the weekend, a wind-down action plan was developed to (1) sell finished goods inventories in the normal course of business to existing customers, (2) restart operations at one plant to convert extensive inventories of scrap raw materials to finished goods, and (3) collect receivables. Had the situation and its serious problems been addressed sooner, there might have been a viable core business. However, the fundamental threshold question of viability, which generally is the starting point and critical branch in the decision tree, had been settled before outside help was sought.

The wind-down plan was presented to secured lenders on a Monday. They approved the advances needed to implement the plan, concluding it was the best basis for obtaining maximum recoveries on the company assets that collateralized loans.

With the concurrence of the company's owner, Chapter 11 proceedings were initiated to provide Bankruptcy Court supervision of the liquidation. Assets of four manufacturing plants were sold and a plan was developed for continued operation of one plant producing more competitive products as a standalone entity.

Responsibility for Diagnosis

We believe that experienced external consultants are the best choice to perform an objective, independent evaluation. To be most effective, they need as much internal assistance as possible, to provide competitive environment information and develop analytical data for areas such as operational evaluations and cash-flow forecasts. While the case can be made that the problem diagnosis can be performed internally, or directed by a new CEO, we have found that in distressed situations it can be very difficult for management and employees to set aside their preconceived views or overcome unconscious attitudes and change their frame of reference, unless guided and supported by a disinterested, objective third party. Furthermore, it is better if this detailed, independent diagnosis is completed before changes in management are made.

If a new CEO is directing the process, he or she will typically have arrived with a vested interest in what the answer should be. Too often, the new CEO will announce a new strategy upon arrival, and whatever diagnosis process follows is intended to identify how to justify and implement the new CEO's directives – *not* to determine what steps are appropriate or achievable. Did we hear someone say, "Ready, fire, aim"? When responding to a hard-charging new boss, employees can easily be intimidated and try to come up with solutions they believe the boss wants to hear, rather than identifying what the boss most needs to know. It is simply human nature for a new executive, who probably got the job by assuring the board that he was just the man to turn the business around, to push on ahead, rather than going back to the board and saying that now that he is place, he can see that the company is not viable and has greater value as a consolidation target than in continuing operations.

Business Cycles

Many scholarly studies over the years have analyzed business cycles and their impact on the U.S. and world economies. Business cycles vary significantly among industries in terms of the timing and severity of being affected by general economic slowdowns. At many consumer businesses that sell food or other consumables, sales may be little affected by business cycles. In sharp contrast, manufacturers of heavy capital equipment used in production processes will have deep volume downturns that last well past the end of a typical recession.

In diagnosing the turnaround potential of a financially troubled business, it is essential that all parties come to understand the business cycle of the industry in which the troubled company is participating. Are problems of declining volume specific to the company or characteristic of the entire industry? These economic or business cycle-related volume fluctuations must be clearly differentiated from volume declines related to loss of competitive market share or to a general decline of sales volume for a mature or declining industry.

We have generally found that the external problems of the Overburdened Workhorse category of business were heavily driven by business cycle issues. When, in hindsight, it develops that they were overleveraged, these businesses develop financial problems during business downturns.

Chapter Summary

To execute a turnaround effectively, a company's problems must be correctly diagnosed and a realistic plan of corrective action developed. The objective of the diagnostic process is to facilitate informed decision-making by identifying realistic alternatives and credibly assessing their risks and rewards.

Internal problems are generally easier to fix than external problems resulting from changes in the competitive environment. Significant differences exist in the nature of and potential for fixing internal and external problems.

One essential element of the diagnosis is an understanding of the business cycle of the company's industry and where the company stands in its lifecycle. This book categorizes the lifecycles of troubled companies as:

- **Undisciplined Racehorses:** Dynamic, growing but immature businesses susceptible to internal problems.
- **Overburdened Workhorses:** Mature, stable, profitable businesses that are overleveraged with debt.
- **Aging Mules:** Businesses on the downward slope of their lifecycle that often exacerbate external market challenges by stubbornly persisting in unsuccessful strategies.

Always, the objective of a troubled company workout should be to maximize realizable enterprise value. In some cases the maximum value will come from a sale or liquidation.

Chapter 4

THE CHALLENGE OF MANAGEMENT
Knowledge, Understanding, Insight, and Leadership

As noted in the Introduction to Part I, credit executives and business writers often loosely opine that 80% or so of business failures are due to "bad management." The business is failing. It may be failing to meet budget. It may be declining precipitously from historical earnings. It may be failing to respond to commodity price changes or foreign competition. Whatever doesn't matter: it's failing. These guys (*i.e.*, existing management) are in charge. It happened on their watch. Ipso facto...they must be the problem. Get rid of them.

In our opinion, not only is this view wrong, it's counterproductive and damaging. Attributing all or most business failures to bad management is a "cop-out" that hinders diagnosing and addressing the real business problems that exist. The only way it is reasonable to blame the bulk of all business problems upon the quality of management is if one can assume that:

1. Good managers should always be expected to make good, *correct* business decisions despite often having to act quickly on the basis of very sketchy, *often incorrect,* information;
2. Good management can readily foresee and easily control or quickly react to changes in the external business environment.

Our experience does not support those assumptions.

Certainly, management decisions, whether errors of commission or omission, play a part in business problems. But errors are not proof of incompetence or mismanagement any more than good luck is evidence of superior intellect. A decision that hindsight reveals to have been a mistake is not necessarily bad management. Neither is the situation in which future changes in external circumstances were not foreseen at the time a course for the future was charted.

Based on extensive experience and observations, it is our opinion that *bad management is much less of a cause for business failures than is commonly believed.*

So, what is the relationship between bad management and business failure? First, let's talk about what we believe constitutes good management. Business management revolves around two interrelated objectives: establishing strategy and direction and effective planning and execution of goal-oriented tasks. Peter Drucker described these very different tasks as "Doing the Right Things" and "Doing Things Right." It's unreasonable to expect that even the best managers will get strategy and direction right the first time, every time. It is, however, necessary to demand that they be able to learn from their mistakes. Good management is demonstrated by long-term effectiveness in providing strategic direction and executing plans, combined with an ability and willingness to learn from mistakes.

Because most successful managers have demonstrated sound strategy choices and execution skills, at least for a limited period of time, the challenge to their success and effectiveness arises in the question of *how they deal with change.* Good management are alert and responsive to changing circumstances, whether they arise from internal mistakes of execution or judgment, or from external influences in the marketplace.

Time and time again in our experience with troubled situations, we have observed that the greatest obstacle to success is an inability to recognize and respond to changing events. Success in dealing with a financially troubled business starts with identifying and accepting reality. Provided with an objective analysis of the facts of a situation, *which they accept as reality,* managers of most businesses have the ability to make good judgments about actions that should be taken. But identification and acceptance of changing realities often come slowly.

Acknowledging and accepting change requires setting aside preconceived views and challenging basic assumptions. When we arrive at a troubled company, we start with the recognition that there are no "cookie-cutter solutions" and no "magic bullets." We cannot pretend we bring prepackaged solutions. Nor can we accept without critical challenge the situation as described by the participants. Our task is to seek either to see something that somebody else has missed or to recognize, accept and respond to something that other people are denying.

Over the years we've developed a disciplined approach to this process that we think constitutes a basic prescription for sound management. This is more than a formula appropriate only for application in a third-party evaluation; it is our view of a highly effective general management process. If you like acronyms, call it KUIL (pronounced "cool"):

- Knowledge
- Understanding
- Insight
- Leadership

Note that, in this view, leadership, although extremely important, comes last. A lot of hard work, detailed analysis and careful consideration must precede it. The ever-evolving marketplace continuously presents pressures, changes and temptations to veer off the right path. A premature rush to action that bypasses or truncates the diagnosis-and-analysis process runs the risk of succumbing to those pressures. We also believe that leadership is situational. Different leadership characteristics are required for different circumstances: "different horses for different courses," as they say in the racing world. Therefore, a board of directors shouldn't select a new leader until the objectives he or she will be charged to pursue are clearly understood.

The concept of KUIL is not rocket science. It's primarily the application of common sense and logic. Much of the discipline dates back four decades to what co-author Steve Hopkins was exposed to in General Electric's management training programs. But KUIL is a discipline and perspective that is easily lost, particularly in stressed situations when management becomes consumed with fighting fires as they stumble down the wrong path toward unattainable goals.

To be effective, management must *continuously* be:

1. Well-informed about the facts of the company's situation, both in its internal operations and in the external marketplace and competition;
2. Able and willing to convert the factual data into reliable and meaningful information and understanding about its business, *even when it conflicts with predisposed beliefs and preferred interpretations;*
3. Insightful in assessing the implications, risks, opportunities and potential rewards of the company's changing situation;
4. Prepared to act as leaders, motivators and coaches, providing vision, resources, support and guidance while simultaneously measuring and reassessing both progress and direction as the situation continuously changes.

In our normal role as consultants and advisors, we have the luxury of addressing situations with fresh eyes, stepping into a new problem situation and assisting with evaluations, strategy and planning. Often our scope of activity includes an active interim-management role during which we guide and direct implementation of our recommendations. Occasionally, we have assumed board positions in which we have continuing longer-term advisory roles and oversight. But our active day-to-day hands-on role is typically a two-to-eight-month timeframe and very seldom extends much beyond 12 months.

We could, of course, describe how our superior innate intelligence combined with decades of broad-based experience allows us to identify patterns of problems far more efficiently than everyone else. But in point of fact, the objective, unbiased, "fresh eyes" aspect of our role is nearly as important as the experience and discipline we bring to the process. That is because for management, the process needs to be a continuous loop of reassessment, which is very difficult to maintain. Two of the most difficult challenges that management have to face are changing direction and acknowledging mistakes.

Inertia is a fact of life. It affects human nature just as inevitably as it does celestial bodies. People tend to gravitate toward consistent interpretations of the facts, and often, once they've formed an opinion and perspective, they unconsciously filter new information; disregarding, discounting or misinterpreting facts that don't fit their pre-existing view of the situation. The more strongly held and carefully conceived their opinions and plans are, the more difficult it is to see that the situation is changing and the more likely management will be in a state of denial (psychologists call these processes *selective attention, selective perception* and *selective retention*). Sometimes implementing change requires both a crisis and an external catalyst.

THE CHALLENGE OF MANAGEMENT : "KUIL"	
Knowledge	Assemble a reliable and complete fact base
	⌃ Utilize Internal and External Information Sources
Understanding	Convert the factual data into meaningful information; examining and evaluating
	⌃ Internal and External Problems
	⌃ Expectations of Various Constituencies
	⌃ Profitability/Contribution by Segment
	⌃ Competitive Environment
	⌃ Management, Organization and Business Processes
	⌃ Cash-flow and Financing Requirements
Insight	Assess the situation and establish a future course based upon this disciplined factual evaluation, with full consideration of:
	⌃ Objectives
	⌃ Risks and Opportunities
	⌃ Resource Requirements
	⌃ Commitment and Authority
	Develop and document a measurable plan of action
Leadership	Execute the Plan
	⌃ Communicate the "Vision"
	⌃ Secure Required Commitments
	⌃ Provide Support, Guidance and Encouragement
	⌃ Measure Progress and Accomplishments
	⌃ Flexibly Reassess Direction Along the Way

So back to the relationship between business failure and bad management: If we describe our primary role as helping management see the need for change, doesn't that mean we view management as the primary cause of business failures? No. While management often need assistance in reassessing their path and responding to changing circumstances, or even recognizing and solving specific functional operational problems, incompetent management *per se* have been a fundamental cause of the decline in only a small minority of the problem situations we've encountered. The fundamental cause of problems is usually a set of changing circumstances to which management could not or did not adapt effectively.

Very good managers are often viewed as incompetent because they have been focused in the wrong direction, most usually pursuing the same objectives that were successful for them and the company in the recent past. Such management may or may not be up to the necessary task of a future response to these changing conditions. But misinterpreting management as the inherent cause of the decline can lead to delays and false starts in responding to the underlying business challenges.

When a board of directors' first reaction to major problems is to focus on hiring new management as the solution, without fully understanding the circumstances of problems to be solved and the reasons they continue to exist, that strategy often leads to major disappointment. What is needed first – before assuming that the fix needed is new, better management – is a careful analysis of the problems, the situation that led to the problems and the best alternatives for solving the problems. The fact that hindsight shows a decision to have had unfortunate consequences does not, of itself, indicate that decision-making skills are worse than the normal expectations for management. If someone is forced with no information, or faulty information, to open one of two doors and chooses the one with the tiger behind it, that is bad luck, not bad management. Arguably, what *is* bad management is allowing oneself to be put in the position of needing to choose one of these two doors without the information needed to make a better decision. In our opinion, the quality of decisions and choices is a function of facts used in the decision-making process much more frequently than it is a function of poor judgment.

Hindsight bias together with a desire to punish the guilty drives too many conclusions that a company has bad management, potentially leading to less qualified replacements and delays in addressing the real problems that exist. Despite conventional wisdom, the individual who "caused and *experienced* the problem" may well be the proper choice, if properly supported, to lead a business turnaround.

KEY QUESTIONS

Some key questions that need to be answered in evaluating the CEO and other top managers include:

The Good
- Do management have a realistic long-term vision for the company?
- Are capital, technology and human resources available within the company being used to maximize advantage?

The Bad
- Are management in denial about the brutal facts of their situation?
- Are resources of the company being misallocated into poor return areas to satisfy management ego or to continue trends of the past?

The Ugly
- Are management causing harm by arrogance, greed or generally erratic behavior?
- Are operating results being manipulated in a fraudulent or illegal manner?

Unfortunately, the perception that bad management cause most business problems is perpetuated by new management's standard practice of blaming everything that went wrong on their predecessors. This helps buy time while the new management figures out what they want to do, but it is not particularly helpful to the process of finding real business solutions.

Randomness of Results

The fallacy of always expecting management to achieve superior results is demonstrated by looking at mutual fund investment results. In general, mutual funds are managed by highly intelligent, well-educated, experienced and knowledgeable managers. On average, they would likely fall in the top quartile of U.S. business management both in terms of intelligence and knowledge of their businesses. Unfortunately for them, they work in a business where results are easily measured and compared.

Logically, the best and brightest fund managers should consistently achieve superior investment results and easily beat the market averages over extended periods of time. However, with a very short list of exceptions, there is little evidence that the average fund manager consistently achieves results any better than could be expected by random coin tosses. This was demonstrated a few years ago when *The Wall Street Journal* had people throw darts at the stock tables and used the companies thus "picked" as a portfolio. When those "selections" were tracked over time, their performance fell *right in the middle* of those of most mutual funds. Clearly, luck plays an enormous role in investment outcomes and, likewise in our opinion, in achieving good or bad business results.

If only a very few individuals can deliver superior stock market returns over time, isn't it illogical to expect the majority of business managers to outperform their peers for extended periods of time? This may not be a politically correct position at the nation's business schools, but we conclude that luck or randomness of results is a much bigger factor in business success and failure than commonly acknowledged. Highly competent individuals are likely to be subject to random bad results due to unforeseen events or to be outperformed due to the good luck of competitors.

Woody Allen said that "80 percent of success is showing up." That's probably not true in the creative arts, where Allen has made his mark. But in the business world, if you add the caveat that you must both show up and *do no harm*, we believe that it's a lot truer than most CEOs would care to admit. Later in this chapter we explore at length those management characteristics that we believe do harm.

Managing Expectations

What is sometimes defined as "bad management" is the failure to achieve the unrealistic expectations of investment analysts, private equity funds or some other third party. An understanding of this expectations game is critical to an evaluation of results, particularly for a financially troubled company, and is a significant reason not to make replacing management the first strategy employed in fixing problems of a troubled business. (The subject of appropriately defining expectations is discussed in depth in Chapter 9.)

Among the difficulties in establishing appropriate expectations are these:

- In booming, rapid-growth market conditions, it is very difficult to define the market top and cut back before it is reached. Trend reversals are much more clearly seen in hindsight.
- While a company is making rapid progress, its competition doesn't stand still. A competitor may prove to be moving even more rapidly than you are.
- Obtaining new resources for a troubled company becomes progressively more difficult as a history of low returns continues.
- Sometimes the coin flips of life's random results come up tails one time too many in a row, despite good management's best efforts, plans and risk assessments.

Aside from the difficulty in setting expectations, it is important to note that many factors will dramatically affect results measurement before the question of good or bad management comes into play:

Risk factors involved in either existing or growing in the industry, the markets and the product lines in which a business competes. High returns are often related to the assumption of high risks; without the advantages of diversification over the long term, high failure rates are almost inevitable for high-risk businesses as a group, despite good management.

Sudden market and competitive environment changes, including rapid supply increases or cost decreases. The effects on the travel industry of the 9/11/01 attacks are a dramatic example.

Resources, both technical and financial, available with which to do battle. The economics of larger, newer, more efficient plants and equipment can provide overwhelming advantages in certain industries. A financially troubled company with low market share typically does not have such advantages and even the superior manager is likely to fail.

Definitions of success in meeting objectives of the business and its industry. Profitably managing to be the last survivor in the buggy whip business is a very different expectation than growing market share in a rapidly developing medical devices market.

The level of competition must be considered: Are your basketball opponents from the NBA or the local high school? General Motors' management looked very tough before the Japanese arrived.

The ever-increasing issue of globalization reinforces many of the above points. Globalization changes the boundaries and rules of markets. It opens the door to low-cost foreign producers. If finished-goods production shifts overseas, many components markets are likely to follow. As an example, when production of television sets began moving from the Mexican border region to Southeast Asia, the North American plastic molders that supplied components saw their market erode sharply.

AUTHORS' CASEBOOK: Communicating the Real Story

A leading manufacturer of metal buildings was not meeting earnings and cash-flow projections made in connection with a highly leveraged management buyout and was in default under loan covenants. Because of changes in fiscal reporting in a somewhat seasonal business and in write-ups of asset valuations, management was having great difficulty measuring results on a consistent basis and providing meaningful reporting to lenders. Profit shortfalls from the highly aggressive plan could not be explained satisfactorily and management lost credibility.

Critical Challenge: Establish viability of the business to the satisfaction of secured creditors and determine a reasonable basis for a financial restructuring.

Evaluation of the situation consisted primarily of a viability review of the company's operations, its business strategy and projections of future cash flow compared with historical results. Although the highly optimistic projections made at the time of the buyout were not being achieved, there had been no actual deterioration in operations of this historically profitable business.

The diagnosis work documented basic strengths of the business and provided detailed approaches to future profitability improvements. With outside advisors providing credibility, the company refinanced its debt with paydown schedules much more likely to be achieved. The company continued its profitable growth and subsequently went public with a highly successful IPO.

Key Management Deficiencies

Bad management occurs when personal characteristics or experience weaknesses are doing harm or when no attempt is made to adjust to changed circumstances. In the worst case, there is a redoubling of unproductive efforts and costs despite their clear failure to correct the problem in the past. Put another way, understanding the problems of a business often evolves to evaluating issues of management's agenda and personal characteristics rather than their capability.

We view the most important real management deficiencies as **denial, arrogance, greed, complacency,** and **lack of leadership.**

Denial that unfavorable events are taking place or require responsive action can trigger long-term negative impacts. Most frequently, denial involves recognizing that certain events are happening but refusing to accept that the effects will be more than temporary. This "refusing to face the brutal facts" is the critical management failure common to all categories of business. Management can't and won't solve a problem that they don't recognize exists. The classic denial of self-evident facts is a common human trait, widely practiced in forums such as the United States Congress and in millions of personal relationships. So there should be no surprise that denial happens at least occasionally to almost every business manager. With the best managers, denial doesn't happen often or for very long – particularly when major risks are involved. In a sign of the natural human bias toward hearing good news, top management and entire organizations often hear what they want to hear and believe what they want to believe despite extensive evidence to the contrary. The American automobile companies denigrated their Japanese competitors for years while gradually losing share – and may be doing so again amid the burgeoning market for hybrids and other "green" cars.

Denial, as we intend the term, means the inability to accept, process and respond to levels of information that, in other circumstances, would be sufficient to ensure recognition of problems and spur corrective action. Acceptance of the brutal facts wins out when the weight of evidence finally overwhelms an individual's capacity for either blocking it or somehow pretending that less painful conclusions are the correct ones to be drawn. The difficulty is that, as long as denial persists, it is likely to preclude development of a corrective action plan, because identification of the crisis and the need for such a plan is being rejected. Too often, the reaction is to kill the bearer of bad news.

When management of a business can be convinced that a crisis actually exists that must be faced and that there are viable, albeit highly unpalatable, options and alternatives for action available, progress can begin to be made. The key is developing a specific plan of action that the knowledgeable, competent business manager can execute. The greater the crisis, the easier it is to overcome denial. Creation of a crisis, usually by third parties such as directors or lenders, is often the first step toward a solution.

Management denial and the related longer-term problem of "myopia" are the principal reasons for business failure. This applies both to the failure to address directly and correct operating problems until it is too late and to the related unfavorable effect on liquidity. In addition to destroying credibility with lenders, the bleeding of negative cash flow, if not stopped soon enough, may leave a company with no resources to invest in correcting problems or financing an exit strategy. This liquidation of asset values is not recoverable and only makes an operational turnaround more difficult. In addition, the continued focus on short-term results to solve liquidity crises at the expense of long-term opportunities may ultimately make an operational turnaround impossible.

A particular added danger of denial is misstatement of financial reports. There may be the bona fide belief that bad receivables will really be collected, obsolete inventories will really sell, or that next quarter's scheduled shipments, which were pulled ahead to improve current quarter results, can be made up. To think otherwise would confirm the facts of past misjudgments. Therefore, the necessary write-offs get pushed off into the future. At best this is wishful thinking or bad judgment; at worst it can be reasonably interpreted as fraudulent financial reporting. Developing some type of inoculation against denial would probably do a lot more for good corporate reporting than the Sarbanes-Oxley Act.

Andrew Grove's book *Only the Paranoid Survive*[4] is valuable fuel for anyone's thought process about overcoming denial. The focus is technology, where change is rapid, but Grove's points apply to all situations. Of particular pertinence to a troubled company situation is his point about listening to the Cassandras

---

[4] Andrew S. Grove, *Only the Paranoid Survive: How to Exploit the Crisis Points that Challenge Every Company and Career* (New York: Currency-Doubleday, 1996).

who bring things to management that they don't want to hear. These are the messengers that you really don't want to kill.

> ### Denial at WorldCom
>
> After stringing together a series of telecom acquisitions, WorldCom CEO Bernard Ebbers oversaw a $40 billion merger with MCI in 1998 that was the largest in history at that time. Four years later, Ebbers resigned and the company filed for the largest bankruptcy in U.S. history. Ebbers was later convicted on federal charges for orchestrating the biggest accounting fraud in corporate history and making false filings to the Securities and Exchange Commission.
>
> While WorldCom stock was rising in the 1990s, Ebbers was buying shares, using borrowed money and reportedly owning up to 27 million shares worth well over $1 billion. And when the stock price started to fall and created margin calls in his account, Ebbers didn't bail out of the stock while he still had positive net worth. Instead, he borrowed an additional $400 million from WorldCom so he could keep his shares, something the Sarbanes-Oxley Act would later outlaw.
>
> Among other things, this made Ebbers a good example of management in denial. Convinced that his ability to build a bigger and bigger company would pay off eventually, Ebbers traded an opportunity to retire as a billionaire for better odds he would wind up broke. Unwilling to accept the facts facing his industry, his company and his own finances, he did not change course, but waited for circumstances to adjust to his thinking. As a result, when WorldCom spiraled into bankruptcy amid a general collapse in telecom and Internet stocks, Ebbers saw the demise of his company, his stock portfolio and his personal freedom.

Arrogance leads to excessive risk-taking due to failure to consider alternative points of view or other input in making decisions. The hubris that leads an individual to think "I am too smart, lucky and good-looking to have anything bad happen to me" is most commonly found among management of successful growth businesses. Success sometimes feeds ambitions that become all-consuming.

Arrogance and its outsized ego-gratification needs often develop after a series of successes that may, in fact, be totally random. The result is a successful entrepreneur who adopts autocratic, one-man rule without the checks and balances of listening to advice from either second-level company management or external advisers. He continues to think that "drawing to hit another inside straight" is a rational business decision. The company is an Undisciplined Racehorse and becomes financially troubled when this highly successful business experiences growth-management difficulties and lacks the business structure and administrative controls to deal with them.

Replacing founder-CEOs is very difficult, because they will not go quietly and are particularly not interested in hearing an assessment that they have been lucky rather than good. If the problems of the business are internal, relating specifically to failure to manage growth, the CEO may be convinced to bring in external resources for a fix of the problem area and can be successfully retained. However, the turnaround of a company where a founder-CEO is still in control often requires a management change.

Arrogance as we define it includes mental laziness, lack of sensitivity to input from others and an excessive reliance on intuition for decision-making. In general, people with big egos find it hard to listen to others; if they don't listen, they can't understand what is really happening. The experienced business manager usually makes many good decisions based on the pattern recognition derived from experience, but it is highly important for major decisions that analysis and input from others be used to consider the best available facts. Arrogant management facing a complex problem that do not want to "get confused with a lot of facts" are likely to make bad decisions and certainly will not optimize solutions. The worst of it is that some decisions turn out to be "bet the company" issues.

Arrogance at Enron

As Enron grew from a simple Texas gas-pipeline company to a $100 billion corporation that owned power companies across the globe and traded up to a quarter of the gas and electricity in the United States, its management naturally seemed proud of its accomplishments. However, that pride came before a huge fall for founder Ken Lay and his successor as CEO, Jeffrey Skilling.

Simple Enron contracts for delivery of energy at a fixed price and time gave way to more complex formulas for hedging risk. Those led to internal trading books, in which Enron generated increasingly complex deals and bought and sold all sorts of other commodities and financial contracts. At the same time, the company refused to disclose its trading details and the amount of risk it undertook, arrogantly claiming that only Enron insiders understood its systems, markets and financials.

While the company's deals were exceedingly complex, not all of them were profitable. As losses began to mount, assets and debts were shifted to separate private partnerships that traded with Enron, as a way of getting them off Enron's books. The company reported a loss of $638 million for the third quarter of 2000 and within a month announced that it faced $6 billion of debt due within a year and would revise its financial statements for the past four years.

Yet even then, the arrogance remained. "People who raise questions are people who have not gone through [our business] in detail and who want to throw rocks at us," Skilling told *Fortune* in March 2001. By December, the company had filed for bankruptcy and Lay told *The Washington Post*, "I just want to say it was only a few people at Enron that were cocky." As of early 2006, several Enron executives had pleaded guilty to criminal charges, and the top executives were on trial.

While 16 Enron employees pleaded guilty to criminal charges, the company's top executives, Ken Lay (now deceased) and Jeffrey Skilling, protested their innocence all the way to the courthouse. In May 2006, they were convicted on multiple counts of fraud, conspiracy, and insider trading. Early comments attributed to Skilling - suggesting that Enron's financial transactions were just too complex for outsiders to understand - may have represented the absolute epitome of arrogance.

Greed leads to excessive risk-taking for short-term gain and, longer term, tends to destroy both internal and external relationships. Greed can be associated with both a desire for money and for power and ego satisfaction. This often leads to a focus on sales and growing the biggest possible business volume, rather than profit, return on investment and best returns for the least business risk. Excessive risk-taking may be controllable by a good board of directors. However, when greed is combined with a lack of integrity, as it often is, this can lead to the inaccurate reporting that requires a management replacement. In solving the problems of a financially troubled company, credibility with all stakeholders is a key to both operational and financial restructuring. Once lost, it is very difficult to regain.

Another aspect of management greed is the development of a trading mentality as a basis for business growth. Building market share and improving profitability based on internal resources becomes too slow a process. Therefore, growth through acquisition becomes the goal. Deal-making becomes the route to growth; it is fast-paced and may be quite profitable but tends to lead to a lack of discipline as rapid profit growth hypes the stock price. Deal-making often diverts management attention from the need to fix the core business. The acquisitions treadmill has to go faster and faster to keep ahead of expectations of the momentum investors.

Greed at Sunbeam

When Al Dunlap was hired in 1996 to turn around the troubled Sunbeam Corporation, the company's stock immediately jumped 49% on expectations that "Chainsaw Al," as this cost-cutter was known, would save the company by slashing expenses and jobs. The author of a book called *Mean Business*, Dunlap started his push for profits by shutting 12 of Sunbeam's 18 plants and eliminating almost half of the company's 12,000 employees. In 1997, he acquired Coleman, Signature USA and First Alert and announced another 6,400 job cuts. But less than two years after he was hired, Dunlap was fired.

Dunlap's critics said he cared only for short-term profits and had no plan for long-term growth. Although that strategy led to a run-up in the price of Sunbeam's stock during Dunlap's first year and helped him secure a three-year, $70 million employment contract, the company's sales numbers began to be questioned. Reports of heavily discounted products being shipped to retailers began to concern the company's board and after investigating Dunlap's actual performance, the directors decided he needed to go.

The Securities and Exchange Commission later investigated financial conduct at Sunbeam during Dunlap's tenure and found that improper accounting methods were used to inflate profits and sales. The SEC settled with Dunlap in 2002, permanently barring him from serving as officer or director of any public company and requiring him to pay a civil penalty of $500,000, in addition to $15 million he paid from his own funds to settle a related class action suit.

Complacency is characterized by a lack of urgency in tackling problems, making decisions and executing definitive solutions. This is the dithering of management that knows a problem exists, may well understand what needs to be done, but can't or won't execute the changes required to fix it.

Complacency is often found in a declining, bureaucratically oriented business, one of those we categorize as "Aging Mules." In this situation, past strengths of the business have been dissipated, but the organization stubbornly persists in refusing to acknowledge or address the decline. Management promotions are often based on relationships and seniority. In such circumstances, the CEO and other top management may have a very limited understanding of the competitive environment and problems in the marketplace. Expertise is likely to be largely functionally oriented, and the gradual decline in competitiveness has not been addressed. The company may not yet be financially troubled because it is living off the liquidation of resources from past successes. In such circumstances, it is unlikely that management has the motivation to drive a turnaround, let alone the expertise required for actual execution of changes required.

The inertia that underlies this complacency is illustrated in the frequently used example of the "boiled frog." You cannot cook a frog by dropping it in boiling water. The frog will jump right out. But if you put a frog in a pan of cool water and then gradually turn up the heat, the frog will stay put until it dies. All too frequently, unless confronted by a crisis, successful business management ignore slowly developing dangers and do not change in a timely manner. Eventually the ability to change may be lost and new management required.

Complacency at General Motors

The erosion of General Motors' market share in the United States didn't happen overnight. The dominant U.S. automaker, once the largest private employer in the world, spent years watching its share of domestic vehicle sales fall from a dominating 60 percent to less than 30 percent. In the 1970s, when customers wanted smaller, more efficient cars, management in Detroit refused to change G.M.'s strategy and allowed Japanese and European automakers to capture sales.

Clinging to the status quo came back to haunt the company. In the 1950s, after becoming the first American company to make $1 billion in a year, G.M. president Charles E. Wilson famously stated, "What's good for General Motors is good for the country." But failure to recognize changing needs and tastes in the country was reflected in a downward spiral in market share.

While it may have taken years and cost the company billions, the message seems to have gotten through. In fact, current chairman Rick Wagoner used the word "complacent" to conclude his 2003 annual report: "We know that the road ahead is still full of challenging twists, turns and surprises. We've driven through plenty of those already, and we've adapted and learned along the way. Now we're shifting into high gear – celebrating our successes on the run, never satisfied, never complacent, but always moving, always forward." As G.M. is faced with a multitude of both internal and external problems, including high-cost union contracts and legacy costs, the jury is still out on its future.

Lack of leadership overlaps with complacency to some extent, but our focus is the manager who will not or cannot execute a plan for improvement despite understanding the need for change. There is a lack of decisiveness in either choosing a path for the future or focusing resources on moving down that path. This lack of leadership may come from a fear of change due to the inherent uncertainties in deciding on a course of action or from an unwillingness to confront the specific difficulties inherent in bringing about change. In effect, management is not showing up and has become detached from taking responsibility for day-to-day business operations. Being a leader means offering solutions to problems; if no solutions are offered, the leader will have no followers.

Behaviors such as the following are usually an indication of lack of leadership:

1. Failure to replace subordinates whose poor performance is severely impacting company operations;
2. Excessive focus on non-strategic deal-making and financial maneuvers;
3. Failure to "mind the store" because of time devoted to charitable, civic, political or personal activities;
4. Displacement activities such as continuing to focus on performing the duties of a functional position previously held.

The result is that necessary change is not effected, while resources are wasted on continuing to pursue failed objectives of the past or those that are important only to the building of empires of functional managers. In the Aging Mule business, typified by this lack of leadership and procrastination, we see extensive use of committees for decision-making, expensive consulting contracts for strategic studies that gather dust after delivery and an abdication of responsibility for selecting and developing management talent.

Lack of Leadership at Morrison Knudsen

Sometimes expected leadership from new management never materializes. That's what Morrison Knudsen discovered when it hired William Agee as its CEO in 1987. The Boise, Idaho, construction company had been built on large successful projects like the Hoover Dam, the San Francisco Bay Bridge, and the Trans Alaska Pipeline. By the time Agee was fired in 1995, Morrison Knudsen was in bankruptcy.

Agee, who previously served as CFO at Boise Cascade and Bendix, was more interested in deal-making and accounting maneuvers than in the company's construction operations. Assets were sold to generate investment capital, with the intention of leveraging future earnings by aggressive bidding on large public transportation projects. Preoccupied with finances, Agee ignored management of the company's historical core competencies. By 1993, the company had lost talented construction management staff and operations were generating huge losses. In addition, Agee was criticized for focusing on his personal affairs rather than the company's future. He turned the company's boardroom into his personal office, worked often from his Pebble Beach home, made questionable personal use of a corporate jet, and placed his new wife (who had previously been installed as strategic planner of the business) in charge of the company's charitable foundation.

The Board of Directors' Role

A weak business may either fail quickly or rebound and thrive for years, depending upon whether good internal business processes and strong guidance and control by a board of directors can provide adequate backup for management and prevent major investment errors. Returning to our two defined tasks, we believe that the board's responsibility is to actively assist management in the establishment of strategy and direction (doing the right things) and to monitor and measure management's performance, holding them responsible for effective operational execution of that strategy (doing things right).

The board has responsibility for establishing strategy, rather than simply serving as a rubber stamp for management. A knowledgeable, objective board of directors should define business success and how it is to be measured. The truism that "you get what you measure and reward" can be harnessed by a good board to focus the organization on appropriate objectives. If the directors play an active role in evaluating strategy and providing operational oversight, the board can sometimes be very effective in reducing the impact of inertia and denial that can cause management to become stuck on the wrong path. The board can minimize and alleviate many problems at troubled companies by requiring the type of problem diagnosis advocated in this book and then participating actively in understanding the results and recommendations before taking actions relating to management replacement.

Sometimes highly capable, visionary leaders are doing the wrong things and simply will not change direction. In that case a management change will be required, but the information and understanding gained from the business evaluation should facilitate making an appropriate choice as replacement. However, if the right things to do can be identified and are accepted as the best path to the future, the current management may be quite capable of executing the changes required to achieve a turnaround. The keys are the ability to overcome denial and recognize the need to change strategy and priorities *and* a willingness to accept the required new direction, even when it may conflict with management's personal goals and self-image.

As a general observation, we believe that private equity firms with a financial incentive are more likely to hold management accountable and to provide appropriate guidance than the typical directors of a public company, without such personal investments at stake.

It's the Processes, Stupid!

Evaluation of management normally focuses almost exclusively on results compared with expectations – despite the fact that, as we've noted, there may be very limited logic to the setting of these expectations. In addition, as we've seen, actual results are often skewed by randomness, particularly over short periods. Superimposing these two factors on an obsession with quarterly results can lead to less than optimal long-term performance and poor short-term decision-making.

However, another factor is significant in understanding management performance: whether management are constantly improving business processes. Such processes are generally recognized in terms of productivity and cost reduction, but they also relate to increasing market share, improving product quality and expanding market applications served. The expenses of these business process improvements enhance long-term business viability and value, but typically are slow to be reflected in quarterly results and easy to cut back in order to meet earnings objectives.

Quality improvement was an area overlooked for years by most American businesses as a major goal. Acceptance of poor quality permeates a business organization with the wrong message. It leads to higher overall costs and the potential for a deteriorating market position when someone in the industry finally starts down the quality improvement track. Bad quality can even permeate an entire economy, as it did in the Soviet Union.

Although too difficult to measure for most external and many internal observers, improved business processes are crucial to long-term business success. Bad managers focus solely on business results as measured by reported earnings and not on management of the value-added processes that are the real key to long-term results.

Chapter Summary

Bad management is much less of a cause of business failure than is widely believed. Replacing management as the one-step solution to solving business problems is highly speculative and often not the best solution.

The greatest obstacle to success in dealing with a struggling business is an inability to recognize and respond to changing events. Success in dealing with a financially troubled company starts with identifying and accepting reality.

The key to sound management is organized problem-solving and a continuous re-evaluation and improvement process of:

- Knowledge
- Understanding
- Insight
- Leadership

Hindsight is always 20/20, but it is essential to remember that one or more major wrong decisions is not necessarily an indication of bad management. Even good management carrying successful strategies to excess can lead to business problems as the competitive environment changes.

Failure to achieve unrealistically high expectations is commonly viewed as bad management, but often has little to do with realities of a situation.

Among the most prominent management deficiencies are personal characteristics of denial, arrogance, greed, complacency and lack of leadership.

The prospects for long-term success are greatly improved when management focuses on improving business processes, not reported short-term financial results.

RECOMMENDED READING

Fooled by Randomness: The Hidden Role of Chance in Life and in the Markets, 2d edition (Thomson/Texere, 2004) by Nassim Nicholas Taleb.

Taleb has spent a long career as a mathematical trader specializing in the risks of unpredicted rare events. As it says on the book jacket, "Writing in an entertaining and narrative style, the author succeeds in tackling three major intellectual issues: the problem of induction, the survivorship biases and our genetic unfitness to the modern world."

In terms of diagnosing financially troubled companies, Taleb provides excellent observations and examples relating to the dangers of assuming that rationality and good leadership are normally the drivers of business success. Or, conversely, that the lack of same must be what caused business failure.

Moneyball: The Art of Winning an Unfair Game (W. W. Norton & Company, 2003) by Michael Lewis.

Starting with *Liar's Poker*, about Salomon Brothers, Michael Lewis has shown an extraordinary talent for describing the innermost working of a business. Although not related directly to business in the normal sense, *Moneyball* has some very interesting observations about getting the best baseball results for the least money while assuming the least risk of unproductive, high-cost investments.

The book examines the success of the Oakland Athletics and their general manager, Bill Beane, in fielding a successful baseball team with a low payroll. His secret was heavy use of statistics and a refusal to buy into a lot of conventional baseball wisdom. Beane's method was to focus on the process of improving the chances of winning the most games over a 162-game season. This is very different than focusing on specific outcomes, which are heavily skewed by randomness, be they quarterly results (before smoothing) or winning the World Series.

Harvard Business Review on Change (Harvard Business School Press, 1998.)

This book consists of eight articles originally published in the *Harvard Business Review,* all offering discussions of approaches to business change. From our perspective, the greatest value is in reminding anyone contemplating a business turnaround how difficult it is to accomplish even when adequate financial resources are available.

In our opinion, the most useful and insightful article in diagnosing future opportunities to effect change is by John P. Kotter, "Leading Change: Why Transformation Efforts Fail." The article details eight major errors that lead to failure.

Part II

MANAGING THE CRISIS

INTRODUCTION

One of the biggest obstacles to developing a disciplined evaluation and diagnosis in a troubled business situation is the sheer volume of crisis activities that scream out for attention. As someone lost in history once observed, "When you're up to your ass in alligators, it's hard to remember that your objective is to drain the swamp." Prioritization of issues is essential, and stabilizing the crisis must come first. In Part II, we address three topics that we believe are fundamental to the task of stabilizing the crisis:

- Pitfalls specific to operating in a financially stressed or insolvent condition that must be considered in order to avoid making the situation worse;
- Liquidity issues and cash-flow management requirements;
- Evaluation of the many and conflicting agendas that typically exist among the various stakeholders in a troubled business and must be addressed.

The crisis must be managed for there to be longer-term potential for maximizing the value of the business entity. How the value of this business pie gets split among the stakeholders is not the first concern. The first concern is *making sure there is a pie to divide.*

Chapter 5

FIRST DO NO HARM:
Legal, Operational, and Political Pitfalls

The only thing worse than a meltdown that results in a zero recovery is a meltdown that triggers incremental contingent liabilities and results in claims or litigation that extend beyond the assets of the estate. One key reason why troubled businesses (as well as investors in, and lenders to, troubled businesses) need to seek experienced legal and professional advice is that there are a variety of ways in which the actions of management, the board, the lenders or professional advisors can destroy existing protections or create new liabilities.

As the realization hits that an investment is failing, the urge is to try to hit a home run, obtain an advantage in a difficult environment or simply survive for one more day in the hope of getting luckier tomorrow. This urge can tempt parties down dangerous paths marked by often unforeseen hazards. We are not here raising the issue of fraudulent behavior, but rather of the potential to inflict harm inadvertently, either as a result of ill-considered precipitous action or the failure to understand fully the rules that apply to a business facing insolvency.

As a company struggles, fiduciary responsibilities shift and adversarial relationships develop, creating a minefield of potential claims and liabilities. Errors and missteps will be subjected to review with the clarity of hindsight and, in many cases, through a lens wielded and focused by damaged parties evaluating litigious options. It is a time for caution.

The dangers of inadvertently doing harm come in three classifications:

Legal: In our litigious society, business enterprises are subject to a variety of laws and governmental regulations that define a company's rights and obligations, as well as the rights of others. Unless great care is exercised in advance, the intricacies and pitfalls of those laws and regulations may become the basis for challenges and litigation instigated by claimants long after the events occurred.

Operational: Exposure to serious operational errors can involve taking actions that destroy value by making the situation worse, or *not* taking action and allowing a deterioration of value to the detriment of creditors or shareholders. When a company is operating in a troubled situation, care needs to be taken not only in the exercise of operational choices but in the documentation of the analytical and decision-making process used to evaluate and initiate those actions.

Political: For lack of a better word, we define certain dangers as political. These involve either triggering, or failing to anticipate and manage, foreseeable damaging acts and responses from third parties. These dangers overlap in part with legal and operational errors, but in our mind are notably distinct in that the damage itself comes from third-party actions in response to tone-deaf or bull-in-the-china-shop behavior. The triggering behavior usually arises from failure to understand or show respect for the relative rights, interests and leverage of other parties. These dangers typically entail misguided communications that lead others into making incorrect decisions or acting in such an aggressive, insensitive or unfair manner that future ability to negotiate rational decisions among various stakeholders is compromised.

To reiterate a basic premise of this book: Always address and document as much of the fact-finding and diagnosis process as possible before initiating actions that have the potential to do harm. Let's look at each of these areas in turn:

Legal Issues

Insolvency Law: The scope and objectives of this book do not allow for, nor are we qualified to provide, a full discussion of the considerations and implications of state debtor/creditor laws or federal bankruptcy law in relation to financially distressed companies. Nevertheless, no discussion or analysis of the options and alternatives available to a financially troubled company is complete without providing at least a cursory examination and understanding of the role and process of the bankruptcy court.

Bankruptcy is, first and foremost, an adversarial legal process. It is a tool, available under varying circumstances to either or both debtors and creditors, that provides a controlled process and highly organized set of rules and principles for dealing with the resolution of competing rights relating to a distressed company and its assets.

A bankruptcy proceeding can be initiated either voluntarily by the debtor or involuntarily by its creditors. In simplistic terms, business bankruptcy comes in two flavors, two alternative sections of the federal legal code under which a bankruptcy filing can be initiated, Chapter 7, Liquidation, and Chapter 11, Reorganization.

In a Chapter 7 proceeding, the debtor is removed from control of the business and a trustee is appointed and charged with liquidating the assets and distributing the proceeds to the company's creditors in accordance with their statutory priorities. Typically, a Chapter 7 filing will be involuntarily initiated by the creditors specifically for the purpose of removing the debtor from control. Voluntary Chapter 7 filings by the debtor occur infrequently and are essentially an acknowledgment of complete failure, of "throwing in the towel." Chapter 7 filings are of little practical use to the debtor (or to consultants) in crafting solutions for problems or in maximizing value. But moving to force an orderly liquidation by initiating an involuntary bankruptcy filing can be the only real leverage that creditors have in a situation where they believe the value of the assets is being dissipated or they believe their rights are being ignored or compromised. In situations where unsecured creditors appear to be "out of the money" (i.e., where the value of the business is less than the value of secured claims), the threat to force a liquidation by initiating, or converting the case into, a Chapter 7 proceeding may be used as an aggressive strategy with which to seek some "compensation for their cooperation." It is a threat or option that cannot be ignored.

The more pertinent and useful section of the bankruptcy code is, for our purposes, Chapter 11. A filing that takes place under Chapter 11 is generally described as "the debtor seeking the protection of the court." Occasionally, creditors may seek to have the court appoint a trustee within a Chapter 11 proceeding, but more typically the debtor retains control of its estate, subject to the rules, guidance and oversight of the court. The basic concept of a Chapter 11 proceeding is to provide an orderly process whereby the debtor is given the opportunity to maximize its value and resolve its obligations and its creditors are given certain protections aimed at ensuring they receive fair treatment, consistent with their contractual and statutory rights. The end-product of a Chapter 11 proceeding is intended to be a "Plan of Reorganization" for the business. It is sometimes described as "rehabilitation of the debtor," intended to "allow the debtor to use future earnings to pay off creditors."

In theory, a bright and shiny line is drawn upon the bankruptcy petition date, following which the debtor loses its right to act independently and becomes a "Debtor-in-Possession," meaning that, from that date forward, the debtor is operating subject to specific rules and oversight of the court. This includes extensive factual disclosures, regular and detailed operational reporting, and the appointment of an official creditors' committee. Pre-petition litigation, judgments, and enforcement actions are stayed and the bankruptcy court is established as the sole forum through which pre-petition creditors can seek to enforce their rights and claims. But the fact that Chapter 11 is defined as a reorganization process intended to facilitate the rehabilitation of the debtor does not ensure that the debtor will emerge from bankruptcy with its operations intact. If a business has reasonable and reliable operating earnings but is overburdened with debt, a bankruptcy filing may facilitate a financial restructuring, particularly if the company has elicited the support of its key constituencies in advance of the filing. However, a bankruptcy proceeding is a very expensive and disruptive process, and will, almost without exception, have adverse consequences for business operations. In many cases, particularly if the filing is precipitated without adequate preparation, the primary benefit of a Chapter 11 filing may be simply that it allows time for the company to orchestrate an orderly business sale in a situation that otherwise might have degenerated into a liquidation of the assets.

Bankruptcy may or may not be useful in effecting a specific strategy. In our opinion and experience (to be discussed more fully in chapter 12) bankruptcy is a much more effective tool for managing liabilities and resolving claims than it is for maximizing value. There are, of course, situations in which the continuing exposure to liabilities and legal challenges is so severe that it becomes imprudent for a company not to promptly seek the protections available from and provided by the court process. However, a rush into a bankruptcy filing without adequate preparation should be avoided whenever possible. Many, perhaps most, of the objectives leading to a reorganized, standalone operating entity that might be sought within a bankruptcy proceeding can be more effectively implemented if they can be achieved through consensual negotiations outside of the court process or, at least, "pre-packaged," with key terms and the support of major constituents being substantially negotiated in advance of filing.

In any situation in which the company is either facing a precipitous interruption of its operations, or a prospective liquidation or sale of the company is threatened in which the likely proceeds are anticipated to leave the company insolvent and unable to satisfy its creditors, bankruptcy counsel should be consulted promptly. The bankruptcy code is very complex and fact-specific, and both experienced advisors and competent bankruptcy counsel should be consulted to advise upon the risks and protections that a bankruptcy filing offers in any seriously troubled situation.

AUTHORS' CASEBOOK: Protecting Business Viability

A European electronics equipment manufacturer acquired a larger publicly held U.S. manufacturer of various industrial electronics products in a highly leveraged transaction. Although it was expected that the U.S. management team would continue to manage the combined entity, several key executives resigned within a short time. There was little integration of the acquired business and expected cost-reduction synergies did not develop. Due to inability to meet debt service requirements, no further funding under the company's working capital financing line was available. A Chapter 11 bankruptcy filing was anticipated within days.

Evaluation of the situation led to the conclusion that, due to clearly defined production difficulties, the company would not survive to reorganize if there were an immediate Chapter 11 filing. The company's principal operational difficulties were due to inventories that were totally out of balance, with many long lead-time, single-source components out of stock. Inability to obtain delivery of only a few such components would shut down production with a likely loss of business from several major customers.

Critical Challenge: Convincing secured lenders that unless unsecured trade creditors were protected, the business could collapse.

After reviewing analysis details, company management and its working capital lenders were convinced of the need for better advance planning for a Chapter 11 filing and additional working capital advances were negotiated. An interim chief operating officer under direction of co-author Steve Hopkins became responsible for all manufacturing and logistics functions. Improved cash management and forecasting systems were installed to control disbursements, provide appropriate reporting to lenders and maintain the ongoing business while component inventories were analyzed and balanced.

In addition, plans were developed and implemented for major operational improvements that were incorporated into business plans used for DIP financing agreements. The Chapter 11 filing required to restructure debt occurred three months after the start of the project. Based on stabilized operations, post-petition agreements with vendors required to ensure continued production were negotiated. New capital was infused by creditors that assumed equity control under a Plan of Reorganization approved four months after filing the Chapter 11.

Deepening Insolvency: It is fairly easy to understand the concept that a company cannot solicit or accept goods and services for which it has no ability or intention to pay. When a company becomes insolvent, the fiduciary responsibilities of management and the board of directors, heretofore pledged to the shareholders, shift and expand to include the interests of the multiple other constituents of the company, including creditors, both secured and unsecured, and employees. If asset values are eroded because of continued operating losses or if actions are taken that exacerbate losses or damages to creditors, employees or other third parties, the officers and the directors of the company may be held responsible.

The question, of course, is, "When does a company become insolvent?" Unfortunately, no bright, shiny line lies there, waiting to be crossed. Lawyers will debate for hours the various indications that a company has entered the ill-defined Zone of Insolvency, but a specific determination unfortunately comes only in retrospect, usually after adversarial argument.

In the hindsight analysis of a creditors' committee and trustees, theories can be constructed and offered as to what should have been known and what actions should have been taken. If management moved too soon, shareholders will line up to file claims. If management waited until it was too late or acted carelessly or too aggressively in pursuing high-risk strategies, the creditors will be clamoring.

So, as we've said, take great care not just to act properly but to document the basis and reasonability of the decision-making process.

Equitable Subordination: The typical company's capital structure may have several tiers of debt or investment, some with secured interests in all or part of the company's assets. Equitable subordination refers to the potential for unwinding those security interests. To the extent that wrongful actions have been initiated in a manner that would benefit the secured parties to the detriment of the unsecured or general creditors, a challenge to the secured interests can be initiated. If proven, claims can be retroactively adjudicated to be "equitably subordinate."

We have found two typical circumstances in which such equitable subordination claims can be successfully pursued:

1.   When a senior creditor exerts undo influence over a debtor's business operations, to the detriment of unsecured creditors' recoveries;
2.   When a lender in an arguably insolvent entity infuses new secured debt that leaches out value that might otherwise have been available to pre-existing unsecured creditors.

Again, these challenges result in a retrospective legal review that, if it goes against the secured creditor, can result in the loss of its secured status. For this reason and others, secured creditors seeking to exercise their rights often prefer a Chapter 11 filing where the bankruptcy court is approving and providing oversight of significant operational actions by management and where new loans advanced to the Debtor in Possession are similarly subject to advance approval by the court, as well as to senior liens and super-priority claims.

The equitable subordination danger to secured creditors can result from actions to manage a company's operations either through direct orders or by retaining a turnaround management consultant who issues such orders to company personnel. For this reason, interim management of a troubled company must be engaged by the borrower, not the secured lender, and both the lender's advisors and its direct agents and employees must be extremely careful about the nature and form of "advice" provided to the company about its operations.

Preferential payments: The bankruptcy laws are expressly intended to provide protection to the debtor and offer a chance to organize an orderly resolution or restructuring of its affairs, as well as ensuring that the creditors receive fair and equitable treatment according to their respective rights and interests. Provisions of the Bankruptcy Code attempt to extend equitable protection to the period immediately prior to a bankruptcy filing. An extensive body of law governs the protection of creditors that might be disadvantaged by payments to others outside the normal course of business. Conceptually, this means that unless goods or services representing new value are received contemporaneously with the payments, unsecured creditors should have their receivables reduced proportionately in the days prior to a bankruptcy filing. The company cannot arbitrarily allocate its resources and disbursements, selectively reducing the damage borne by some creditors while increasing the exposure of others. Payments outside the ordinary course to creditors during the "preference" period can be reclaimed for the benefit of the other creditors. The general preference period for unsecured creditors is 90 days. With regard to insiders, the period for which payments can be reclaimed is 12 months.

Fraudulent conveyance: It is illegal to transfer company assets to another business entity, particularly one controlled by insiders or selected creditors, in an effort to shield the proceeds from the company's creditors. A potentially insolvent company cannot sell assets without incurring potential risk that the transaction can be reversed, particularly if the value of the transaction is depressed by the company's financial situation and its need to raise cash quickly. Because of this threat that a transaction could be unwound, in many cases a potential buyer of distressed assets will demand that the transaction be effected with protection of the court after a bankruptcy filing.

The **Sarbanes-Oxley Act of 2002** imposed requirements for financial reporting that can be difficult and costly for a financially troubled company that is publicly held. A new CEO or turnaround management consultant who takes actions with the best of intentions to reduce expenses in a way that results in a failure to comply with Sarbanes-Oxley does so at his peril. Similarly, an existing management that overvalues assets, whether by misplaced optimism or overtly pushing the envelope in its analysis, faces significant liability exposure. (As an aside, allow us to assert that the combination of a large supply of private equity available to purchase companies and the high cost of compliance with Sarbanes-Oxley and other regulations is likely to result in a significant decline in the number of public companies in the United States over the next few years. This might increase economic productivity, because long-term investors provide better oversight than government organizations whose focus often seems to be protecting short-term speculators.)

Outstanding litigation and contingent claims: Whether involving government agencies or private parties, such actions must be taken seriously and addressed appropriately; even if management view them as frivolous and a drain on resources. Usually, the most appropriate approach for a troubled company is delay and deferral, attempting to limit expenditures while not increasing potential exposure by letting critical defenses drop.

Contracts and commitments: These represent future performance guarantees, and they must be identified and understood in terms of the ramifications of failure to meet obligations. Particularly where ordinary-course contract negotiations and renewals are taking place as the company approaches insolvency, care must be taken not to misrepresent the company's financial situation or to provide inappropriate inducements that later might be viewed as actionable, or even fraudulent.

Operational Issues

In the context of this chapter, two key risks exist:

- Failure to act
- Acting wrongly because of inadequate information and analysis

Operational changes may hold the potential to improve a company's situation, and the status quo should not be regarded as an option. However, the unintended consequences of precipitous action present the risk both of deteriorating performance and of subsequent criticism and attack. Acting without adequate facts can sometimes do irreparable harm, but delaying action until all facts are known is usually not practical.

The best approach may be to act as quickly as possible on relatively unimportant matters, to set a tone of decisiveness, and to proceed cautiously on major issues until a decision can be justified on something other than past experience in different circumstances.

Among the most challenging crisis decisions is that of management and control, as we noted in the previous chapter. Obviously, certain circumstances – such as a precipitous resignation or when management's actions are determined to have been fraudulent or obstructive – demand a rapid and complete change in control. But beyond such extreme cases, a trade-off exists between continuity and the value of information and relationships, on the one hand, and the financial and operational costs of maintaining that continuity. This is true even where a change of management may ultimately be required. As we've said frequently – and will continue to assert throughout this book – significant benefits can be realized in engaging existing management in the critical evaluation and diagnosis process that must be the first key step in any turnaround. The diagnosis-and-evaluation process should clarify the risks or benefits of changing management, as well as making it easier to identify and evaluate the appropriate qualifications of a suitable replacement.

As we discuss in detail in Chapter 9, operational evaluations should be completed before making major decisions, and we have found that inadequate management reporting systems often provide very misleading results – even if total business profitability and asset values are being reported properly. Guard particularly against over-optimism in initial assessments and conclusions, because in a troubled company, things are often worse than they appear, and the causes are not usually as obvious as they first seem. It is unwise to start expending a lot of effort treating symptoms without understanding their root causes. For example, analyses may determine that new, disruptive technology in the marketplace is causing a shift to a less-profitable product mix, or that minor changes in internal factory processes or material used is having major effects on product quality.

Political Issues

In the sense that we use the term here, political issues refer to the desirability of treating all stakeholders fairly in a troubled situation. The temptation may be great to achieve quick results by exerting power against the perceived weakest constituencies. Sometimes this works, and sometimes it leads to a disaster of unintended consequences.

Key suppliers can stop production of sole-source, long-lead-time parts, labor unions can stop or interfere with production, terminated employees can depart with essential knowledge, reduced customer service from engineering personnel can lead to the loss of key contracts. If the new guy on the block has a big ego and a lack of sensitivity to the legitimate rights and needs of others, a host of bad things can happen. While risks must be run if a turnaround is to be achieved or even contemplated, big political risks should not be taken for small rewards.

Effective communications to all the company's constituencies may help deter future claims and disputes. To the extent practical, facts should be fully disclosed to all interested parties – and particular care should be taken to ensure that disclosures are not selectively released, and are accurate and even-handed:

- All public filing disclosures should be made in as complete a manner as possible;
- Potential conflicts of interest should be fully disclosed;
- Over-optimistic projections about future results should be avoided;
- Information released should be assumed to be public. Never give different parties different answers to the same question.

Improper attention to any of these areas can sometimes lead to what is perceived as failure.

AUTHORS' CASEBOOK: Oops! Did I Say Too Much?

In 1997, co-author Steve Hopkins was one of three people whose names were provided to the board of directors of Centennial Technology as a potential replacement after Centennial's CEO was jailed following accusations of financial manipulation.

After spending a half-day reviewing Centennial's public financial statements, Steve advised the board that he believed that the problems appeared to run far deeper than had yet been acknowledged and hypothesized that the company might never have had any real profits in the 2½ years since it went public. The board retained interim management which expressed a more optimistic view of the situation.

Critical Challenge: Exercising care with communications when the information is incomplete.

Promptly after he was retained, the new Interim CEO was publicly quoted as saying the company faces an "easy turnaround," triggering a 300%, 10¼ point run-up in the stock price before trading was halted. Before trading resumed three days later, the company announced that it would restate its earnings for the prior four years – wiping out all reported earnings during the period. The stock plunged 11¼ points.

The extensive litigation that followed now included charges emanating from after the change in management control as well as before.

Chapter Summary

The dangers of inadvertently doing harm fall into three categories: legal, operational and political. The legal dangers can increase liabilities both contingent and real, and often emerge after the fact, as supposedly aggrieved parties benefit from hindsight. Operational dangers can involve failing to act or taking actions that make the situation worse or prolong the duration of losses. Political dangers arise from not fully understanding or acknowledging the needs and points of views of various stakeholders. To protect against these dangers, we strongly advise our clients to obtain and rely on qualified legal and professional advisors, complete the organized diagnosis process before taking irrevocable actions, and document the factual evaluations and basis of their decision-making process.

Chapter 6

LIQUIDITY FIRST
Try Not to Bounce the Payroll Checks

One major difficulty in doing a proper diagnosis of a troubled company's problems is management's lack of time and focus. Anyone with responsibility either for directly managing the business or assisting management in the role of a consultant becomes consumed with "fighting the alligators in the swamp you are trying to drain." Few things are more disruptive to a business than having employees go out on their lunch hour and discover that the bank won't honor their paychecks. If for no other reason than because some of them won't come back from lunch.

For a financially troubled company, the immediate cash-flow situation must be the first and highest priority. Among the cash-flow problems that arise are:

- Lack of cash to make the next payroll
- Loss of control over cash management and payment priorities
- Shipments "on hold" as vendors refuse to honor purchase orders
- Inability to negotiate competitive material pricing with vendors
- Management and employee defections
- Lack of funds for capital expenditures and product development
- Competitors point out the company's financial problems to customers
- Excessive receivable deductions by retailers to protect against future returns
- Difficulty in negotiating long-term customer contracts
- Threatened cancellations of insurance coverages

A review of cash flow and financing must rapidly determine how bad the liquidity crisis is and what opportunities are available to reverse the trend. A reversal may not prove possible, but at the very least the review can provide warning to all interested parties. Nothing is more embarrassing (and destructive to everyone's credibility) than to have a consultant spend two days conducting detailed interviews, listening to senior management describe its strategic challenges, only to learn at 7 A.M. on Day 3 that the company issued $5 million in disbursements the day before without advising lenders that it had initiated a $3.5 million unapproved over-advance.

In order even to attempt to control a looming liquidity crisis, it is critical to obtain a firm grasp on near-term cash-flow projections, borrowing base and availability restrictions, and loan administration issues. Once the broader situation has been diagnosed and evaluated and the external constituents adequately educated about the company's circumstances, it may be possible to justify and obtain incremental support and relief. But, at the onset, when everybody is operating in the dark, the company typically has to live on its internal resources. Thus, if a liquidity crisis is looming, early-stage priorities often focus upon the potential for generating additional cash from such internal sources as excess inventories or receivables.

The options may well vary. Unpledged assets may be available or the borrowing base formula may undervalue some assets. If the liquidity situation is very tight and little or no borrowing availability exists, the alternative of a bankruptcy filing and debtor-in-possession financing must be contemplated. Be warned that this evaluation may result in a conclusion that the company is not likely to survive the bankruptcy process.

Liquidity Crisis

The term "liquidity crisis" is often used in discussions of financially troubled businesses. In common usage, it refers to situations where a company cannot meet its payment commitments in the normal course of business, usually because of negative cash flow from operations. The company may or may not be technically insolvent from a legal standpoint. The situation is often compounded by some combination of:

- Short-term borrowing that has been used to finance investment in long-term assets;
- Significant long-term borrowing that will become due in the near term without a clear path to refinancing;
- Situations in which rapid revenue growth requires rapid increases in inventory and receivables, but the company doesn't have enough liquidity to cover the deficit from working capital advance rates;
- Short-term cyclical or seasonal borrowing requirements that exceed debt capacity.

Many hidden legal traps and contingent-liability issues lurk among these issues, and they may have the potential to disrupt totally any turnaround plans. As part of the liquidity crisis analysis, a logical, disciplined approach to identifying these issues is very much needed.

We have found the most comprehensive, well-organized source of checklists for such an evaluation is *The Business Workouts Manual – The Practitioner's Guide*[5], edited by Donald Lee Rome. Its chapter on "The Debtor in the Workout" offers 63 checklists for evaluating the financial condition of a troubled company. These checklists include overview questions about many operational issues, extensive lists of potential liabilities and litigation expenses, and 12 checklists relating to preparations for a bankruptcy filing, should it become necessary.

Cash-Driven Management

Even when a company is facing a cash crisis, most CEOs do not become sufficiently involved in understanding cash flow. They often continue to focus on managing reported earnings results right into bankruptcy court. The CFO or Treasurer is expected to worry about what actions are necessary to keep from running out of cash. But without CEO involvement, disbursement priorities often become established by political power within the organization rather than by true business necessity.

When a CEO is forced to review cash receipts and disbursement forecasts in detail and to understand what negative borrowing availability means, good things usually begin to happen. The old saying "income is an estimate, cash is a fact" begins to hit home. More realistic priorities are established, secondary cash needs are deferred, and cash flow begins to turn positive. If no cash is available, unpalatable decisions are made and sometimes the bankruptcy court is avoided.

The key to making this happen is a realistic, fully detailed cash-flow forecast. But as this critically important analysis is under way, the preliminary evaluation of business viability discussed previously must be done *simultaneously*. This helps determine whether:

1. Opportunities are available to achieve a standalone turnaround;
2. Certain product lines or other assets should be sold;
3. The entire business should be sold;
4. Liquidation is the only logical option for best preserving whatever asset values exist.

---

[5]Donald Lee Rome, *The Business Workouts Manual – The Practitioner's Guide*, 2nd ed. (Boston: Warren, Gorham & Lamont, 1992).

Accounting systems used in all sizable companies provide information on an accrual accounting basis. But the key to good management control in a tight liquidity situation is getting back to the tried-and-true, easily understandable, cash-is-king method of looking at things. Operations can be better managed by removing the accounting underbrush of accruals and cost allocations to focus on managing actual cash receipts and disbursements in a way that keeps cash flow positive. (See Appendix A, *Better Management Through Control of Cash*, which details the reasons that weekly cash flow forecasting in a receipts and disbursements format is essential for a troubled company.)

We advocate a rolling 13-week cash-flow forecasting system that:

- Centralizes control over cash as a basis for setting priorities;
- Clearly defines forecasting responsibilities;
- Establishes the source and extent of negative cash flow;
- Carefully monitors associated changes in current assets, liabilities, loan balances and collateral;
- Sets disbursements priorities to "stop the bleeding";
- Improves credibility with lenders by establishing and achieving realistic forecasts;
- Educates both creditors and management about reasons for cash needs.

Inherent in the process are variance analyses to compare actual with forecast. This is an extremely useful management education tool and is required to develop accurate forecasting processes. Two questions need to be asked in analyzing each significant variance:

- What should I have known that I didn't when I made the forecast?
- What has changed that causes the variance?

Our approach to cash-flow control in many ways resembles the simplified production control systems that many manufacturers have installed in recent years. One underlying principle, as detailed in *Lean Thinking*[6] by James P. Womack and Daniel T. Jones, is that control is best achieved by making key information readily and regularly available to all employees who can affect the improvement process.

Our approach is targeted specifically to cash-flow control. It is not driven from a multipurpose accounting system, which typically is ineffective for real control of cash flow because of accounting complexities and which lacks adequate

---

[6] James P. Womack and Daniel T. Jones, *Lean Thinking: Banish Waste and Create Wealth in Your Corporation* (New York: Simon & Schuster, 1996).

focus on cash receipts and disbursements. If no cash-flow projection system is in place in a financially troubled company, it must be started at once, even if the initial period covered is only two to four weeks. If the total picture cannot be seen, the squeakiest wheel will get the grease – and that may be absolutely the wrong priority.

A clearly defined understanding of cash flow is essential for establishing credibility in negotiations with lenders relating to the potential for future debt service, either in bankruptcy or as an ongoing business. Credibility about cash needs is one of the most critical but least understood requirements of the financially troubled company process. Lenders tend to be bureaucratic institutions with several levels of approvals required. Surprises and new "bites at the apple" – additional cash needs – are not appreciated.

The overall objective is a total company cash-flow summary at the level where total borrowing is managed. But summaries should be prepared at the business unit level, so the cash-flow winners and losers can be seen clearly and business priorities can be set.

One would think that the results of the cash-flow analysis by business unit would be consistent with information developed during the analysis of where the company is making and losing money. But sometimes major surprises develop, particularly when a profitable growth business is a major consumer of cash to fund such items as large working capital increases, facilities investments, capitalizable software development, store-opening expenses or a major promotional campaign.

Although we like cash flow to be discussed in terms of a rolling 13-week forecast, to the extent that a business is seasonal or has significant longer-term investment needs, the forecast must be carried out for more extended periods on a monthly basis. But *always* the first priority is understanding the extent of the near-term crisis. As a starting point, if the only realistic forecast covers a two- to six week period, work with that until it can be improved. In extreme crisis situations, daily cash forecasts for the next 10 days or so may be essential.

AUTHORS' CASEBOOK: Squeezing Out the Excess Assets

A family-owned Mexican manufacturer of metal cans and other containers with multiple plant locations was experiencing a severe liquidity crisis as it attempted to meet debt service requirements. The company's mature markets were suffering from a downturn in general economic conditions and competition from lower-cost alternative packaging approaches was increasing. Although the company was a market leader, had operated successfully for many years and had valuable real estate, it was highly leveraged due to heavy capital expenditures to serve changing markets and achieve state-of-the-art quality. Crisis managers were retained by the company's owner to develop an improved cash-flow management system, assist with working capital reductions and provide organizational guidance to third-generation management.

Critical Challenge: Release excess assets employed in the business in order to reduce debt and improve return on investment.

Actions taken included:

- Installing a series of rolling 13-week cash-flow forecasts by business segment that became a management responsibility of each business;
- Analyzing receivables in detail to provide a basis for improved collection efforts;
- Developing improved inventory management and purchasing controls;
- Analyzing where the company was making and losing money by product line, with a particular focus on allocating charges for working capital investments.

Based on profitability and working capital requirements by business, a series of priorities was developed related to price increases, exit from certain product lines, reduced inventory stocking, restriction of receivable terms, and commitments to suppliers. In addition, numerous business-process improvements in receivables collection, inventory control and cash management were implemented by the company.

The major working capital reductions that were achieved provided funds to reduce debt and cover ongoing debt service. Subsequently debt was reduced significantly by asset sales, and the company continued as a leader in its industry, earning a reasonable return on assets employed.

Receivables Management

Growth businesses with weak administrative controls frequently end up with major receivables problems (Appendix A provides guidance on setting up trend reports to understand what is happening to receivables balances and related agings). For some reason, many growth-oriented CEOs have a blind spot when it comes to receivables control.

It is difficult work to control receivables. It can alienate customers, and often old balances represent disputes, not weak credit, so the problem is ignored if collections personnel have no authority to settle the disputes. For two key reasons, the problem diagnosis process should aggressively focus on excessive receivables:

1. Harvesting the excessive investment can have a major impact on cash flow and sometimes even solve the immediate liquidity crisis.
2. Uncollectible receivables detail is a treasure trove of information about what is wrong with the company's business processes – issues that must be addressed to improve the company's operating results.

Among the issues we have found in analyzing receivables are:

- Poor collection routines
- Progress collection documentation issues
- Credits due for excessive product returns

- Uncontrolled advertising allowances
- Incorrect invoicing routines related to pricing or documentation
- Undisclosed extended terms or consignment shipments
- Late shipments or failure to follow shipping instructions

Fixing receivable-related problems can sometimes be the key to a turnaround of a basically viable business. So determining whether this area is a major problem must be done as quickly as possible. If a problem is found, secure the internal or external resources needed to fix it. No area produces a higher and quicker payoff, and these changes can be undertaken independent of other actions.

> **AUTHORS' CASEBOOK: Fixing Broken Receivables Processes**
>
> A provider of home nutritional services was acquired by its publicly held parent company as a small, rapidly growing entrepreneurial business. However, continued rapid sales growth had not translated into growth in operating earnings, due to large and erratic requirements for receivable write-offs. Health insurance companies paid slowly and frequently discounted claims. As a result, the company was experiencing severe cash-flow problems and uncertain earnings. This resulted in loss of credibility of the founders, major disputes over payments due under earn-out provisions of the acquisition agreement and serious consideration by the parent company's board of directors of liquidating the business.
>
> Evaluation of the situation led to the conclusion that the business had an attractive future in a rapidly growing market if information systems and business processes related to billing and receivables management could be brought under control.
>
> **Critical Challenge:** Upgrading the billing, receivable and accounting functions in order to maximize collections and accurately report earnings. Services to patients were being performed effectively and professional staff was highly competent, leading to high revenue growth rates. However, the medical doctor managing the business had ignored the need for growth in capacity and professionalism of administrative functions.
>
> Interim financial management assistance was provided to develop and install new computer systems; the credit and collections function was strengthened by additions of both personnel and management; and appropriate, conservative procedures were developed for detailed evaluation and realistic adjustment of receivable reserves on a monthly basis.
>
> As financial reporting became credible, a settlement of the final acquisition price with the company's founders was negotiated. They continued to manage the company while it regained stability and continued its rapid sales growth at profitable levels. The business was subsequently spun off to shareholders of the parent as a standalone publicly owned company with a highly attractive market value.

Borrowing Capacity Deterioration

Debt of businesses with strong balance sheets is usually unsecured, or, if secured, does not require borrowing base reporting. As a company's financial strength deteriorates and it becomes more overleveraged both in terms of debt-to-equity ratio and of interest coverage tests, loan agreement covenants will trigger defaults. This gives lenders the opportunity to require security, renegotiate interest rates and impose additional restrictions on the company, including limiting loan availability under a borrowing base formula.

The first renegotiation of loan terms should be perceived by management as a strong message that the future course of events has to change dramatically. Yet we have found that, in many cases, management remains in denial and thinks the future will bring brighter days as this minor, temporary problem goes away. Many times, management deliberately obscures the visibility of the problem, restricting knowledge of the "bump in the road" to a few select personnel in the finance area. Rarely is outside professional assistance retained this early in the process or meaningful adjustments made that will improve company operations.

Unfortunately, for many companies the problems do not go away and the lenders take tougher stands trying to maintain or enhance their loan-to-value ratios. Their objective is to keep loans off the "classified" status when reserves will have to be set aside, resulting in charges to the lender's earnings. As interest coverage ratios drop, more pressure will be exerted. In some cases, usually those of cyclical businesses in which the market turns more favorable or those where serious internal problems are resolved, profitability returns, the long-term picture brightens and the business disappears from the lender's problem-loan portfolio.

In many situations, however, the problems are not fixed and begin to feed on each other. The downward spiral of operating profits begins, which can lead to a cash crisis and the bankruptcy court. Clearly, at some point in this process, and the sooner the better, the problem diagnosis that is at the heart of this book must be started. In every situation in which we have become involved, that process started later than it should have. Started early enough and acted upon appropriately, the company would avoid entry into our troubled company universe.

Borrowing Base Availability

The concept of borrowing base availability is of pre-eminent importance in any discussion of the status of a financially troubled company.

All asset-based loans and many other secured loans will have started with a regular, at least monthly, reporting of a company's borrowing base. Typically, the borrowing base consists of a company's eligible receivables and inventories. Eligible means that various categories of low potential value balances are excluded, *e.g.*, receivables past due over 60 days, or those due from foreign entities, or excess or obsolete inventories. Borrowing advance rates against these eligible assets usually run 75% to 85% for receivables and 25% to 60% for inventories, depending on liquidation potential. For some readily tradable commodities like petroleum products, inventory advance rates can run up to 90%. As further protection for the lender, a company may not be permitted to borrow the full amount of the calculated available funds (eligible assets multiplied by the advance rate). In these situations, additional reserves will be established against certain assets, or a minimum undrawn availability will be required.

In addition to working capital borrowings, a term loan is often available from the same group of lenders, collateralized by fixed assets or cash flow.

Lender Negotiations

When a financially troubled company must negotiate with its lender, the talks may occur at one of three levels of seriousness:

Level 1: Relatively routine, first-time waivers of minor "technical" covenant defaults. Such negotiations are usually conducted with lender marketing personnel who value the long-term relationship.

Level 2: Subsequent loan amendments waiving additional, more serious covenant defaults, but continuing original principal payment schedules, likely with some combination of significant amendment fees, higher interest rates, granting of security interest in company assets and restrictions on borrowing ability under a revolving borrowing facility. The bank's workout department usually becomes at least a consultant to the process at this point. Lenders will almost always ask equity holders in non-public companies to inject new funds to cover these "temporary problems."

Level Three: The loan is transferred to the workout or special assets department of the bank with the objective of an exit from the credit. At this point the company can assume that the lender will exert every effort to reduce its exposure, improve loan-to-value ratios and convert the loan to a secured position, if that is not already the case.

The "crunch" on the business comes when lenders recognize that cash flow is not great enough to meet debt service requirements. This usually places management in the position of needing to make very unpalatable decisions that they have been avoiding. After the first knee-jerk action of delaying payments to vendors, the other short-term options are typically to:

- Reduce the number of employees
- Expedite collection of large balance receivables
- Temporarily shut plants to reduce inventory
- Reduce non-critical outside services
- Delay capital expenditure projects

These generally temporary actions often provide immediate relief and may see the company through its initial cash crisis. To the extent that permanent overhead or other cost reductions are achieved, that will extend the interlude until the next crisis arises. If the problem is a cyclical downturn, no further actions may be necessary for a viable company to survive, provided that a financial restructuring to reduce or defer debt service payments can be negotiated.

If the seriousness of the liquidity situation escalates, management will come to realize that no matter how profitable lenders have found their past relationships with the company, these regulated institutions are subject to review by federal examiners and must not be confused with venture capitalists. Except in the most unusual cases, the company cannot expect to receive "new money" from the lenders unless it can maintain an acceptable collateral position, regardless of how attractive a case the company appears to be making for anticipated future improvements.

Once a loan has turned bad, the lender is motivated to reduce risk. Lenders have little incentive to extend or increase their risk in an effort to mitigate the negative effect on the company's equity values or employees. Even where there is no equity value and the company is cooperating in a consensual process from which proceeds will ultimately go to the lenders, it can be very difficult for banks to rationalize advancing additional cash into a struggling firm without a bankruptcy filing. Debtor-in-possession financing, subject to super-priority liens, will probably be made available following a filing to facilitate a Plan of Reorganization or an orderly wind-down.

Liquidation Analysis

During this interim period, while a company waits for the next crisis or prepares for a bankruptcy filing, it must either take, or at least develop a plan for, the permanent actions necessary for an operational restructuring. At this point, lenders will typically insist that, as part of the most current loan agreement amendment, a financial consultant to the lenders be hired at the company's expense to review the company's business plan.

One of this consultant's projects will be to develop a liquidation analysis for both an orderly and a forced liquidation. Although thinking in such terms is distasteful to management and the equity owners, it does help concentrate the mind on one potential alternative to continuing further dissipation of value through operating losses. This lender's liquidation analysis is not likely to be made available to the company, but company representatives will provide most of the data and should be able to construct their own comparable analysis fairly readily.

Developing a realistic understanding of the ranges of the company's liquidation values should become a common base point for negotiations. The lenders will have a perspective on the likely maximum loan loss, if any. Company representatives will likely understand the lack of residual equity should a liquidation become necessary and will face some quick decisions in order to preserve what does exist. They will also need to acknowledge that the bargaining power is held by lenders. If a loan has been classified as non-performing under bank regulation guidelines and is in "workout status," the lender may show little flexibility in restructuring its terms – particularly if the loan value is generally in line with liquidation value. Lenders tend to be highly motivated to reduce their nonperforming loans, and especially when they believe that liquidation will get them out whole, they may press for a prompt resolution.

However, counterintuitive as it may be, if the liquidation value of a company's assets is worth far less than the outstanding loan, the banks may show more flexibility. Typically, they will not be receptive to putting in more "new money," but if a prompt liquidation would result in a large loss that could be mitigated by their patience and forbearance, the lenders might be open to a debt restructuring that preserves existing "loan-to-value" ratios while promising a significantly enhanced recovery at minimal incremental risk.

Alternative scenarios for enhancing value to justify a financial restructuring are reviewed in more detail in Chapter 9. The measurement of enhanced value in lender negotiations is not normally based on reported operating results, but rather is the ratio of liquidation value of the collateral to the outstanding loan. That is why lenders require that borrowing base reporting be prepared using discounted liquidation values of receivables and inventories compared with the revolver loan balance outstanding.

Crisis Actions

Although this cycle and the decision-making involved are typical of many troubled companies, it comes far later in the process than the lenders and the company should be addressing the underlying problems. In fact, a crisis can be defined as a delayed turnaround. Turnaround management consultants are typically hired by either the lender or the company (or sometimes separately by both) at about this point in the process, or sometimes even later, after a Chapter 11 filing. Unfortunately, they are almost never brought into the process before a company's loan is transferred to the workout department. As a result, flexibility of action is very limited and the pressure for a timely completion of the business viability analysis is tremendous. The options most frequently available for addressing the crisis and receiving temporary debt service relief are these:

- Developing a plan for significantly reducing receivables or inventories to generate cash;

- Exiting segments of the business that have negative cash flow;
- Selling assets, such as surplus real estate and poorly performing business units;
- Obtaining new money from current equity holders or other third-party sources.

If management accepts and agrees with its lenders that one of these actions is a potential solution, then completion of the action will be required as part of the next loan agreement amendment. This will be part of a business plan believed to have the potential to return the company to a proper financial footing and can be the basis for a long-term financial restructuring.

Often, however, that plan does not work, because the business was not inherently viable. Critical operational problems were not properly addressed by management, or asset sales did not take place as scheduled. Frequently, asset sales or working capital reduction proceeds that were supposed to be applied to debt are not available because they were consumed in the financing of operating losses.

Chapter Summary

Management of companies in a liquidity crisis tend to become consumed with the day-to-day battles of managing negative cash flow, when they should be focused on understanding and solving core business problems. But critical to the problem diagnosis process is an understanding of cash-flow problems. A regularly prepared (usually weekly) rolling cash-flow forecast can be used to reevaluate disbursement priorities, focus on improvement of the most critical areas of negative cash flow and establish credibility with lenders and other stakeholders. Using this tight cash-flow control should facilitate managing temporary improvements to mitigate negative cash flow while longer-term operational and financial evaluation and restructuring can take place.

Receivables management is one of the highest priority items to be addressed in the cash-flow review, because improvements on this front can help cash flow *and* identify poor business processes.

Another essential element of the analysis is understanding and managing borrowing base availability. This is critical to maintaining credibility with lenders and, ultimately, for business survival.

EXHIBIT 6-1
LIQUIDITY AND FINANCING RISK ASSESSMENT

Question	Low		Average		High	
	0	1	2	3	4	5
Liquidity						
• Cash crisis (negative availability) is likely within 60 days?	N	N	??	??	Y	Y
• Debt service exceeds cash flow from operations?	N	N	??	??	Y	Y
• Large operating earnings declines are occurring?	N	N	??	??	Y	Y
• 50% or more of accounts payable are over stated terms?	N	N	??	??	Y	Y
• Significant non-cash financing is required, *i.e.*, LC's, bonding?	N	N	??	??	Y	Y
• Significant increase in working capital (no. of days)?	N	N	??	??	Y	Y
• High seasonal working capital needs?	N	N	??	??	Y	Y
• Total assets employed are increasing significantly?	N	N	??	??	Y	Y
<u>TOTAL SCORE</u>						
Number of 4's and 5's						
Financing/Lender Relationships						
• Borrowings are on a secured basis?	N	N	??	??	Y	Y
• Borrowing base reporting is required?	N	N	??	??	Y	Y
• Loan covenants are out of compliance?	N	N	??	??	Y	Y
• Relationship with agent is strained?	N	N	??	??	Y	Y
• Loan has been transferred to workout?	N	N	??	??	Y	Y
• Debt service payments are delinquent?	N	N	??	??	Y	Y
• Financials have "going business" opinion?	N	N	??	??	Y	Y
• Bankruptcy counsel has been retained?	N	N	??	??	Y	Y
<u>TOTAL SCORE</u>						
Number of 4's and 5's						

KEY to scoring – Circle most accurate:

N = No   Y = Yes   ?? = Uncertain; not clear-cut

0 = No, without exception   3 = Generally yes, with regular exceptions
1 = Generally no, minor exceptions 4 = Yes, but not a crisis
2 = Generally no, with regular exceptions   5 = Yes, creating a crisis

Chapter 7

WHO WANTS WHAT? AND WHY?
Identifying Conflicting Agendas and Objectives

Diagnosing the problems of a financially troubled business would certainly be easier if one could assume that all key stakeholders were motivated by the same goals. In healthy, profitable, soundly capitalized companies, this is generally true. All the stakeholders have a common, mutually beneficial interest – maximizing the ultimate value of the enterprise. Control of the situation is generally not in doubt. Risk is aligned with reward. Secured lenders are adequately protected. Unsecured lenders or creditors can rely upon the structural protections and stability that existed when credit was extended. And the management and board direct the company for the benefit of the owners, whether they are private or public shareholders.

Of course, there are examples, several of which have been highly visible in recent headlines, of management and boards whose view of fair compensation puts them at odds with other constituents. But as a general rule, in a healthy, viable entity a commonality of interest in seeking increased growth and profitability tends to minimize conflicts among the parties.

However, when a company is financially stressed and operationally in decline, interests begin to diverge, sometimes widely. For the most part, these conflicts and divergences arise out of competing interests that are clearly identifiable within the capital structure and are motivated by logical economic motives. But not always. In many cases, stakeholders have developed strongly held beliefs or agendas that are not so logically driven.

In either case, a failure to identify, assess and respond to the different perspectives and goals of the various parties can result in disastrous and highly contentious conflicts, often effectively precluding reasonable negotiations and making it difficult, if not impossible, to address the underlying issues of the business.

Getting out of the mess requires not only diagnosing and addressing competitive and operational problems but identifying the alternative paths to a resolution of the situation. Such paths to resolution can't be identified and evaluated without understanding the conflicting agendas, objectives, and values that must be considered in any negotiations.

Capital Structure

Many, probably most, of the motivations that drive the stakeholders of a troubled business are fundamentally rooted in the varying rights and interests of the capital structure and, as such, can generally be anticipated with reasonable confidence. That stated, it's surprising how often even highly experienced management and sophisticated investors will make the mistake of believing they can force secured lenders to undertake equity-style risks.

It is not within the scope of this book to try to convey all of the nuances and permutations that underlie today's common and complicated capital structures. But it is surely worthwhile to review the basics.

Capital structures can be simple or complex, but fundamentally they revolve around a single driving concept – *the greater the risk, the greater the reward.* The greater the protections provided the lender, the cheaper the financing. Teams of lawyers, accountants and advisors spend their careers seeking to provide their clients with structures, covenants and default provisions that define the protections and compensation related to their investments – but the basics are simple. Safe money is cheap. Money at risk comes dear. Priority of claims and payments, pledged collateral values, default triggers and recourse, all are variables adjustable to control and to define risk and movable in sync with pricing. Some people view the risk/reward continuum as a subjective art; others believe it to be objective science.

While nearly everyone understands the concept in a theoretical sense, when things go wrong it's important to realize how strongly the different positions and perspectives of the players influence their views of the situation and contribute to sometimes insurmountable conflict. Participants in different layers of the capital structure generally have very different expectations and appetites for risk. When a deal turns sour and their expectations are broken, their reactions can be highly emotional, even when they are grounded in logical financial considerations.

A wide variety of issues bear consideration in evaluating agendas that may be driving the decision-making processes of different stakeholders, particularly the creditor classes that have much different motivations and objectives than top management and equity owners. We have categorized these groups as follows:

- Secured Creditors
  - Senior working capital and cash-flow lenders that may be secured by all or only a portion of the assets

- Noteholders or bondholders that may hold first or second security positions on some or all of the assets
- Real estate mortgage and lease holders
- Equipment lease holders

- Unsecured Creditors
  - Suppliers and other trade creditors
  - Unsecured noteholders or bondholders

- Related Parties
  - Top management
  - Other management and employee groups, including retirees
  - Board members

- Equity owners
  - Public or private
  - Controlling or minority
  - Tiered with multiple classes

- Other
  - Customers
  - Key alliance partners
  - Governmental and regulatory agencies
  - Licensors

Under worst-case conditions, any of these stakeholders can be the "show-stopper" in precluding the turnaround of a financially troubled business or at least be a factor that forces a Chapter 11 bankruptcy.

In general, agendas will be rational and financially driven for the specific group involved. For example, most of the interested parties will greatly prefer for the ongoing enterprise to be preserved. However, if the company's proposed attempt to preserve the enterprise requires that secured creditors increase their exposure or allow their collateral values to erode, it is likely to be met with significant resistance.

It is our strong belief that the most effective way to bring conflicting viewpoints into proper focus is the detailed problem diagnosis advocated throughout this book. If the facts of a situation are presented in writing, in an organized and logical manner, there is a basis for objective discussion. Both the facts and conclusions leading from those facts can be debated in a rational, rather than emotional, manner by all parties at interest.

This does not mean there will be an instantaneous meeting of the minds, but the diagnosis serves as a basis for understanding which of the "brutal facts" may need further verification and the actual impact of various economic factors in dispute. To the extent there is disagreement, the order of magnitude of the dispute should be clarified. It is very difficult resolving conflicts defined by exaggerated claims based on emotion rather than facts. It is much easier to trade off a claimed loss of $1 million for other certain well-defined benefits than it is to trade off this claimed loss if the perceived value is $10 million.

Although usually not well articulated or defined, another agenda runs through the various disputes and negotiations of a financially troubled company. That is a desire to punish the guilty. Everyone involved in the situation has suffered losses to some extent. Even if a party can expect no monetary benefit for itself – in fact, *particularly* if it can expect no monetary benefit for itself – there is often a desire for the emotional satisfaction of causing bigger losses for the perceived guilty party. This "punishment" factor greatly sharpens the focus on identifying "bad management." Fact-based analysis can help bring out all of the economic issues and mitigate the effect of fighting over the trivial.

Secured Creditors

Secured creditors, whether their exposure consists of bank debt, letters of credit or other security such as equipment leases, are generally believed to hold the strongest hand in any financially troubled company situation. Their primary motivation, usually, is to exit a situation with the lowest possible write-down of their credit exposure. For them, 100% recovery with full interest is a win and is often achieved. Typically, secured creditors have limited interest in preserving the ongoing enterprise or protecting values of other stakeholders. They just want to get out as quickly as possible, with minimal losses and without the loan officer losing credibility in the bureaucratic institution in which he or she is employed. Assuming they've structured their covenants carefully and properly evaluated their collateral, if secured lenders move promptly and aggressively upon the initial default they generally can "get out whole."

However, this general institutional objective is easily subverted, because the personnel responsible for the impending losses tend to postpone the inevitable as long as possible. Loan agreement covenant waivers are granted, and initially these may result in additional funding being provided. Denial exists just as surely among lenders as it does among the management of troubled businesses. On larger syndicated loans, the denial tendencies are supposed to be overcome by federal banking regulations and loan examiners who classify loans and require that adequate loss reserves be established.

This tendency toward denial is a key reason that lending institutions establish internal "loan workout groups" to take over the proceeds recovery function. Whether called special-assets managers or some other euphemism, workout specialists have the task of getting maximum proceeds for their institutions while "letting the chips fall where they may" as far as other stakeholders are concerned. The sympathetic ear of the loan officer with the long-time relationship with the company is gone; the "kneecap breakers" have arrived. We describe them as such warmly and without rancor. Over the years many of these people have become our friends. But their jobs as workout officers are not to develop cozy lender/borrower relationships. Their task is to reduce outstanding loan exposure and improve loan-to-collateral value ratios.

However, four key restrictions limit overly aggressive action:

1. Creditors can't assume management control of the company's activities in a way that would impair values of other creditors. In the event that it can be established in a bankruptcy court that such wrongful actions have occurred, their claims could be adjudged as "equitably subordinated" and the secured position in their collateral voided; presumably, a major loss in recovery value of their loans would ensue. This is widely understood among bankers to be very bad for their job security.

2. To the extent that the secured creditor's actions dramatically impact the company's ability to continue normal operations, value of collateral can be severely eroded: receivables become uncollectible, inventory values deteriorate and single-use plant and equipment may become worthless. The valuation of assets in a "going concern" is generally substantially higher than in a forced sale or liquidation. Thus, precipitous actions are undesirable, if avoidable.

3. Secured lenders usually have an extreme aversion to bad publicity. Arbitrary actions that result in significant job losses at borrowers can trigger unwelcome calls from politicians and news organizations to top management of the secured creditor. Smaller loans escape much of this detailed scrutiny and place borrowers in a much more vulnerable position.

4. Continuing to work with the company while loan-to-value ratios are improving can be quite lucrative for a secured lender. Interest rates will be higher and substantial fees can be extracted from each new amendment to the loan agreement. If risk is going down while return is getting better, this is a win.

In larger loans and syndications, there will be a "lead" established to manage the workout process. If this individual is experienced and a strong leader, this helps the workout process considerably and has the advantage of developing a cohesive group with a clearly defined focus. However, such lender groups often are not cohesive and not focused on a quick, effective process of resolution. Although generally unsuccessful, one or more members of the group with relatively small exposure may use the requirement for a 100% vote on certain matters to attempt to get their loans purchased by larger members of the group. Such attempts to enhance relative position can delay the process and, as a potential problem, should be identified as early as possible.

Despite what we have said about the motivation of secured creditors to exit the situation, they are also motivated by economic considerations and can be induced to have patience if management has credibility and an adequate risk-adjusted rate of return is being earned. As indicated above, this means loan-to-collateral value improvement, a higher interest rate and significant fees for all loan amendments and covenant default waivers.

AUTHORS' CASEBOOK: Orderly Sale vs. Disorderly Liquidation

A private equity firm acquired a joint venture manufacturing several types of food product additives. In addition, rights were acquired to a series of animal and human nutrition products in various development or startup stages. Projections indicated that the existing business would fund the further development and release of multiple products acquired. Shortly after the transaction was closed, prices declined sharply on some of the company's traditional products and it became impossible to both service debt and fund development expenses related to the various other new products. The equity holders were unable to infuse additional capital and the senior lenders were threatening to abruptly cease further funding.

Critical Challenge: Convincing secured lenders that continued advances in excess of formula availability were justifiable as protection of collateral. The equity holders were prepared to facilitate an orderly liquidation for the primary benefit of the secured lenders, but only if the secured lenders would continue to provide ongoing borrowing requirements to preserve maximum value, if any, for the equity.

Nineteen separately identifiable product and market segments of the company's businesses were analyzed to provide the basis for evaluating alternative strategies and values. A comparison of asset liquidation and orderly sale values was prepared and documented. Analysis demonstrated that liquidation would result in major losses for the secured creditors due to the specialized nature of high-value inventories and potential environmental liabilities if manufacturing facilities were shut down.

Improved cash-flow forecasting and management control systems were installed for each of the company's divisions in order to provide the ability to control cash, use borrowing capability effectively and assign responsibility for improvement to the most appropriate management levels. Sale strategies for each business segment were developed and incorporated into an extended-term debt forbearance plan with *strict milestone measurements of results.*

In return for agreeing to the forbearance and continuing advances, lenders were paid significantly higher interest and fees. While maintaining tight control over cash and borrowing base availability formulas to ensure compliance with loan covenants, company management liquidated lower-value assets while selling major product lines and businesses in a series of three separate transactions. All secured and unsecured creditors were paid in full with equity owners and management retaining the potential for future recoveries from certain residual intangible assets and developmental products.

Subordinated, Mezzanine and Unsecured Debtholders

It has become increasingly common for U.S. companies to capitalize themselves through structured financing transactions that use multiple levels of tiered debt, each carrying different rights, risks and incentives. In return for higher coupon rates of return, these second- and third- (and sometimes lower-) tier lenders accept progressively higher risk, weaker security and less stringent performance covenants. In some cases, the same holder may participate in multiple tiers.

The existence of these multiple tiers of debt can vastly complicate the dynamics of managing a workout, because establishing the motivations and leverage of these debtholders is sometimes not a simple task and requires understanding both the existence of and adequacy of any security claims and the specific covenants and recourse provisions of the loan documentation. Many cases where the debt has been trading at a discount may be further confused by the fact that multiple holders in the same tier may have widely different investment costs. This trend toward ever-more-complicated debt structures has been accelerating rapidly over the last several years with the aggressive expansion of non-standard lenders and hedge funds in distressed companies and high-yield securities.

To the extent that a secondary lender does hold security, whether a shared lien, subordinated lien or selected assets, the first task is to evaluate the adequacy of that collateral, both for the direct holder and for any senior secured lenders that exist. Occasionally, such analysis may reveal that the senior secured lenders' claims are over-collateralized and a secondary tier lender has a reasonably strong position of influence and control, acting very much like any other secured lender. More frequently, however, subordinated or unsecured lenders will find themselves in a very vulnerable position should a liquidation of the business occur. The primary agenda of such creditors will be to get paid out without forcing a Chapter 11 bankruptcy, which in many cases would wipe them out.

It is among these tiers of unsecured or under-secured debt holders that an out-of-court financial restructuring of the business is most likely to occur. This can take many forms, including debt-to-equity swaps, interest rate reductions or even a reduction in outstanding debt. Such financial restructuring should not be negotiated without doing the detailed problem diagnosis that is advocated throughout this book.

Increases in value of the business enterprise as an ongoing entity will most likely produce the greatest benefit for the unsecured or under-secured creditors. This is based on the assumption that secured creditors are usually reasonably safe and equity is typically going to get wiped out. It is the middle area of the priority pyramid where there is the greatest uncertainty and the most opportunity for gain or loss. Unfortunately, restructuring negotiations often tend to focus less on improving the enterprise value of the business and more on either exploiting or defusing the leverage of those with ability to do harm to other parties. The position of the unsecured debtholders may be improved by threatening a "scorched earth" policy that will reduce recoveries from secured debt or higher classes of unsecured debt.

In large cases, the debt is publicly held or institutionally held, which tends to lead to a trading mentality. In recent years, it has become easier for the original debt issuer to get out, albeit at a loss, than to spend extensive time and energy on a workout. The secondary market trader of the debt usually has no more vested interest in long-term success of the business than if the trade involved a commodity like corn or soybeans.

Top Management and Equity Owners

As used here, top management consists of the CEO and board of directors, which are responsible for providing guidance and direction to the business, exercising their joint judgment and control, and, nominally at least, focused on the task of maximizing the value of the business. As noted earlier in this chapter, so long as a company is successful, healthy and well-capitalized, there are few substantive issues of conflict that arise relative to this goal. Management and the board have a great deal of latitude to set the agenda, particularly in a private company. If the CEO wants to own a corporate jet to facilitate his daily responsibilities over the company, and if on the weekend he may desire to use it go to Scotland for a golf outing, the board either approves or rejects the proposed travel policies and budget and no one else has standing (or in most cases, desire) to argue otherwise. A company may be sharply focused on maximizing short-term profits, it may be more strategically focused on long-term investments, or it may choose to dedicate a portion of its profits and resources to pursuing charitable or other non-financial goals. Setting aside the complex issues that surround a proxy battle in public companies, so long as the company satisfies its contractual commitments to the other constituents of the company, management and the board control the agenda.

In theory at least, the board holds the ultimate power and control, with management serving subject to the board's guidance and direction. But in practice, it's a bit more complex, typically controlled by closely woven interrelationships among and between the parties. For the most part, management and the board should and do act in concert. When management's performance falters it is the board's responsibility either to provide guidance and direction or to initiate a change. It's worth repeating that we believe the best path to resolving conflict between the CEO and the board is the fact-based diagnosis. Facts, properly documented, should speak for themselves. If top management are in denial of the facts and refuse to take appropriate action, the board and third parties will need to insist on change. Secured lenders generally can't name a replacement CEO, but they can refuse to fund working capital advances until someone they consider as satisfactory is in the position.

The conflict of agendas between the company and its creditors or other constituents arises when performance of the business begins to fail. At this point, the interests and desires of the various parties may diverge and both the judgment and latitude of management and the board begin to be questioned.

Normally, the objectives of top management at a financially troubled company are to preserve control and autonomy of the business entity with as little change as possible and to protect the value of the equity. Preserving control may or may not be entirely consistent with protecting value. While generally not acknowledged directly, the desire to maintain control is frequently driven by more personal concerns and objectives involving status and power both within and outside the organization. Loss of position means loss of power and status and so tends to evolve into a fight over money, severance, continuation bonuses and other issues. At the extremes, these conflicts may cause a total loss of focus on the need to fix operations.

Within the organization, many attributes of bad management (discussed in Chapter 4) affect the ability to focus on economic rather than personal objectives. If maintaining growth and size of the business are management's key criteria for success, maximizing value of the business may become secondary. Managing a smaller, more profitable company may be such an unsatisfactory outcome that it cannot be objectively considered. Although irrational, failure may be a more preferable outcome because it can be blamed on "the banks," "the unions" or others. This can occur even though a financially troubled company's equity is controlled by this same top management with its irrational focus on uneconomic factors in reaching critical decisions. This involves all of the management failure actions discussed in Chapter 4.

In a troubled situation, both the defensive maneuvers of management, whose reputation is becoming tarnished, and the focus on preserving the value of the equity are likely to come into conflict with the interests and agendas of the company's creditors. The reason for the conflict is quite simple. Excepting those rare occasions when new equity is available to fund a response to the company's problems, which seldom happens in truly troubled situations, attempts to preserve equity value typically require either increasing risk or the use of "other people's money," or both, because as the financial situation deteriorates it becomes increasingly difficult to justify the new funding requirements. Management can find themselves tempted to try "swinging for the bleachers," pursuing increasingly higher-risk options in the attempt to hit a home run and recover from the brink. As they pursue ever more aggressive strategies, they may fail to stop negative cash flow while waiting for the turnaround that is believed to be just around the corner. Such hope-and-delay agendas may lead to accelerating declines, resulting in a bankruptcy filing, when an earlier, out-of-court financial restructuring would have been much more appropriate.

As financial difficulties deepen, the natural motivations of management and owners can also present a conflict with their fiduciary responsibilities to creditors, which may be the real owners of a business. One step in the problem diagnosis process is to ensure that such conflicts are clearly identified. Lack of credibility, specifically, confidence that creditor interests are being protected, may become the reason that a management change is required even though management is capable of taking actions necessary to achieve a turnaround. If expected benefits of the turnaround are being directed to the equity holders in an inappropriate manner, a Chapter 11 filing that is not in the best interests of maximizing business value may be forced.

Intangible Benefits?

How far can the values and objectives of some business owners stray from what might be considered rational economic motives? A branded luxury consumer products company with relatively low market share was owned by Middle Eastern investors and had its headquarters in an attractive Manhattan office building overlooking Central Park. A major operational restructuring had reduced annual operating losses from nearly $10 million to under $2 million annually, but the business could not support the high-profile corporate presence and attendant overhead. However, the brand had value and sale to a strategic buyer was recommended as an exit strategy.

The owners' response was, "No, thank you very much for improving our operations, but we like owning the business and having the New York offices. It's a lot cheaper than our racehorses."

Other Management and Employee Groups

Middle-management professionals, using the term in the sense of functional managers of the marketing, sales, engineering, manufacturing and finance staff, will normally have somewhat different agendas and objectives than top management. They are interested in continuing the business entity, but they also have a vital interest in maintaining their professional reputations and in upward career trajectories. They typically will do the right things with regard to maintaining the business but will also be on the lookout for an exit from a career-threatening situation.

At this level, managers are less likely to be motivated by the arrogance and greed of some top management and more likely to be focused on protecting a source of income and expanding opportunities for future professional growth. There is likely to be someone in this group who clearly understands the problems and knows exactly what to do about them. One key objective of the structured management interview process (discussed in Chapter 8) is to identify this person, understand what he or she has to say and evaluate whether this person should be moved up to manage the entire business.

A key issue with middle-management professionals is whether they are focused, or can be focused, on total business results and priorities rather than on individual functional goals and budgets. At this level, there is often strong resistance to making the trade-offs among different business functions that are a key to retaining financial viability. So, the ability to move this group out of its cultural attachment to the status quo is an essential component in achieving a turnaround – or sometimes the key limiting factor. Determining the extent of this resistance to flexibility should be one objective of the structured management interviews. This attitude among middle management is a key reason that business strategy change in the turnaround of a mature business is so rare. It is much simpler to dump the losers and cut back to concentrate on a profitable core business, without seeking to effect a radical change in culture.

Much of what we've said about middle management applies to other, less well-paid employees. Career objectives and resistance to cultural changes are quite similar in these groups. And in mature, troubled heavy industry companies, there are often unionized employee groups that can be the limiting force in developing a turnaround plan. This occurs when, as in businesses such as steel or automotive manufacturing, compensation of highly paid unionized employees and legacy commitments to retirees are major components of total costs. Reducing such compensation becomes a primary management focus – the easiest way to cut costs. In these situations, the long-term agendas of the union leadership may become more important than short-term needs of the members whose jobs and income are on the line. To achieve the goal of cost reduction without the bitter infighting that can destroy a business, a detailed diagnosis (discussed in Chapters 8-11) is needed. With this information in hand, hopefully a facts-based solution can be negotiated. Sometimes the real problems are more issues of productivity, business structure and management rights than actual wage rates.

In terms of conflicting agendas and objectives in dealing with a unionized business, management often seems to focus on reducing compensation rates rather than on improving productivity, while union representatives are interested in preserving jobs even though, in the long run, this is counterproductive to business survival. While such conflicts were occurring, Nucor and the mini-mills were taking increasing shares of steel markets and Southwest and other low-cost airlines were eating into market share of the majors.

AUTHORS' CASEBOOK: Resolving Labor Issues

A foundry producing high-quality heavy steel castings for sale to construction and farm equipment manufacturers was being operated for the benefit of creditors. The company had a strong position in the marketplace and was selling at competitive prices. But a sale could not be concluded due to operating losses stemming from excessive manufacturing costs and low productivity of the union workforce.

Critical Challenge: High costs resulting from almost 100 different job classifications in place within the plant. Certain employees were idle a large part of the day but could not be reassigned to other available work.

As a prerequisite for purchase of the business, a local business group negotiated with the union to develop a consensual revamping of the cost structure to allow a return to profitability. In addition to wage reductions, job classifications were reduced to six. A sale of the business based on asset values was concluded, and the business continued as one of the city's significant employers.

Customers and Alliance Partners

As a class, customers are usually the most economically rational group in any turnaround, with the exception of their limited tolerance for rapid change. Customers usually view the financially troubled company as a "good supplier" or they wouldn't continue to use its goods or services. In some situations, continued purchases result from longstanding personal relationships, but relationships don't last if the buyer is not satisfied.

One key to any turnaround is a clear understanding of the competitive environment. Since the company has survived to date, a mature business must have been delivering value to its customers for an extended period of time. If this remains true despite the financial risks that are developing, it is important to understand the components of this value. It may be that the value is lower prices or product advantages not matched by competitors that provide a future opportunity to improve margins. When a company's customers continue to value the relationship despite the company's financial weakness or operating failings, it is a very favorable indication that there are core components of the business that continue to hold value. Where this is true, identifying those components and cutting back to that core business is often the most effective turnaround strategy.

On the other side of the coin, if there is no long-term customer loyalty and customers are falling away as fast as they can arrange new sources of supply, a company faces an entirely different and much more difficult problem. To effect a turnaround, not only must this erosion be stopped, it must be reversed and new customers added. This is a very difficult for any financial troubled company, and it is impossible to develop a business turnaround strategy without addressing and understanding these issues.

Customers have a need for reliable, consistent, low-cost suppliers. If the financially troubled company can make the case that it can continue to fulfill this expectation, there is a starting basis for a turnaround. If it cannot pass this preliminary threshold test, there is no basis for a turnaround.

Alliance partners can be involved in a wide variety of different situations, but the ones that will likely have the greatest and most immediate bearing on a troubled business situation are exclusive supplier, distribution or licensing arrangements.

In some situations, the company's very existence may depend on continuing the alliance, for example if the company has a licensing agreement with Disney to manufacture and sell consumer products with likenesses of the Disney characters. If these licensed products represent a major portion of sales volume, cancellation of the licensing agreement could put the company out of business almost immediately. The option of finding alternative licensing agreements is likely not available to a financially troubled company.

In such situations, all creditors of the troubled business must recognize that this licensing agreement may be the most valuable asset of the business. The details of trademark and licensing laws are far beyond scope of this book, but we have been involved in a number of situations in which extensive litigation was needed to resolve the rights involved. Such litigation is a value-deteriorating proposition no matter which side ultimately prevails.

Recognize that either a licensor or a manufacturer of products being sold under an exclusive distribution arrangement needs a strong partner to achieve the best possible financial results. Financially troubled companies don't fit the model, and it is almost certain that the other party will be looking for an out. Defending this key partnership to whatever extent possible must be considered even as the balance of business problems are being diagnosed.

Suppliers

Suppliers should want the company to survive and prosper for two reasons. First, from a debt-priority standpoint, they fall behind secured creditors in a liquidation and typically lose most of their receivable value when a business does not survive. Second, to the extent that purchases from the supplier continue, profit margin will continue to be generated, and there is at least some opportunity for reduction in outstanding receivable balances. In any event, a supplier should have significant incentives not to force a financially troubled business into bankruptcy – while at the same time having no incentive to allow receivables from a financially troubled company to increase.

Although each supplier of a business will be trying to obtain some reduction in its receivables, the long-term advantage if the company files for bankruptcy may be offset by recovery of excess payments by the debtor estate as "preferences," i.e., payments made for which either there was no new value received in the normal course of business or which were paid in advance of terms required by the original contract.

In dealing with a financially troubled company, suppliers quite rationally will attempt to enhance their returns with higher prices to offset increased receivable risks. This may be the limiting factor to achieving an operational turnaround where costs of purchased material are increased for a business that was already losing money.

If raw material or critical services cannot be obtained at competitive prices, there can be no turnaround. From the supplier's viewpoint, if alternative markets are available, there is little incentive to take the risk of not collecting receivables from a financially troubled customer. This may lead to a decision by the supplier to provide only a very small line of trade credit, restrict terms to C.O.D. or cash in advance, or, in a worst case, to refuse to supply product. Onerous trade terms place an extremely heavy burden on continuing normal operations and often, particularly in retailing, are the trigger for a Chapter 11 filing.

AUTHORS' CASEBOOK: Reducing Excess Inventories

A leading wine and spirits distributor with stable, profitable, multi-state operations was failing to meet debt-reduction goals established at the time of its acquisition by a private equity firm. Unexpected credit line over-advances put loans in default with secured lenders. A crisis management team was engaged to conduct a detailed business viability review with particular emphasis on profitability by location, inventory investment by supplier and inventory planning processes related to seasonal and other special promotional-period supply requirements. It was concluded that the operating costs and marketing programs of the business were being managed very effectively. However, lack of consideration of expense trade-offs involving inventory carrying costs combined with loading pressure from suppliers at certain times of the year resulted in large excess inventory balances. In general, negotiations with suppliers had been confrontational showdowns focusing on "loading the shelves" on one side and maximum possible promotional discounts on the other.

Critical Challenge: Develop negotiating tactics with suppliers related to inventory stocking practices, such as accepting somewhat lower purchase discounts in exchange for ordering flexibility. This would significantly reduce peak inventory investment and related borrowing requirements.

The improvement process was started by quickly designing new inventory control systems that provided detail needed for better decision-making in working with suppliers to improve their market penetration. Management's new negotiations with suppliers were then conducted in an objective, market data-focused manner and were generally successful in accomplishing the desired objectives of both parties. Major inventory reductions were achieved and debt was reduced significantly below levels required for compliance with loan agreements.

Professionals and Advisors

Understanding the motivations and agendas of various professionals and advisors of a financially troubled company is sometimes the key to diagnosing problems. In the context of our use of the term we would include:

- Corporate and bankruptcy attorneys
- Public accounting firms
- Financial advisors retained by debtors or creditors
- Investment bankers
- Strategic and operational consultants

In most situations, professionals and advisors act in a responsible manner, but their allegiance is to their clients, not to maximizing value of the business. Each set of advisors is convinced that billing $1 to collect $2 more for their client is a very good deal, regardless of the impact on total costs of several other groups with the same objective. This most often happens after a Chapter 11 bankruptcy filing and leads to very high reorganization expenses as each stakeholder jockeys for position. It often seems like a prolonged Kabuki dance held at great time and expense leading to a pre-ordained conclusion. Representing a client in a Chapter 11 case usually generates a significant steady stream of service billings, and unfortunately this provides a built-in incentive for legal and financial advisory professionals to push for a bankruptcy case rather than an out-of-court turnaround.

Prior to a bankruptcy filing, the operationally troubled business is often overrun with strategic and operational consultants, rather than legal and financial advisors. These firms tend to focus only on their narrow specialties and assume that the company's principal problem is the one that requires their pre-fit solution. In some cases, this is true, but more often the balanced approach that comes from a good problem diagnosis and facing business realities is more appropriate.

Landlords

Except in retailing, landlords are not usually a significant factor in most troubled company situations. The position of landlords is reasonably well defined in the bankruptcy process. If a lease is assumed in accordance with bankruptcy court rules, the owner is entitled to all unpaid rent. If a lease is not assumed, then the future stream of rental commitments becomes an unsecured claim calculated under well-defined rules.

Outside a bankruptcy filing, there may be an opportunity to renegotiate rental payments, but in our experience only rarely is this the real driving force in effecting a turnaround in profitability. The real driving force in an operational turnaround where real estate is a significant expense comes from effecting a consolidation by closing facilities used in the business. This is particularly true with retail operations but can also involve manufacturing plants.

With a troubled retailer, the typical "four wall" profitability analysis will yield major variances in profitability by store, with some modification of the 80/20 rule usually applicable – that is, 20% of the stores are providing 80% of the profits. Careful analysis of this data will demonstrate that some significant number of stores should be closed. In these circumstances, a Chapter 11 filing can truly become part of the solution to a turnaround. Leases can be rejected, stores closed and business profitability improved via a true operational restructuring around a profitable core.

Chapter Summary

As part of the diagnosis of problems of a financially troubled company, it is important to understand the conflicting agendas and objectives of the parties involved in the situation. The first major conflict relates to whether there is a viable business, either in whole or part. Resolving this issue will determine whether the objective is debt restructuring or an exit.

Among the stakeholders whose agendas must be acknowledged are:

Management and **the board of directors** or other parties with the power to replace management will have conflicting motives and agendas. One key to resolving these issues is a good problem diagnosis to preclude acting prematurely. Establish the business objective, then make management and restructuring decisions, using the fact-based problem diagnosis to bring parties together to understand the situation and develop a solution that yields maximum total value. Argue about splitting up the pie after figuring out how to make it as large as possible.

Secured creditors often hold the key to maximizing total value, but usually have little motivation to act for the benefit of other parties involved. The best motivation for secured creditors to see the situation through to the highest value solution for all parties is high return on their loans and improving loan-to-value ratios.

Unsecured or under-secured debtholders are extremely vulnerable in a financially troubled company. They are often the group with the most to gain or lose as attempts are made to enhance total enterprise value.

A significant part of the process of a troubled company turnaround is ensuring that all **management** and **employee groups** below the CEO are focused on the total business, not their own functional agendas.

Relationships with **key customers** and **alliance partners** must be preserved if a business is to be viable. Unless **suppliers** are operating at capacity and have alternative customers, there is a mutual interest in maintaining a continuing relationship as long as the supplier's risk is not increasing.

Professionals and **advisors** become extremely costly after a Chapter 11 bankruptcy. To hold down costs, the excessive use of professionals to improve rearrangement of slices of the pie should be avoided where possible.

Part III

THE DIAGNOSIS PROCESS

INTRODUCTION

Understanding the drivers and problems of a business, separating the wheat from the chaff and developing a plan for maximizing the value of each are the objectives of the diagnostic process. In Part III, we lay out a step-by-step process to obtain and organize the factual knowledge and understanding of the business required to develop an effective response to its problems. The process involves:

1. Conducting organized and thorough interviews with management to rapidly obtain access to valuable corporate knowledge;
2. Evaluating operating trends and drivers of the business and assessing potential for operational improvement;
3. Assessing the competitive environment as the key to determining if the business is viable and what its prospects are for long-term success;
4. Reviewing and assessing the company's management, organization structure and business processes to determine if they are adequate to the requirements of the business.

This four-step, disciplined information-gathering process will provide the basis for the subsequent development of alternatives and assessment of risks.

Chapter 8

CONDUCTING MANAGEMENT INTERVIEWS
The Quickest Source for Identifying Problems and Solutions

Typical Management Views of Consultants	
#1	#2
Those who can, do.	*A consultant is someone who borrows*
Those why can't, teach.	*your watch to tell you what time it is.*
Those who can't teach…consult.	

It can be hard not to bristle when a CEO greets you with attitude No. 1. But, quite frankly, there is some validity to attitude No. 2.

As newcomers on the scene, consultants, in order to be effective, do indeed need to obtain and rely upon information provided by the company. They don't bring fresh facts. Rather, as we have said previously, they bring *fresh eyes* – to assist in the reinterpretation of facts that have been, or could have been, available to management before their arrival.

When we arrive at a troubled company, we start our evaluation by attempting to obtain and evaluate the full scope of those facts. We also identify gaps in or disputes over the information available and how and why company personnel have interpreted them. Unless this initial background review is performed thoroughly, we risk developing the same tunnel vision or myopia that often has contributed to the company's stressed situation

An essential early step in our process is the confidential structured interview of selected management and employees of the company. These interviews can quickly provide useful information about a business and, if conducted in an inclusive and objective manner, begin to dispel management's understandable defensiveness or distrust about outsiders asking questions.

These interviews should include the CEO, the CFO and other key managers reporting directly to the CEO, as well as at least one employee each from the marketing, sales and manufacturing functions. As appropriate, try to include long-service, lower-level managers who have broad-based knowledge of company operations, such as the internal audit manager, purchasing manager, product line sales managers and so on. Within this group, there is usually some individual who is generally acknowledged as the company historian, and that person is another "must interview." It is important that all functions of the company be represented.

The objective is to obtain background information from a diverse sample of company employees who have meaningful historical knowledge relating to the company's operating trends, problems and opportunities. Combining organizational-effectiveness knowledge from confidential management interviews with operational reviews and an evaluation of the competitive environment, as defined by both internal and external third-party sources, provides a powerful set of diagnostic tools.

Although these interviews will provide many useful specifics, the intention is to build an overview understanding of the situation, not to solve specific problems. The action plan for solving specific problems comes only after an understanding of the total business situation has been achieved in a way that allows appropriate setting of priorities. These priorities can then be communicated in context to all constituencies. A consultant particularly does not want to spend a lot of time:

1.   Solving future problems of a business likely to be liquidated;
2.   Rehashing the guilt for mistakes of past management;
3.   Focusing on relatively minor business process problems.

The example interview guide (see Exhibit 8-1, at end of chapter) provides a long list of questions intended to elicit an objective general discussion of how the business works – not a litany of complaints. Summarizing and comparing the results of different interviews should provide an overview of the company's operations and culture and a basis for evaluating its organizational effectiveness. Those managers being interviewed who cannot get past the complaints stage generally tend to be part of the problem.

Company personnel want problems solved, generally know what is wrong and will tell a sympathetic listener what they think needs to be done, if they are interviewed in a non-threatening environment. Discussion of the practicality of proposed solutions is left for another day when better facts are available. Often, the interview process becomes one of shutting down excessive detail in order to focus on the highest priorities, rather than getting people to open up and talk. However, it is critical to the diagnosis and decision-making process that a broad base of opinion be obtained and evaluated. Representatives of different functions will have diverse opinions on the situation and what key future priorities should be: marketing will blame manufacturing and manufacturing will blame marketing.

The interviewer's job, after the interview process is completed, is to sort out the various facts and opinions and develop an objective, reliable summary about the views expressed. The interviews may reveal the need for facilitating communications across the organization or even mediating disparate views, but the primary tasks during the interview process are to gather information and attempt to establish a cooperative rapport with the company's management and staff.

It is best to structure the specific interview questions only after obtaining some preliminary general information about the company. The highest priority of the first day or two should be to gain an understanding of operating trends and deviations from projections in order to ensure that the interview focuses on these specific issues. As new information is developed and other questions arise, they can be included in subsequent management interviews or supplemental sessions with people already interviewed.

The key objectives of the confidential structured management interview are to:

Obtain general knowledge and opinions about the industry's competitive environment and the company's strengths and weaknesses in the marketplace. The interview provides an excellent forum for evaluating the extent to which company personnel are focused on the external environment in contrast to internal business processes; discussing industry and market trends; and understanding the company's position on market growth and life-cycle curves.

Obtain alternative views and historical perspectives on company operating trends and past changes in strategy and management focus, including perceptions of how and why a financially troubled company got that way. This material provides an opportunity to contrast internal perception of the company's problems with objective external data sources and the independent analysis of operating result trends.

Identify management's primary agenda to the extent possible and compare it with that of other stakeholders. If the CEO is interested primarily in volume growth as a means of ego gratification, that interest is not likely shared by other stakeholders.

Identify dysfunctional organizations and management in terms of:

- Agendas being driven by internal politics or outside third-party forces that are not consistent with business focus and needs;
- Lack of consistent vision of company strategy;

- Organizational weaknesses in defining accountability and responsibility;
- Adequacy of company planning and decision-making processes;
- Poor operational measurement and control systems;
- Communication improvement needs, both internal and external;
- Bureaucratic cultures and processes that are inhibiting business change.

The people with the best understanding of the business and its organizational culture are likely to have an understanding of how to fix internal problems and more appropriately operate in the external environment that exists. They are most likely to be forthcoming in a non-threatening environment that focuses on facts, challenges and opportunities. Later, there will be time to search for the guilty and incompetent, when better-prepared analytical facts are available.

Ideally, the interview will be conducted in a conference room away from the distractions of the individual's office and telephone. The discussions should be confidential and not disclosed, without the interviewee's permission, except as disguised general findings. The interviewer – and only one should take part – must be a willing listener and learner. This is not the place for an interviewer to attempt to demonstrate superior knowledge and experience while jumping to conclusions about the company's problems and potential solutions. Although it is sometimes difficult, the interviewer should also attempt to minimize the time spent listening to war stories and complaints not directed at answering the questions asked. As we've said, the objective is a broad-based understanding of the business, not a series of unrelated anecdotes.

Try to complete each interview in 1½ to 3 hours. Let the interviews run longer, though, if the interviewee is opinionated and talkative with a broad base of knowledge about the company and has the ability to discuss most of the questions in some depth. The extra time is well worth the effort if the interviewee is focused on the questions asked. At the same time, always bear in mind that it is better to talk to more people than to have fewer longer interviews, which become counterproductive in terms of breadth of the management staff that can be covered.

Management Interview Guide

The Management Interview Guide (Exhibit 8-1) we have developed over a number of years is split into the main sections discussed below. It provides a comprehensive set of questions that can be edited down to a shorter list of probable key issues depending on the circumstances (it would take far too long to ask all the questions on this list). The interview should be tailored to solicit opinions only when they fit the specific business and when interviewees are knowledgeable about the subject matter.

Company History or Work Experience

With long-time employees or general management, the interview should focus on key events in the company's history and how the business got where it is. With relative newcomers, discussing their work experience and why they came to the company is a good "ice breaker."

General Competitive Environment

The objective is the best possible knowledge of the industry's playing field and where the company fits in. It is critical to obtain a good understanding of key business drivers and measurements of success in the company's business environment. It is also important to use the interview process to determine how much, or little, management knows about its competitive environment. When management displays a weak or limited understanding of its competition, it may be losing touch with its market and customers as well. An objective general discussion of the industry may bring out that the company does not have the products, market position, business processes or human resources to continue as a viable ongoing concern.

Company Mission/Strategic Direction

Discussions in this section should focus on the company's business model and the strategic direction that is expected to bring future success. These discussions should produce an understanding of whether the company has anything resembling a long-term strategy or vision for the future and, if so, whether there is general management consensus as to what it is. If the industry is subject to major new competitive forces or disruptive technology, major disagreements may be disclosed about what the strategy should be.

Competitive Strengths/Market Opportunities

This is the *positive side* of the Strengths-Weaknesses-Opportunities-Problems (SWOP) analysis (discussed fully in Chapter 10). Sometimes, this discussion will identify a hidden jewel within the business. This may be one individual's understanding of a major opportunity that is being ignored by the management consensus or that is not receiving the resource commitments necessary to support growth. Likewise, it may identify critical changes needed to continue or enhance core business success.

Competitive Weaknesses/Problems

This is the *negative side* of the SWOP analysis. These discussions may trigger an understanding of the best opportunity for a turnaround. In a financially troubled company, often the quickest way to improve operations is to dump the losers. Even in a company with extremely bad accounting and reporting systems, line management usually has a clear understanding of which product lines and markets are losers and why. Because they fight the problems every day, middle managers are less inclined to be in denial about this than senior management. These discussions should identify both the big losers that could be dumped and the major internal problems that have the potential to be fixed – keys to a quick turnaround. As with discussions of strengths and opportunities, the emphasis is less on understanding the conventional wisdom and more on finding the insightful viewpoint as to why weaknesses exist and how they can be fixed.

Profitability/Revenue Issues

This represents another opportunity for the interviewer to smoke out the economics of the company's conceptual business model in a way that most managers, particularly in financially troubled companies, don't focus on. There is a tendency to be caught up in the details and miss the forest because of all the trees. Questions about where the company is making money and/or growing and why often bring out interesting and thoughtful answers. It is particularly important to bring out opinions on the driving forces in leveraging profitability. This includes Pareto's law, often referred to as the 80/20 rule (see Chapter 9), the concept that a very high proportion of results from any organizational function result from a small portion of the activities involved in producing total business results. The discussion should also include the extent, if any, to which the operating parameters of the business must be structured around seasonal or cyclical limitations.

Management Information and Control

This discussion should provide a basis for understanding how accurate, timely and useful the company's business systems are. Quite frequently these systems are viewed as terrible deficiencies in a troubled company and serve as an excuse for not addressing core problems. But such systems difficulties are often a symptom, not a cause. Excess product-line or market complexity and lack of market focus, not the mechanics of management reporting, may be causing the problem. Occasionally, poorly planned implementation of new computer systems may actually be the main source of the company's problem. Unsatisfactory customer service relating to a botched ERP installation has killed more than one company and badly hurt many others. However, if this discussion indicates timely, effective installation of a useful ERP system, that is "prima facie" evidence of competent functional management. Unfortunately, the good information available is often focused on perceived functional-control needs without properly addressing real problems of the business. Better information about the details of a basically bad business won't stop the losses.

Organization/Culture

These questions get into the soft, "touchy-feely" type of discussions that are difficult for most business analysts and, therefore, tend to be ignored in favor of concentrating on "the numbers." However, these areas may be the crux of the company's problems and must be evaluated carefully (for a full discussion of these issues, see Chapter 11). In some ways, this section is the most important part of the management interviews because there is no other quick way to develop this information. This subject is best introduced near the end of the interview, because responses to previous questions may have already provided some of the information required, and as the interview progressed, a rapport should have grown between interviewee and interviewer, producing honest, forthright, answers to these questions.

Summary Overview

The summary overview questions are an opportunity for the interviewee to reconsider previous questions and discussions. In some cases, the sequence of the interview enables the thinking process to overcome denial of unfavorable facts and may have changed certain of the interviewee's points. On numerous occasions, a second-level manager's answer to "what would you do if you owned the company?" is "I would sell it." This usually turns out to be the proper solution.

The question about what the company will look like in three years is intended to initiate a wrap-up discussion of trends that may be leading toward failure and the need for dramatic change.

A point to keep in mind during management interviews is that the interviewees are drawing on their own experiences, and they will have their own agendas and axes to grind. They sometimes believe passionately in things that are incorrect. Listen carefully, but be thoughtfully skeptical. The primary objectives are a diagnosis of business problems, identification of key challenges and opportunities and access to the corporate knowledge base. It is not a witch-hunt seeking to apportion blame for past mistakes. At the same time, if a significant number of interviewees identify the same person as a major problem within the company, this information is worth investigating in detail.

Evaluating Management

Evaluating management is an essential element in diagnosing problems of the troubled company, and the management interview process is extremely important to this evaluation. The broad-based questions and the answers to them should provide a critical initial perspective on whether the CEO, CFO and other key managers have an objective view of their business, its economics and the industry in general. The questions and answers also provide a basis for evaluating the strength of management. If all 10 interviewees have the same basic view of company strategy, it seems clear the company has an unusually well-directed management team. If the interviewees offer 10 different versions of the company's strategy and direction, the company has serious management deficiencies.

Many troubled company CEOs and their management staffs, particularly in Aging Mule businesses, have tunnel vision and are wedded to historical points of view. Effective management of a financially troubled company requires that strategies, tactics and methods of operation be re-examined. The management interviews help bring out whether managers understand the need for such action.

Some characteristics of bad management that may be observed in the interviews are:

- Rationalization and justification of past events and unsatisfactory operating results, rather than a focus on immediate and near-term problem-solving and corrective actions;
- Lack of facts and understanding about where the business is making and losing money;
- Focus on the revenue line, rather than on operating profits and cash flow;
- Lack of specific plans, timetables and responsibility for addressing and correcting known internal problems; .
- Focus on manipulating reported numbers rather than addressing basic problems;
- The "wishful thinking syndrome" of assuming and projecting favorable future results, in spite of consistently missing previous forecasts and an absence of specific plans for corrective action;
- Inability to consider seriously the possibility of downsizing the business;
- Focus on ego gratification, rather than on decisive business actions and results. Some tip-offs include: excessive use of the word "I," blaming the problem on others and inability to listen to questions being asked;

- Lack of understanding of the need for good management and control systems, including use of clearly defined performance measurements;
- Citing poor performance of previously terminated management employees as the reason for the company's problems.

Summarizing Results

The objectives of the interview process are to determine if a consensus exists regarding the business situation, to solicit ideas for fixing problems and to evaluate the ability of existing management to focus on the need to effect change.

What follows is a report from a project involving a branded consumer products company. This report provides a useful methodology for summarizing results in a way that focuses on generic problems and tells a compelling story to management and other constituencies about actions needed to fix problems. (This report is a condensed version of an extensive report to the company's board of directors based on interviews with 14 management and supervisory employees covering all functions of the business.)

AUTHORS' CASEBOOK: Defining the Problems

CONSUMER PRODUCTS COMPANY
SUMMARY OF MANAGEMENT INTERVIEWS

I. Major strengths are the company's image in the marketplace and its quality products; each was mentioned by more than 60% of those interviewed.

    A. High quality/effective products were mentioned as a major strength by approximately 80% of respondents.

    B. Company image is perceived as a major strength by more than 60% of those interviewed.

II. The company was perceived by approximately 60% of those interviewed as having high-quality marketing management and/or many long-service employees who are loyal and dedicated.

    A. Marketing, advertising and trade show creativity was mentioned as a strength by one-third of respondents.

III. Manufacturing and logistics problems and issues are considered the company's greatest weakness. These problems were mentioned in one form or another by all management employees interviewed. These weaknesses are at the top of everyone's list as the company's greatest problem and undoubtedly obscure focus of attention on other very real issues.

A.   60% of respondents mentioned lack of manufacturing/logistics expertise, efficiency and discipline in one form or another.

B.   One-third reported loss of market share due to continuing shipment problems.

C.   One-third reported deteriorating relationships with suppliers as a result of accounts payable problems and/or need for more capital.

IV. Organizational issues and absence of a clearly defined and communicated business plan are perceived as major problems.

A.   Lack of communication/coordination of plans and organized meetings.

B.   Lack of teamwork, follow-up of commitments, support from other departments.

C.   Ambiguous organization structure/lack of accountability.

CONSUMER PRODUCTS COMPANY
14 MANAGEMENT INTERVIEWS

Number of
Mentions

	Strengths
11	Product effectiveness and quality
9	Company image/community perception
6	Brand franchise strength/leadership position
6	Company knowledge base of products and customer needs
	Weaknesses
10	Lack of manufacturing/logistics expertise, efficiency and discipline
	a. High product costs/lack of manufacturing productivity
	b. Need for improved production forecasting and scheduling
5	Loss of market share due to continuing shipment problems
5	Deteriorating relationships with suppliers due to accounts payable problems
	a. General corporate need for additional capital
4	Lack of communication/coordination of plans and organized meetings
4	Lack of teamwork, follow-up of commitments, support for other departments
4	Ambiguous organization structure/lack of accountability

The company that is the subject of this report was a major turnaround success because it was able to fix its internal problems. As with most other successful turnarounds, the company had significant core strengths:

- High-quality, competitively priced products
- Established brand with good market image
- Good knowledge of market needs by competent personnel

Problems and weaknesses were greatest in manufacturing/logistics functions of the business and were accentuated by organizational difficulties resulting from a classic entrepreneurial, shoot-from-the-hip culture. The business needed to improve administrative controls and did not have specifically defined authority and responsibility. The report's extensive documentation of both conclusions and specific individual comments provided the impetus for the board of directors to take actions that had not previously been considered to be possible.

Emphasis was moved away from unproductive finger-pointing to management change and installation of effective reporting controls in manufacturing, purchasing and production scheduling. Identification and documentation of constraints to the manufacturing process and purchasing deficiencies allowed a focus on fixing the root cause of problems rather than trying to shift blame. Successes in improving customer service led to successes in increasing sales, better morale throughout the organization and restored pride in being associated with a company with excellent products.

Note that the report is focused on concepts and actions, not on individuals. Certain managers had to be replaced, but this came in the context of hiring individuals with the ability to fix specific problems. This is a far better approach than bringing in a superstar CEO with large-company experience who is often inclined to try to fix problems from his last war with a host of new, "better" people. Experience and know-how is lost, the dysfunctional organization culture continues, the "new guy" fails and, ultimately, so does the business.

Chapter Summary

One of the most successful approaches to obtaining useful information quickly about a business is the confidential and structured interview of members of management. The key objectives of these interviews are:

- Information and opinions about the competitive environment
- Alternative historical perspectives about the business and its problems
- Identification of dysfunctional organizations and management

Done well, these interviews will be of major assistance in evaluating management and identifying potential solutions to business problems.

EXHIBIT 8-1

EXAMPLE

MANAGEMENT INTERVIEW GUIDE

NAME: _____   POSITION: _____

I. **COMPANY HISTORY OR WORK EXPERIENCE**
    - Defining historical events?   • Why working at company?

II. **GENERAL COMPETITIVE ENVIRONMENT**
    - Are markets served generally growing or mature?
    - Are company products/services competitive? Why or why not?
    - Keys to business success in industry/markets served?
    - Near-term outlook for the industry, key market segments and company?
    - Longer-term outlook for the industry, key market segments and company?
    - What major industry/market changes are in process or expected in future?
    - Who are top competitors? Strengths? Weaknesses?
    - Market share position of the company? By market niche?
    - What are the barriers to entry or exit from the industry?

III. **COMPANY MISSION/STRATEGIC DIRECTION**
    - How would you define the company's mission and/or business strategy?
    - Customer/market groups toward which products/services are focused?
    - Who are the company's largest customers? Competitive sales advantage?
    - What is the primary basis for providing customer value?
      - Low cost?   - Leading technology?   - Superior service?
    - Key drivers of decisions: manufacturing capacity, technology, cost structure, brands owned, location, revenue growth, return on assets?

IV. **COMPETITIVE STRENGTHS/MARKET OPPORTUNITIES**
    - Unique core competencies   • Proprietary products
    - Cost structure advantage   • Technology position
    - Brands owned   • Market share position

    What are primary opportunities to increase revenue?
    What are the company's strongest products/market segments?
    Where is the company increasing market share?
    Which customers are increasing purchases? Why?

V. **COMPETITIVE WEAKNESSES/PROBLEMS**
    - Key competitors; why stronger?
    - Product lifecycle/technology change issues?
    - Where are declines in company market share occurring?
    - What are weakest product lines and/or market segments served? Why?
    - What are the primary cost structure disadvantages? Correctable?

- Cause of shortfalls from past expectations; external vs. internal factors?
- Are any major customers reducing purchases? Why?

VI.   **PROFITABILITY/REVENUE ISSUES**
- Describe conceptual business model
- Keys to leveraging long-term profits
        - Revenue growth   - Technology   - Cost reduction   - Service
- What are standards for successful company performance?
- Impact on the company of seasonality and cyclicality factors: Does this result in unusual working capital, equity or financing needs?
- Greatest profit/revenue improvement opportunities: Near term? Long term?
- Are internal performance problems impacting revenue or profitability?
- Should the company exit from any markets or product lines?

VII.   **MANAGEMENT INFORMATION AND CONTROL**
- Does the company clearly understand where it is making and losing money?
        By product, market and customers?
- Are administrative processes generally adequate to control expenditures and commitment to risk?
- Is there an understanding of cash management and control of working capital?
- Are business planning processes useful and adequate?
- Is information provided consistent with needs and objectives of the business?
- What are, or should be, the most important measures of performance?
- Is timely, reliable market information available: product technology, industry sales trends, pricing trends and market share?
- How widely is financial information shared with company employees?

VIII.   **ORGANIZATION/CULTURE**
- Would you define company culture as more entrepreneurial or more bureaucratic?
- Is responsibility and authority clearly defined and communicated?
- Is decision-making timely and appropriately centralized/decentralized?
- How focused is company on external vs. internal issues/problems?
- How does the company implement change? Who makes things happen?
- Key cultural values motivating or de-motivating employees: company reputation, work challenges, personal growth opportunities, team spirit?
- Most valued/important function of business: R&D, manufacturing, sales?
- Who controls key customer relationships? How?
- Who and what type of managers have driven past successes?
- What management/organization deficiencies have caused failures?
- Turnover experience rates: management, salaried, hourly? High or low?
- Principal employee morale issues? Atmosphere of trust and respect?
- Are incentive programs appropriate for industry and business objectives?
- What activities are measured? How is success awarded? Failure penalized?
- Cooperation between organizational functions? Silo management issues?
- Are customers well served by the organization structure? Significant flaws?

IX.   SUMMARY OVERVIEW
- On its present course, what will the company look like three years from now?
- If you owned the company, what major changes would you make to improve growth and profitability?
- Who else in the company should I be sure to talk with for a good understanding of the business?
- The last question: What should I have asked, but neglected to do so?

Chapter 9

UNDERSTANDING OPERATIONS
IMPROVEMENT POTENTIAL
Where and Why Are You Losing Money?

We believe that a first step of investigating and analyzing a company's operations will develop many questions and issues that need to be covered in evaluating the external environment – that might not be evident without the operations analysis. Although the facts of a situation may make cash control the highest priority, gaining an understanding of operating results as quickly as possible is essential to the diagnosis process.

Financially troubled businesses are typically facing one of two key problems that cause them to be in default on loan agreements: either generally satisfactory past operating results have begun to deteriorate significantly or a business plan assuming significant profit growth has not been achieved. In either case, diagnosis of the problem requires a clear understanding of reasons for the decline in results or the shortfall from expectations. Three key operational analyses are used to reach overview conclusions that should point the way to more detailed investigations:

1. Understanding expectations by developing a reconciliation of the differences between the company's business plan (presumably the basis for the current overleveraged financing) and actual results;
2. Identifying unfavorable changes in operating results since satisfactory performance was achieved at some point in the past;
3. Analyzing where the company is making and losing money by product, customer, distribution channel or other industry-specific criteria – developing data that detail how Pareto's Law (the 80/20 principle) manifests itself in operating results of the business.

Specifically *excluded* from the above is a "breakeven analysis." This can be a useful tool for various levels of internal discussions about profitability but doesn't provide much in the way of useful solutions. First, it tends to perpetuate the assumption that the primary route to a business turnaround is cost reduction of existing product lines and business processes, and, second, internal assumptions regarding variable margins used in the calculation are likely to be incorrect. In our view, breakeven charts are much more useful in communicating a call to action to ensure business survival under deteriorating conditions than as an analytic tool for diagnosing business problems.

Results vs. Expectations

In the initial analysis of troubled business problems, it is essential to determine whether the company suffers from real deteriorating results from historical operations or has simply failed to live up to unrealistic expectations. A financially overleveraged company with sound, profitable business operations but unrealistic expectations for future improvements in profits is in a very different situation from an operationally troubled company facing a deteriorating external market environment. In our experience, 10 to 15% of troubled companies are very sound operationally but have managed to persuade lenders that profit growth will be much greater than justified by past experience – the well-known "hockey stick" forecast.

Among the many quite logical justifications and rationales for such optimistic forecasts are:

- New marketing programs will dramatically increase sales;
- Cost-reduction programs will significantly increase profits;
- Market share will be gained from competitors;
- Industry revenue growth rates will improve;
- Delayed synergies will be obtained from a past acquisition;
- New product introductions will be highly successful;
- Commodity material costs will decline.

Sometimes the hockey-stick forecast is actually achieved; more often it isn't. Even when planned actions are successful and revenues and cost-reduction improvements occur as scheduled and expected, profit may not improve significantly because competitors are not standing still, or a tougher competitive environment may drive down pricing with no individual company in the industry actually accomplishing a significant improvement in profitability despite declining costs. In a competitive environment, industrywide operational improvement benefits usually get passed on to customers.

It is critical to identify quickly the operationally sound company that is a victim of excessive leverage based on an unrealistic expectation. The operationally sound, Overburdened Workhorse company is a good candidate for a financial restructuring and is likely to survive by negotiating a fix of the "right-hand" (liabilities) side of the balance sheet while preserving and improving the operational cash-flow value that exists. Unless this financial restructuring need is recognized and addressed promptly, the excessive debt load and drain of cash required to service it may lead to a series of bad decisions and ultimate failure, caused by lack of financial flexibility. Although it may be a difficult negotiation, a financial restructuring should be to the advantage of all parties to correct overleverage as soon as possible.

The process to be followed in understanding shortfalls from expectations (and from financial projections that may have been used in the accumulation of excess leverage) involves:

- Determine details of "base period" operations used in projections;
- Evaluate operating trends prior to start of the base period;
- Compare "pre-base" operating trends to "post-base" operating expectations;
- Carefully identify changes related to acquisitions or other non-recurring events;
- Compare "pre-base" trends with actual results;
- Establish the extent to which poorer-than-expected operating results were due to:
  (a) unrealistic expectations of improvement;
  (b) actual deterioration in internal operating performance;
  (c) a more difficult competitive environment leading to lower pricing, reduced market share or other unfavorable trends.

Information required for this analysis is very similar to that used for determining changes in historical trends. However, the necessary first step is an overview understanding of whether you are dealing with unrealistic expectations or unfavorable operating trends.

Trend Deterioration Analysis

An understanding must be developed of the forces that drove past successes and of subsequent changes in trends as results moved from satisfactory to unsatisfactory. It is particularly important to understand what caused the past successes and to have an overview of the extent to which they can be expected to recur. This analysis often leads to totally different conclusions than those provided by management. In our experience, it is amazing how often even competent management will grasp at straws to explain deteriorating results or failure to obtain growth objectives rather than do the work of performing an objective, detailed analysis. This analysis is the quickest shortcut to a detailed understanding of the "brutal facts" of the situation.

Financial problems frequently result from debt incurred to pay for an acquisition. Almost 20% of the situations included in the selected project summary in the introduction to this book fall into this category. It is imperative in analyzing historical operating trends that growth be clearly segregated between organic internal growth and that resulting from acquisitions. This distinction is often lost in the acquisition financing approval process but is extremely important to better understanding performance of the business.

Likewise, if some major capital project expenditure or product-line addition has improved financial results, this must be identified, because it is likely not a constantly improving trend. Consolidating plants may produce a definable one-time improvement in earnings, but this specific improvement will not be repeated in the future. In troubled companies, cost-reduction actions tend to slow the trend of deterioration, not stop it. Despite the short-term improvement, the balance of the business usually continues its downward spiral.

One of the best sources of conceptual thinking about the goals of an operations analysis is Peter Drucker's *Managing for Results,* first published in 1964. It clearly sets forth the type of detailed analyses required and offers an extensive discussion of the need to focus on opportunities for the future rather than on solving problems of the past.

The first step in evaluating declining trends is to break out the results of the various subsidiaries, business units or product lines that are consolidated into total business results. Often this isolates all of the real trouble in one discrete segment of the business. If this is the case, it clearly defines what the primary focus must be.

Significant changes, if any, in accounting practices must be identified and organization structure/reporting unit changes must be isolated before hard conclusions can be reached. In addition to an acquisition or major project, other examples of changes that may distort comparative results include:

- Manufacturing or corporate overhead expense allocation procedures;
- Intra-company pricing/costing routines;
- Mix of sourcing from different manufacturing plants;
- Organizational changes that alter the base of selling, general and administrative expense calculations and/or allocations.

After determining that results are being reported on a comparable basis for the one or more business units with significantly changed operating results, begin a detailed comparison of changes between reporting periods. To the extent that accounting method changes have occurred, adjustments should be made to report results on a consistent basis. This step sometimes totally changes the perception of what is happening and can provide a major surprise even to very good management. Incorrect cost allocations and non-comparable reporting can be very dangerous to good business decision-making.

Particular care must be exercised in evaluating "extraordinary, non-recurring" events. In many cases it is true that a one-time event, perhaps external, often internal, has imposed a severe but temporary strain upon the business *without effecting its underlying core operations and profitability*. Sometimes, however, "one-time" events become recurring excuses; they may be indicative of internal operating problems or external market risk. It is surprising how frequently we have seen businesses in which year after year management cites a single extraordinary event that pounded the company's bottom line but fails to see that its business model is fundamentally susceptible to such unique and ever-changing exposures.

AUTHORS' CASEBOOK: Integrating a Rollup

Seventeen regional companies providing IT infrastructure development were consolidated into a national supplier in the first quarter of 2000, just prior to the telecom crash. For each of the next three years, despite very soft revenues, the company reported high profitability for 10 months, followed by a "Fourth Quarter Surprise" wherein selected projects were belatedly discovered to have massive cost overruns, wiping out the bulk of prior period reported earnings. Senior lenders became disgusted with management's lack of credibility and were pressing for a liquidation of the business.

Critical Challenge: Overcoming denial and inertia and focusing top management on specific day-to-day project management challenges. In response to the external market forces that dramatically reduced demand, top management was focused almost exclusively on attempts to drive sales contracts and was neglecting operational management. A complex Enterprise Resource Planning (ERP) information and accounting system was purchased but implementation was slow and the result was lots of data with little information.

Initial assessment revealed that, despite the external market decline, the intended strategy of developing access and penetration into large national accounts was proceeding favorably. However, failure to focus on project progress and profitability resulted in neglect of problems until it was too late for effective remediation. The solution, which co-author Doug Hopkins developed with management, was establishment of a carefully prioritized and disciplined weekly reporting process that eliminated the ability of local management to ignore or hide its problems. Issues and challenges surfaced more rapidly, providing not just greater visibility of poor performance, but allowing for timely response and remediation of problems. Senior lenders were provided with greater visibility through third-party monitoring in return for an extended forbearance agreement and deferral of principal repayment schedule.

Volume/Mix

Compare changes in both unit sales and average selling prices per unit. Make this comparison by product, by customer and by any other key volume statistic that might provide insight as to which products or product lines represent significantly high (or low) profit margins. Often, total reported revenues remain relatively constant, with mix shifts toward lower-margin products. The objective of this analysis is to determine the extent to which unit volume or pricing is a major factor in changed operating results.

In a cyclical business, unit volume reductions may be the only real changes in operating results, thereby quickly focusing attention on the competitive environment. Companies that are the victims of global sourcing problems often have, simultaneously, both a major unit pricing deterioration and declining unit volume due to loss of total market share. However, pricing generally may not be a problem in the industry market niches that did not move to lower-cost sourcing.

Total dollar or unit volume declines are not a good basis for understanding what has actually been happening or for taking corrective action. It is essential to carry the analysis forward by major customer, product line and distribution channel to develop a reasonable basis for future action. Particularly with regard to customers, it is important to analyze where the company is gaining and losing volume. Looking at sales trends of the top 20 customers of a business may trigger an understanding that was previously missed by looking at only the total picture. In a troubled company with relatively constant revenue, it is common to find a shift toward lower-margin customers. This occurs when more astute competitors concentrate on those customers buying products with higher margins. Alternatively, there may be a loss of unit volume and related ability to amortize fixed costs, as competitors using a lower-cost "disruptive technology" profitably begin to serve a company's lower margin customers.

Value-Added Margin

In manufacturing businesses, "value added" is the concept of margin over material costs. Direct material and purchased or subcontracted parts and services are deducted from net revenues to determine value added. In many businesses, including some service operations with variable direct labor, this is the appropriate starting point for an operating results comparison. This is particularly important in a commodity-oriented business where raw material costs represent a large portion of total costs and fluctuate dramatically, sometimes on a daily or hourly basis. Two examples at the extremities of product types are meat-packing, where the input is farm animals purchased for slaughter, and steel mini-mills, where the primary raw material is steel scrap. In businesses such as these, margin over material cost, or "value added," can remain consistent as reported sales dollars of revenue fluctuate widely over time even if physical units sold remain constant. Therefore, ratio analysis related to reported sales dollars is not a useful measurement.

Manufacturing Costs

Unless there are dramatic shifts in physical volume, product mix or technology, manufacturing labor and overhead expenses usually do not vary greatly over time. A line-by-line expense analysis will often show little change in actual costs incurred despite significant unit volume fluctuation. Except for the changes in *reported* overhead absorption, this is not typically where a significant change should be expected. More often, it will be found that expectations unrealistically assumed that a major cost-reduction project could be accomplished or that costs would decline in line with volume declines.

Where major unit volume changes have occurred and costs have increased or decreased significantly in total, it is best to understand manufacturing cost details in terms of expenses per unit of production output, i.e., tons of steel, pounds of meat or yards of cloth.

Selling, General and Administrative Expenses

Except for items such as advertising, promotional expenses and commissions, a company's selling, general and administrative costs tend to be inflexible and slow to change under normal circumstances. Consequently, it is important to understand those changes that have occurred, particularly major expense increases in anticipation of revenue increases that did not materialize.

Over time, "fixed" SG&A costs tend to increase as a ratio to revenues despite supposed leverage from volume increases. It is important to identify and understand these increases on a ratio to sales or units of sales basis in order to evaluate both the potential for reduction and the reasons for profitability change.

Working Capital

Working capital used in the business should be evaluated in terms of both absolute dollars of change and changes in number of days receivables, inventories, payables and any other major working capital balances that may exist.

Two key factors are important:

- If working capital employed is declining while number of days sales remain constant, cash is being generated from volume declines that is likely going to fund cash operating losses as conditions of the business deteriorate;
- If reported "working capital used" increases are due to a significantly higher number of days inventories and receivables, this is a major danger sign. It often means that operating profits are overstated due to failure to establish adequate reserves or, in rare cases, to outright fraud

in valuing assets. (In Chapter 11 of this book, we discuss the flaws in business processes and decision-making that can result in such asset overstatements.)

AUTHORS' CASEBOOK: Losing Control of Outsourcing

A publicly held designer, manufacturer and importer of women's wear products expanded rapidly after second-generation management took control. As sales volume more than doubled over three years, sourcing activities were extended to more than 50 countries, with the result that the company lost control of its purchasing and manufacturing outsourcing activities, leading to excess inventory investments and a liquidity crisis.

    Critical Challenge: Understanding the fundamental profitability, which had been obscured by misstated asset balances.

    Although there were many operational problems to be addressed, a key evaluation of the situation consisted of understanding realistic gross margins, which had been overstated by failure to take appropriate inventory write-downs. Exhibit 9-1 shows a five-year summary of operating results and inventory values, including "guesstimated" revisions.

    The company totally lost credibility both in the marketplace as a result of poor service due to loss of control over product sourcing and with creditors due to lack of proper financial controls. It was forced to file for Chapter 11 bankruptcy and, ultimately, was liquidated because of its inability to recover its market position and obtain new financing.

EXHIBIT 9-1
APPAREL MANUFACTURER
COMPARATIVE FINANCIAL DATA
(Millions)

| Reported Results | Year Number | | | | | Total |
	One	Two	Three	Four	Five	
Sales	$366.0	$464.5	$625.9	$806.6	$780.4	$3,043.4
Gross Profit	105.1	129.6	176.6	191.1	144.2	746.6
SG&A	63.6	82.0	116.6	158.4	184.9	605.5
Operating Income	41.5	47.6	60.0	32.7	(40.7)	141.1
% Gross Profit	28.7%	27.9%	28.2%	23.7%	18.5%	24.5%
Inventories	$113.8	$151.8	$227.3	$198.3	$197.1	
Days Inventory -a)	104	125	128	129	102	
Guesstimated Revisions						
Good Inventory @ 56 days [b]	$61.3	$68.0	$99.4	$86.1	$108.2	
Excess Value @ 60% W/O	$21.0	$33.5	$51.1	$44.9	$35.6	
Inventory Adjustment [c]	$(31.5)	$(50.3)	$(76.8)	$(67.3)	$(53.3)	
- Current Yr. Change	$(31.5)	$(18.8)	$(26.5)	$9.5	$14.0	
% Gross Profit – Adjusted	20.1%	23.9%	24.0%	24.9%	20.3%	22.8%

(a- Calculated based on subsequent periods cost of sales.
(b- Unweighted average number of days inventory for Years 4 and 5 of six major apparel manufacturers.
(c- Reduce value to 56 days plus 40% of value over 56 days.

Determining Where a Company Is Making and Losing Money

In diagnosing the troubled company, a detailed understanding of where the company is making and losing money is imperative. This may seem self-evident, but it requires a business analysis of quality and depth often missing in troubled companies. Even where good data appears to be available, the data should be carefully reviewed and verified.

"Making money" does not refer to accounting profits. Money eventually requires the generation of *cash*. Cash is what will keep the company out of bankruptcy court or off the auction block. Our requirement for independent verification of the numbers has little to do with distrust of incumbent management; often honest, responsible managers have been misled by numbers that conform to standards of conventional managerial accounting but may not properly report the reality of the situation in the depth required for taking effective action.

Diagnosis of the troubled company might best be approached as a progression from general to specific. As one gains understanding of the business it is possible to form and test hypotheses, using increasingly specific information and analysis. Keep in mind that the objective is to learn where the company is making and losing money – not to demonstrate one's exceptional cost-accounting expertise. Where is profit being generated at minimal cost and where are excess costs generating losses or "negative value"? Which business activities generate value-added margin contribution and which don't? In addition to the standard array of managerial accounting ratios and breakouts from consolidated reports, there are other helpful intellectual frameworks for the consideration of business efficiency.

Pareto's law, often referred to as the 80/20 rule, has been known and discussed in many business articles over the last 50 years. Simply put, the concept is that a large proportion of results from any organizational function come from a small portion of the activities involved in producing total business results, e.g.:

- 20% of products provide 80% of profits
- 20% of customers provide 80% of sales
- 20% of the sales force generates 80% of sales
- 80% of value added comes from 20% of revenue

Obviously, this is not a hard and fast rule, but whether the proportions are 90/10, 80/20 or 70/30, the concept always seems to apply and must be clearly defined and understood in the business analysis to determine the true sources of a company's profit margins.

The 80/20 Principle[7], a book by Richard Koch, provides an excellent detailed approach to this type of financial analysis (particularly its Chapter 4). Koch clearly discusses both the type of analysis necessary and those questions that should be asked when the financial analysis has been completed. He reinforces this with terminology we like: "the vital few" as being the most effective and "the trivial many" as being ineffective.

Drucker, in *Managing for Results,* discusses many of the same concepts. He particularly emphasizes the need to focus resources on opportunities rather than on solving problems of the past. Concentrating attention and resources on expanding the 80% of high-margin transactions rather than reducing costs related to the unproductive 20% is a better use of management time. The best solution is to get rid of the 20% and *all* its related costs. Determining where a company is making and losing money is not an easy process, but can be approached in terms of several different levels of analytical time requirements and complexity of analysis. Initial diagnosis of a troubled company is best approached on *as simplified a basis as possible in order to develop a preliminary hypothesis that can be compared with information obtained from other steps of the diagnosis process.*

When evaluating contribution to profit of various business segments, it is important to carefully analyze profits in terms of "value added before fixed costs," as we noted above in discussing trend analysis. Value added (which represents revenues less direct material, purchased parts and subcontracted production services) is the starting point. Contribution to profit before fixed-cost allocation by product line should then be calculated. Although the company may have internal reports of gross profit by product line after overhead expense allocations, such data often leads to erroneous conclusions. If expense allocations are prepared on a general basis they should be used with great care. It is not uncommon in a financially troubled company for *accounting systems to be manipulated either consciously or unconsciously to "help the losers" (product lines or customers), so management can rationalize not taking required actions.*

Fixed costs in our analysis differ from most standard cost conventions. The intention is to identify those costs that generally will not change in the short term, regardless of volume. Typically, this would include all facilities-related costs, financing costs, corporate administrative costs, depreciation, research and development and long-term equipment leasing costs. Employee costs related to production should be assumed not to be fixed.

---

[7] *Richard Koch,* The 80/20 Principle: The Secret to Success by Achieving More with Less *(New York: Currency-Doubleday, 1998).*

Value added under this definition then consists of all variable operating costs and expenses plus contribution to profit and fixed overhead. The objective is a realistic allocation of these costs by product, customer or other pertinent and useful category. The conceptual thinking related to this allocation is that most of these costs and expenses, whether reported as indirect labor, factory overhead or selling expenses, do not, in fact, vary significantly from period to period, regardless of how much accounting effort is spent on cost allocation. These cost-accounting machinations often tend to confuse rather than clarify management's and lender's understanding of what is really happening to operating results.

The key to a good analysis is a reasonable rationale for allocating these costs. In *Managing for Results,* Drucker recommends the identification of an appropriate simple transaction base on the theory that the truly directly variable expenses, including direct labor, are in most businesses a minimal part of total costs. Neither factory nor SG&A costs are much different for a large shipment than for a small one. However, cost details should be reviewed by line item to determine those categories that should be allocated on different bases. Some categories of costs that should be evaluated for specific allocations are:

- Advertising and sales promotion of branded products;
- Warehousing and inventory costs for slow turnover product;
- Setup costs on low-volume, build-to-order products;
- Design costs for specially engineered equipment;
- High-cost freight-in on products or parts sourced externally;
- Maintenance service related to high-value, special purpose production equipment;
- Direct labor that is widely variable due to product complexity;
- Selling costs if organized as a separate sales force by line or customer class.

AUTHORS' CASEBOOK: Shedding the Chaff

A well-known international manufacturer of equipment used in the steel industry and other industrial applications was not meeting profit expectations established at the time of its acquisition by a private equity firm. Sales volume and market share were increasing despite a cyclical downturn in end-user markets. However, operating profits were declining despite the higher sales volume, and ability to service acquisition debt was in serious jeopardy.

Critical Challenge: Understanding profit contribution by product line.

The company was not in an immediate cash crisis and its historical competitive strengths remained in place, but without a major improvement in profitability its future was at serious risk. Detailed analysis of product line profitability as illustrated in Exhibit 9-2, demonstrated that all profits were being generated from the parts business and standardized products sold through distributors. High-quality, special-design "Cadillacs of the Industry" installations upon which management was focusing a disproportionate amount of its energies were not price-competitive with simplified standardized designs produced by competitors.

Exhibit 9-2 is a simplified illustration of the problem diagnosis calculations made in connection with an operational review of the business.

EXHIBIT 9-2
EQUIPMENT MANUFACTURER
PROFIT CONTRIBUTION BY PRODUCT LINE
(Millions)

Product Line	Revenues	Less: Material	Value Added	Proposal Cost	Design Engineering	Installation	Controls Labor	All Other-a)	Net Contribution
						Allocated Costs			
A	$100.0	$50.0	$50.0	$15.0	$15.0	$10.0	$10.0	$45.0	($45.0)
B	75.0	37.5	37.5	10.0	5.0	5.0		23.5	(6.0)
C	50.0	15.0	35.0	0.0				14.0	21.0
D	25.0	5.0	20.0	0.0				5.0	15.0
E	12.5	2.5	10.0	0.0				2.5	7.5
F	12.5	2.5	10.0	0.0				2.5	7.5
Total	275.0	112.5	162.5	25.0	20.0	15.0	10.0	92.5	0.0
Parts	75.0	10.0	65.0	0.0	0.0	0.0	0.0	17.5	47.5
Total	350.0	122.5	227.5	25.0	20.0	15.0	10.0	110.0	47.5

Less: Other Fixed Costs 30.0

Earnings before interest, taxes, depreciation and amortization (EBITDA) $17.5

(a – Allocated based on weight of equipment shipped.

The company's product lines C through F, which had been standardized and simplified for sale through distributors without requirement for proposal, design and installation expenses, were highly profitable. Since all products were fabricated from heavy steel, weight of products shipped was considered a reasonable basis for allocation of costs other than proposals, design engineering, installation and high-cost labor involved in custom manufacturing of specialty designed control systems.

Details of data had been captured in the cost-accounting system but were not readily available in a form useful for analysis. What were readily available were gross margins by product, incorporating detailed allocations of all manufacturing costs using direct labor as an allocation base, but such data was not useful for a conceptual thought process about real profitability of the business.

The bottom line was that all profits were being generated from the parts business and from standardized products sold through distribution channels. The decision-making process for corrective action was not as simple as getting rid of products A and B, which were losing money. These products were a key to the company's excellent reputation and to getting a large installed base in place that generated ongoing high-margin replacement parts sales.   However, this simple analysis focused management on the objectives of cost-reducing and standardizing products A and B to eliminate losses and dramatically improve profitability of the total business.

Once again, keep in mind that the objective is an overview diagnosis of where the company is making and losing money, not a demonstration of cost-accounting expertise. The rough estimate of profitability by product provides the basis for many more detailed questions and further analysis. The group providing the analysis must never lose sight of the need for speed and the well-known, but often abused, KISS principle – "Keep It Simple, Stupid." All the data utilized in the example above was available in excruciating detail within the company's own accounting systems. But because it was only viewed irregularly, in isolated detail, by staff members well down the company's hierarchy, it never became actionably visible to management. It is the simplified summary schedule as displayed above that grabs management's attention.

In *The 80/20 Principle,* Koch captures the essence of what drives profitless growth: "The road to hell is paved with the pursuit of volume. Volume leads to marginal products, marginal customers and greatly increased managerial complexity. Since complexity is both interesting and rewarding to managers, it is often tolerated or encouraged until it can no longer be afforded."

Koch was discussing sales volume, but the cost side of the business equation is similar. Size of organization and level of expenditures managed represent status and level of importance in the society that forms the average business. The exceptional business manager is motivated by profits and does a good job of controlling costs. However, until competitive conditions force a change, many managers pursue volume because it is easier than understanding the sources of true value added and cutting out the unproductive efforts and expenses related to "the trivial many."

One key reason that organizations are difficult to change is that the need for sales attention to focus on high-margin products has not been adequately demonstrated. Together with this focus must be an understanding of the effect it has on costs and the re-direction of attention that is required. Across-the-board expense reductions are the refuge of bad management. However, if denial can be overcome, the average manager can effect most of the changes needed.

AUTHORS' CASEBOOK: Sharpening the Focus on Profitability

Due to declining earnings, a major manufacturer and distributor of branded consumer food products goods was in default under covenants of senior notes held by a group of insurance companies. The project involved evaluating the company's proposal to lenders relating to a financial restructuring.

Critical Challenge: Understanding profitability by product line.

While evaluating operations and management structure, significant analytical assistance was developed for company management in areas not previously evaluated adequately, including the need for consolidation of facilities and understanding a series of complex, inter-related reasons for declining profitability. It became evident that certain core brands were steadily losing market share, resulting in excess plant capacity and non-competitive overhead costs.

Exhibit 9-3 is a simplified disguised illustration of calculations of product line profitability.

EXHIBIT 9-3
FOOD PRODUCTS MANUFACTURER
PROFIT CONTRIBUTION BY PRODUCT LINE
(Millions)

Product Line	Revenues	Less: Material	Value Added	Advtg & Prom -a)	Warehouse Distribution -b)	Mfg. -c)	All Other	Profit Contribution
					Allocated Costs			
A	$ 125.0	$ 12.5	$ 112.5	$ 10.0	$10.0	$12.5	$ 4.0	$ 76.0
B	150.0	20.0	130.0	30.0	25.0	75.0	5.0	(5.0)
C	100.0	15.0	85.0	40.0	10.0	45.0	3.0	(13.0)
D	50.0	10.0	40.0	10.0	10.0	20.0	2.0	(2.0)
E	50.0	12.5	37.5	10.0	5.0	50.0	2.0	(29.5)
F	25.0	2.5	22.5	–	2.5	10.0	1.0	9.0
Total	500.0	72.5	427.5	100.0	62.5	212.5	17.0	35.5

Less: Fixed Costs (60.0)

Operating Income / (Loss) $ (24.5)

(a - Allocated based on actual costs by product for advertising and other promotional activities.

(b - Based on cases sold.

(c - Actual costs, excluding depreciation, since each product was produced using equipment in separate, clearly defined plant areas.

In particular, Product E had rapidly lost volume but continued to support a large high-cost manufacturing operation. Product A was under-supported with advertising while growing in volume and generating large profits. This highly valuable brand had greater profit potential on a standalone basis than the total for the entire business. The remaining 75% of the business (product lines B through F) was worth less than zero because of lack of profit contribution and liabilities associated with an exit via liquidation.

The company made significant changes to its operations, a high-cost manufacturing plant was closed, assets were sold and the debt refinanced by a new lender group. Subsequently, the company was merged with a stronger industry competitor with the distribution leverage to generate cash flow and profitability from the declining brands.

The above illustrations focus on two very different types of manufacturing operations, but the principal of understanding where a business is making and losing money applies to non-manufacturing operations as well.

Retail operations must be evaluated on a "four-wall contribution" basis for each store as a starting point for evaluating where the company is making and losing money by volume category, size of store, age of store or geographic location.

AUTHORS' CASEBOOK: Understanding the Financial Reporting

The well-established nationwide specialty chain selling home-decorating products, previously discussed in Chapter 2, was in a liquidity crisis despite attractive reported EBITDA returns. Understanding and managing the situation had become extremely complex due to weak financial reporting.

Critical Challenge: Extracting usable information obscured by overly complex reporting and restructuring reserves.

With the assistance of management, attention was focused on the following key projects:

1. Understanding the financial reporting and clearly defining reasons for long-term negative operating cash flow, which was being obscured by a combination of special "non-recurring" charges, capitalizing of large software and store improvement expenses, the need for continuing store improvements and accounting for debt restructurings (see Exhibit 9-4).

2. Individual "four-wall" analysis of profitability of all store locations in order to clearly define where the business was making and losing money and to assist management in correction of operational problems.

   Evaluation of a four-year history of individual operating results for the more than 600 stores indicated that:

   a. less than 100 stores with revenues over $1.0 million each were generating 80% of the profit contribution;

   b. in general, these most profitable stores were suffering rapid profit erosion due to rapidly expanding "Big Box" competition in the demographically favorable areas that were company strongholds;

   c. operating results were unsatisfactory at more than 1/3 of the company's stores.

The company filed for Chapter 11 bankruptcy to allow termination of leases on unprofitable stores, but deterioration of its competitive position had become so severe that new investment was not warranted and a subsequent liquidation resulted.

EXHIBIT 9-4
HOME PRODUCTS RETAILER
EBITDA TO CASHFLOW RECONCILIATION
(Millions)

	One	Two	Three	Four	Five	Total
			YEAR			
Reported EBITDA	$54.2	$50.6	$60.2	$54.2	$66.0	$285.2
Less:						
Capitalized lease/IRB payment	(8.5)	(8.6)	(8.4)	(8.5)	(9.5)	(43.5)
Capitalized software and development costs	–	–	(4.7)	(9.6)	(12.3)	(28.0)
Utilization of "restructuring" reserves	(10.4)	(9.9)	(9.5)	(10.3)	(16.3)	(56.4)
Working capital (increase)/decrease	–	3.8	(7.8)	(3.0)	(12.9)	(19.9)
Cash flow available for capital expenditures and interest	**$34.7**	**$35.1**	**$29.8**	**$22.8**	**$15.0**	**$137.4**
Less:						
Capital expenditures	(13.6)	(8.8)	(12.1)	(12.4)	(17.2)	(64.1)
Interest	(43.3)	(44.0)	(24.8)	(15.3)	(32.5)	(159.9)
Cash Flow Surplus/(Deficit)	**$(22.2)**	**$17.7**	**$(7.1)**	**$(4.9)**	**$(34.7)**	**$(86.6)**

Initial Conclusions

Assuming that reasonably complete answers can be obtained to questions generated, a preliminary hypotheses regarding business problems can be developed. As applicable, the characteristics of a viable cyclical business or one affected by major correctable internal problems should begin to be identified. Initial conclusions are subject to confirmation while evaluating the competitive environment trend information and the analysis of sources and uses of cash. The combination of results from these three different viewpoints will allow a preliminary judgment about whether the business is viable. In addition, overly optimistic forecasts compared with past trends will have become obvious. If current business results look similar to the base year but reflect a serious shortfall from plan, the company typically has a "wishful thinking" plan that was not backed up by concrete execution plans to bring about change.

At the same time, completing the recommended analyses should have identified the key "profitability drivers" of the business, i.e., product mix, distribution channel, capacity utilization, product yield and so on.

At this point, a useful analysis tool is to take the information developed and prepare a simple, one-page bridge analysis projection identifying conceptually how the company gets from its unsatisfactory present situation to a satisfactory future. If the changes required are extensive in number and generally have a low probability of success, then management may have to reconcile themselves to confronting the reality that the business is not viable without major changes to its business model.

It is important, at this point, to again draw a tentative hypothesis regarding the situation, similar to the summary prepared after evaluating historical operating trends and variances from projections. This involves a bullet-point list of actions that would be necessary both to focus attention and resources only on money-making positions of the business – that is, the 10 to 40 % revenue of the core operation generating the highest contribution – and to abandon or improve significantly the profitability of the money-losing segments of the business – the 60 to 90%.of revenues generating the lowest, often negative, contributions.

Actions that are relatively simple, in concept if not in implementation, can have a dramatic impact. For example, the food products company discussed above (Exhibit 9-3) effected a major operational improvement by discontinuing product E and closing the related high-cost manufacturing facility. However, this was only a temporary fix that did not address other product lines that were following the same downward trend at a slower rate. Ultimately, this business was sold to a competitor that could properly capitalize on the potential of Product Line A while milking cash from other declining products.

A key to identifying effective strategies is finding the constraints to improvement. With a background understanding of where value added is provided at the lowest cost, defining constraints may point to a high-potential, low-cost path to improvement. The objective is to identify specific practical and achievable ways to solve a problem with a reasonable chance of success and to focus attention on the "diamond in the rough" product line that becomes a key to an operational turnaround or enhanced recovery from a business sale.

Dispassionate evaluation of the business model may lead to the conclusion in a significant number of cases that the only logical scenario for preventing value deterioration is a quick exit. In the absence of a clearly identified need for the quick exit, it is usually quite instructive and an effective communicative device with all interested parties to prepare a summary of required actions with clearly defined key assumptions. This defining of key assumptions brings a clarity that is the difference between providing understanding and delivering unintelligible numbers. Data to be presented would normally include:

1. A two- to three-year forecast based on current trends of the business. This will usually present how bleak the future looks based on present trends in order to get management to "confront the brutal facts."

2. A financial "bridge analysis" defining and reconciling differences between the "brutal facts" of past history and current trends, compared with the company's goals and objectives.

3. A short list of key actions and related funding requirements clearly identifying the specific operating and financial requirements necessary to "bridge the gap" to satisfactory performance, with an estimate of the probability of each objective being satisfactorily achieved.

Among the types of actions that might realistically be taken, some of which might be accomplished without substantial funding, are:

- Conversion of production capacity to increase sales of a growing product line;
- Equipment replacement to reduce manufacturing costs or improve quality;
- Product redesign to reduce manufacturing costs or satisfy changing customer demands;
- Plant consolidation to reduce fixed costs;
- Production-control systems improvements to solve customer service problems;
- Promotional spending increases for high-margin products;
- Price increases on mature, niche market specialty products with minimal competition;
- Quality improvements to stop loss of market share;
- Standardizing and simplifying consumer products to reduce price points.

Longer term, installation of lean manufacturing techniques to reduce costs may provide an excellent opportunity, but it won't happen overnight and requires total management commitment and focus.

As an aside, let us observe – and this demonstrates our somewhat prejudiced approach to this type of analysis – that there is often an inverse relationship between the sophistication of tools and techniques used and usefulness of results obtained.

Chapter Summary

Understanding operations improvement potential requires a clear understanding of whether the basic problem is deteriorating operational trends or failure to meet unrealistic expectations. If the basic problem is unrealistic expectations, a financial restructuring is likely to succeed, if it is based on more realistic new projections of future earnings and cash flow. If there is a declining operating-result trend, it is necessary that there be a clear understanding of:

- What segments of the business have been declining?
- Where present operations are making and losing money?

In analyzing the business and its profit results, it is essential to understand and use the concept of value-added margin over material costs and to focus the analysis on unit volume, not just dollar-based revenue.

Working capital analysis is a prerequisite for understanding operations. Increases in number of days receivable or inventories is almost always a sign of trouble and often reflects overstatement of operating results.

In almost all cases, analysis of where the business is making and losing money will disclose that the 80/20 rule is alive and well. Profit improvement can best be effected by operational changes that focus on increasing the revenue streams that generate the most value-added contribution and discontinuing those products that provide the least value added or require disproportionately high overhead costs.

A useful analysis device and communication tool is a simple, one-page bridge analysis projection identifying, conceptually, how the company gets from its unsatisfactory present situation to a satisfactory future. If changes required are numerous and probabilities of success low, the business likely is not viable.

After determining and understanding where the company is making and losing money and its operations improvement potential, the next steps in the diagnostic process are evaluation of the company's external competitive environment and its internal organization and business processes. These are discussed in the following two chapters.

EXHIBIT 9-5
OPERATIONS RISK ASSESSMENT

Questions		Low		Average		High	
	0	**1**	**2**	**3**	**4**	**5**	

Risk Profile

Questions	0	1	2	3	4	5
Operations						
• Unit sales volume trends are negative?	N	N	??	??	Y	Y
• Operating earnings trends are negative?	N	N	??	??	Y	Y
• Income below forecasts due to revenue misses?	N	N	??	??	Y	Y
• Income below forecasts due to cost increases?	N	N	??	??	Y	Y
• Gross margin ratios have declined significantly?	N	N	??	??	Y	Y
• S, G & A ratios have increased significantly?	N	N	??	??	Y	Y
• Return on investment is low?	N	N	??	??	Y	Y
• Union rules restrict production flexibility?	N	N	??	??	Y	Y
TOTAL SCORE						
Number of 4's and 5's						
Business/Organization Stability						
• Relationships have deteriorated with key customers?	N	N	??	??	Y	Y
• Customer base is highly concentrated?	N	N	??	??	Y	Y
• Growth has been largely via acquisition?	N	N	??	??	Y	Y
• Acquisitions have not been well integrated?	N	N	??	??	Y	Y
• Losses have occurred implementing new projects?	N	N	??	??	Y	Y
• Management turnover is high?	N	N	??	??	Y	Y
• Employees with core competencies are leaving?	N	N	??	??	Y	Y
• Directors are insiders or lack business knowledge	N	N	??	??	Y	Y
TOTAL SCORE						
Number of 4's and 5's						

KEY to scoring – Circle most accurate:

N = No   Y = Yes   ?? = Uncertain; not clear-cut

0 = No, without exception   3 = Generally yes, with regular exceptions
1 = Generally no, minor exceptions   4 = Yes, but not a crisis
2 = Generally no, with regular exceptions 5 = Yes, creating a crisis

Recommended Reading

Managing for Results: Economic Tasks and Risk-Taking Decisions
(Harper & Row, 1964) by Peter F. Drucker.

This is one of Drucker's earlier books, a business classic in terms of innovative thinking and useful advice relating to business strategy. Many business books in the 40 years since *Managing for Results* was published seem to continue to be fleshing out ideas first presented there.

Drucker describes his book as a "what to do book...practical rather than theoretical." Part One stresses analysis and understanding of a business, the diagnosis process in our terminology. Part Two focuses on building for the future, based on strengths and opportunities rather than solving problems and prolonging the life of yesterday's breadwinners.

Lean Thinking: Banish Waste and Create Wealth in Your Corporation
(Simon & Schuster; 1996) by James P. Womack and Daniel T. Jones.

This book, built on the authors' earlier work about the automobile industry, includes a number of excellent case histories documenting cost improvements. In our view, its most valuable parts are detailed definitions, explanations and examples of what can be accomplished in creating customer value.

Womack and Jones provide an excellent context for thinking about the company's value stream in an overburdened workhorse manufacturing company. There is no better source for thinking about the potential for process improvements if time and resources are available. Their advice is simple in the telling, if not necessarily in the execution. "To hell with your competitors; compete against *perfection* by identifying all activities that are *muda* [waste] and eliminating them."

The 80/20 Principle: The Secret to Success by Achieving More With Less (Currency/Doubleday, 1998) by Richard Koch.

Pareto's Law (the 80/20 Principle) was postulated in 1897 by the Italian economist Vilfredo Pareto. This book may be the first devoted to this subject, although the concept has been discussed in many other studies and articles. As defined by Koch, "the 80/20 Principle asserts that a minority of causes, inputs or effort usually lead to a majority of outputs or rewards."

A great deal of this book is devoted to the history of the use of the 80/20 Principle and potential applications outside the field of business. However, Koch's excellent discussion of business analysis by identifying the "vital few" and "trivial many" point the way to innovative thinking about operational turnarounds of troubled businesses.

Chapter 10

EVALUATING THE COMPETITIVE ENVIRONMENT
Business Cycle and Competitive Issues

While looking inward can often illuminate a great deal about a company's problems, businesses don't operate in a vacuum. External challenges typically have the potential to be more devastating than internal stumbles, and the competition refuses to stand still. Understanding the competitive environment is, therefore, critical.

The starting point for evaluating the competitive environment is to understand the industry, its historical trends and the company's position within it. Industry data should be obtained from both company and external sources. The latter may not exactly fit the company's niche in the market, but it is a reasonable starting point. Among the key general questions are:

- Market maturity and growth rates: Are markets for the company's products growing?
- How cyclical is the business: What factors drive the peaks and valleys?
- How easy is it for new domestic or international competitors to enter the market?
- What are the long-term profitability trends of the industry?
- How important is seasonality or a fashion cycle to the business?
- What are industry requirements for heavy capital expenditures?
- How rapidly is industry and product technology changing? Is there a "disruptive technology" attacking low-end portions of the market?
- What is the industry's leverage with regard to the distribution channel?

Background information and analyses relating to the above data can be obtained from a variety of sources. For a quick industry overview comparison of financial statistics, we generally use Value Line reports. More in-depth information can be obtained from reports by security analysts and trade associations and by analyzing the financial reports of public companies.

The other, most readily available source of information about the competitive environment is, of course, company personnel (see the management survey questions in Chapter 8, Exhibit 8-1).   In these interviews, the questioning should drive deeper than top management. It is not uncommon in an operationally troubled company to find widely divergent views of the industry and the company's position in it.   Second-line managers are likely to view the industry and the company from their different functional perspectives, which can be useful.   At the same time, a discordance of views may be an indicator that a company lacks a coherent strategy.   This is particularly true when company plans are built around increasing volume by means of market share growth.

Many excellent books discuss business strategy and the changes needed to bring about long-term growth.   As we've said, the key objective of *this book* is to examine and emphasize the earlier and broader task of identifying opportunities and evaluating risks, rather than the development or implementation of detailed action plans for a turnaround.   If conclusions are reached that the business is not viable as a standalone entity and that a turnaround is unlikely, the next question is, what exit strategy will yield greatest value?   The goal is separating the wheat from the chaff and then determining how best to maximize the value of each.

Developing an understanding of the general competitive environment, coupled with other diagnostic tools discussed elsewhere in this book, makes possible a reasonable evaluation of:

1.   The odds of achieving an operational turnaround, or at least continuing survival for a reasonable period;
2.   The general action steps required to achieve a turnaround, or, alternatively,
3.   The best course of action to maximize the value of company assets when a survival attempt does not justify projected costs and risks.

Market Maturity Issues

During periods of rapid growth, products typically generate high margins and increase a company's profitability.   In contrast, mature markets like steel and textiles offer very slow growth, with many, if not most, products becoming commodities with little or no pricing power due to both domestic and global competition. (To a significant extent, organization issues are a result of the stage of the company's product and market lifecycles, as previously discussed in Chapter 3.)

If an industry is mature it will typically be consolidating, as the weaker players drop out or are acquired.   In mature industries, it is important to understand the company's position and where it stands relative to the No. 1 and No. 2 participants. If a mature business does not have a No. 1 or 2 position in any profitable market niches or have a clearly defined cost advantage, its prospects are likely to be poor. In evaluating market maturity and growth cycles of products, it is essential to consider that products are not commodities *if* a strong brand image and product preference have been established that maintain good margins, even in an industry and market that may be mature.

Conversely, low market share, weak brand recognition and low perceived value are major weaknesses in consumer markets. In such situations, a business is at a major competitive disadvantage in dealing with larger retailers. If this situation results primarily from lack of past support for a brand, it is difficult to correct and probably too costly for a financially troubled company. Even with good prospects and a well-defined implementation plan, creditors are unlikely to support this type of "investment."

In certain businesses, mature low-growth markets for heavy industrial equipment can bring increasing profits from after-market sale of parts and service to a constantly increasing installed base. The parts tend to be proprietary and after-market service pricing generally yields higher margins than the base business. This is both a good opportunity if the base business has a large market share and a risk if competitors are being provided an excessive pricing umbrella.

In general, if physical volume of an industry is declining due to reduced market demand, it is extremely difficult to maintain a viable business when a company is not a market leader. Jack Welch is well known for his philosophy of being No. 1 or 2 or getting out. One alternative is a move into new product lines selling into a different market, but very few companies seem to make this change successfully. Most continue on the downward volume curve, unsuccessfully trying to reduce operating costs fast enough to stay ahead of falling revenue and value added.

With proper management the market leader can sometimes "milk the business" for an extended period as it declines, while generating good cash. General Electric, for example, did just that for many years with a profitable vacuum tube business in which it held a No. 1 position. As products in which tubes were used converted to transistors, management clearly articulated their vision of being the last manufacturer to survive in this declining business. High labor-cost operations were transferred to new plants in Southeast Asia to maintain cost leadership, other cost reductions were rigorously pursued and technical resources were devoted to technology involving higher-priced, low-volume products that continued to be used in military electronics applications. Very little profit was left for other industry participants, which gradually closed their plants and exited the business. These competitors were generally financially troubled businesses that addressed the need for an exit strategy far too late.

However, taking the actions required to pull off this process for an extended period of time is anathema to most management teams, because, in their view, revenue growth is where the glory is. The highest value option for a troubled business is often to address needs for required cost-cutting by sale to a strategic buyer that may be more prepared for or capable of implementing what is required in a declining market.

As products or services become commodities in mature markets, low costs become the key to success. In retailing, the Big Box retailer took share from the smaller, higher-cost chains and "Mom and Pop" standalone stores. In meatpacking, the large, efficient plants built near the best sources of supply wiped out the old multi-story, inefficient plants of Chicago. In branded consumer products, the No. 1 and 2 brands with the marketing, advertising and distribution cost leverage are usually the winners.

The alternatives are few for turning around a financially troubled Aging Mule business in this competitive environment. A well-planned exit via strategic sale or liquidation is likely to provide the highest value. If the decision is made to hang on, it should be made with clearly defined rules that investment spending for the business is to be subjected to diligent cost/benefit analysis and minimum return thresholds.

Roger Lowenstein's *Buffett: The Making of an American Capitalist*[8] contained an enlightening description of how Warren Buffett milked cash out of Berkshire Hathaway, the textile company he acquired in 1965 that became the base for his mammoth holdings. The company's textile mills in New Bedford, Mass., in long-term decline, were operated on a cash-positive basis for 20 years until 1985, when they were finally closed. During that time, Buffett exercised aggressive discipline, approving capital expenditures only when justified by reliable, short-term paybacks.

AUTHORS' CASEBOOK: DUMPING AN AGING MULE'S LOSERS

A publicly held manufacturer of specialty chemicals and pharmaceuticals had lost market share to lower-cost competitors in key segments of its historical mature core business and was experiencing large operating losses. As a result of its failure to achieve a restructuring of bank debt, the company filed for Chapter 11 bankruptcy.

Critical Challenge: Analyzing product and market segments of each of the company's businesses to provide the basis for operational and financial restructuring upon which to base a Plan of Reorganization.

The following actions were implemented by existing management, including co-author Steve Hopkins as CFO:

---

[8]Roger Lowenstein, *Buffett: The Making of an American Capitalist* (New York: Random House, 1995).

> • Sale of the parent company's historical business in a series of four separate product-line divestitures to maximize recoveries;
>
> • Transfer of responsibility for manufacturing and marketing of selected high-margin products with growth potential from the parent company to profitable subsidiaries;
>
> • Decentralization of most business-support functions to subsidiaries, allowing the company's headquarters to be sold and corporate personnel relocated to another state with a 90% staff reduction.
>
> The company emerged from bankruptcy with a Reorganization Plan that provided for 100% payment of debt with interest. Debt was paid in full several years ahead of schedule.

Profitability Trends

What are the long-term profitability trends of the industry? Is profitability of the industry and its major participants improving or deteriorating? What pricing power is available? Are there any "gatekeeper" or "toll-bridge" characteristics in the market that increase pricing power? Pricing power of established communications businesses in setting advertising rates is reportedly what led to Warren Buffett's interest in Capital Cities Communications and his purchase of the daily newspaper *The Buffalo Evening News*. Similar pricing power exists with well-known brands like Coca-Cola and Gillette. Daily newspapers are a prime example of businesses that historically acted as a "gatekeeper" to the market. However, with the disruptive technology of the Internet, they are losing some of their clout.

These questions typically lead to lifecycle issues (discussed in more detail in Chapter 11). Are you dealing with a growth industry in which profitability is high because products are differentiated and improving in value? Or, conversely, are markets mature, with products becoming more like commodities, followed by globalization of sourcing and deteriorating profits? If industry profitability trends are bad, it is unlikely that prospects are good for any financially troubled individual company within that industry. Exceptions may occur, but generally only for market leaders.

Typically, the keys to good long-term profitability trends include:

1. High share in a growing market;
2. Continuing technology improvements to differentiate products;
3. Brand position that hinders entry by competitors.
4. Lower cost structure than competitors.

If none of the above exist, long-term prospects are not good and risks of attempting a turnaround are high.

Industry Cycle and Capacity Issues

In evaluating a troubled company, understanding industry and market demand cycles is critical. This affects both commodity pricing (discussed below) and product demand.

It seems to be the case that the cyclical business is most often found in mature markets. Such a business becomes financially troubled as the low point of the cycle approaches. Diagnosing problems of such businesses will, of necessity, be heavily focused on obtaining the best possible knowledge and forecasts of when the next upturn will start and how fast the growth is likely to be.

A key issue in evaluating risks and opportunities is how much the peaks and valleys of the cycle vary from the normalized trend. Sales of heavy capital equipment used in plant expansions can easily drop 50% or more during a recession.

In heavy fixed-cost industries like paper manufacturing, some plants must either be operated full-time or shut down. In an economic downturn, the high-cost producers will obviously tend to drop out first. In an upturn, new investment in more cost-efficient capacity often comes on-line, which makes obsolete, high-cost plants even less profitable. Many never restart production.

Effectiveness and the cost of the critical overhead structure compared with the competition can be either a key to long-term success or a competitive disadvantage. In certain businesses, technical design engineering and sales support can be as important a fixed cost of capacity as the manufacturing plant itself. Cutting back this structure as revenues drop becomes as difficult a decision as closing a manufacturing plant. If technical skills and ability to react to customer needs are not competitive, business will go to those who are.

There is a tendency for management to think that its technical support functions are the best in the industry and well worth the high cost. This is an area where benchmarking the competition, if possible, is critical. Outsourcing as many non-critical functions as possible, both domestically and internationally, to reduce fixed costs can be a significant protection for profitability during down-cycles.

When a financially troubled cyclical business has good market position and a management that accepts the need for dramatic cost-cutting to survive, chances of a profit turnaround and realistic debt restructuring are quite good. The key is overcoming denial and acknowledging that action is necessary. Among the major turnarounds we have seen in cyclical industries were a manufacturer of foundry equipment for automotive parts applications, a commercial and industrial tempered glass manufacturer, a foundry serving heavy industrial machinery markets and the time-share resort developer described below.

AUTHORS' CASEBOOK: Riding Out a Real Estate Downturn

Fairfield Communities, Inc., a major real estate time-share developer, filed Chapter 11 bankruptcy in October 1990 with $850 million of liabilities. The company's problems were primarily a heavy debt load resulting from acquiring a savings and loan bank used for receivables financing and initiating a series of new development projects that became unprofitable during a downturn in the economy. Co-author Steve Hopkins was an advisor to secured creditors; his assignment was to review and evaluate business viability and provide bankruptcy court testimony regarding valuations and plan feasibility. Particular attention was focused on a review of future prospects for each time-share development location, including valuation of outstanding installment receivables.

Critical Challenge: Convince the bankruptcy court and other parties to the case to require certain modifications to the Plan of Reorganization that would more adequately protect secured creditors and preserve enterprise value.

Proposed changes to the plan that included discontinuing development at selected locations were opposed by the company, which feared that long-term growth would be reduced. However, convincing arguments were presented based on the facts of the situation, and compromise adjustments to the plan were negotiated.

The modified Plan of Reorganization with existing management continuing in control was approved. Restructuring actions implemented by the company proved highly successful, and profitability improved dramatically as the economy improved. Secured creditors were ultimately paid in full and shareholders of the reorganized company subsequently achieved major gains.

Commodity Pricing Issues

Cyclicality, a key issue in many troubled businesses, occurs on two levels: increasing unit costs as volume declines, due to failure to utilize manufacturing capacity, and the effect of global supply trends on pricing of commodity products.

Unprofitable commodity pricing is extremely difficult to deal with in an overleveraged, financially troubled company. Particularly difficult is the extreme uncertainty involved when global forces such as exchange-rate fluctuations, government-subsidized operation of uneconomical facilities and drops in demand reduce pricing for a U.S. producer below its cash costs of production. Consider these two examples:

A costly, well-engineered, carefully analyzed facility was built to provide a low-cost alternative to using scrap as the raw material for steel mini-mills. Historical levels of scrap metal prices were analyzed over a period of many years to justify the large investment. Unfortunately, shortly after the plant began operations in the late 1990s, companies in Russia, India and other countries began to deliver an alternative to scrap metal. Pig iron, produced in underutilized government-subsidized mills, began to be imported into the U.S. at prices 25% below equivalent scrap metal prices, making the new plant totally uneconomical until the market turned, much later.

The primary component in the manufacture of ammonia fertilizer is natural gas, so fertilizer plant location becomes a trade-off between comparative costs of natural gas and the costs of fertilizer transportation to the big Midwest farm markets. Due to these economics, significant production expansion occurred in Trinidad and Venezuela, where low-cost natural gas was available. When domestic natural gas prices spiked dramatically in 2000-2001, operation of U.S. ammonia plants became uneconomical and many plants shut down temporarily with natural gas commitments being sold for other higher-value added uses. A major windfall occurred for the Caribbean producers.

When evaluating cyclical businesses it is important to understand the history of the cycles and to allow a large margin for error in forecast assumptions. Assumption of a straight-line continuation of past trends leads only to trouble and over-optimism. Even looking at the past history of the cycles at their worst may not be adequate. Changes in global trends of supply and demand can dramatically change the competitive landscape in ways not seen previously. Murphy's Law – "what can go wrong will go wrong" – is usually fully operative. In troubled companies, "O'Toole's view" that Murphy was an optimist also often proves correct. However, when the market swings there is dramatic upside potential, as was evident with copper, nickel, oil, coal and even steel during 2004 and 2005.

Ease of Entry Issues

Certain businesses have trouble maintaining profitability because it is easy for competitors to enter cyclical businesses in good times when margins are high and then "hang around" until driven out in the next downturn. This can be particularly troublesome in service industries. At one commercial and industrial roofing installation company, a local branch manager told us his competitors were "anyone with a pickup truck and pair of scissors." This was a gross exaggeration considering the scale of projects on which this company worked, but is an indication of a business in which it was easy to add capacity to skim some small high-margin projects when demand increases caused pricing to improve. A new competitor in the market is always reluctant to leave until losses become untenable. We have seen this with in many businesses, including:

- Plastic molded parts, costs of which are driven primarily by equipment capability. Competition is both the alternative manufacturer and vertical integration by a user to produce a plastic molded part that is a component of another finished product.

- Metal trash containers assembled with low-tech cutting and welding equipment.

Somewhat related to the ease of entry question are issues of geographical location and the need to be "local" to service the market properly. Although a program was in place to effect change to a more standardized approach, the roofing installation business was local in the sense that transporting experienced work crews long distances to do installation work is not cost-effective when competitors are closer to the project. Freight, too, can be a significant factor in some businesses, favoring those that have local, or at least geographically dispersed, production facilities. Prefabricated steel buildings and metal trash containers, for example, carry high delivery costs because of their weight and bulk. Good market position in a local or regional market is likely to produce higher profits than a larger volume of business that is geographically dispersed.

The other side of ease of entry – the difficulty of exit – will be taken up in more detail in Chapter 12, as part of a discussion of developing and evaluating alternatives. In some situations, it is more costly to exit than to continue existing operating losses.

Seasonality, Fashion and Fads

By their very nature, some industries and businesses are subject to fashion and seasonality issues that lead to major swings in revenues and income month-to-month and year-to-year. Such businesses are subject to risks uncharacteristic of other businesses and must be very carefully evaluated if an assumption is to be made that they can survive on a standalone basis. A sound capital structure with solid equity is required to protect against these abnormal risks. The fact that the business has become financially troubled is usually more an indication that the economics of the business model have changed than that leverage was excessive at the time debt was incurred.

Frequently, such businesses are both fashion-oriented and seasonal in nature; consider the new hit toys or games that sell primarily during the Christmas season. Mattel has survived and generally prospered for many years with the Barbie doll as its leading product, but this is the rare exception. A new entrant to the market faces many hurdles, starting with an order cycle that must be essentially complete by April 1, scheduling and financing of product sourcing from East Asia under a very tight frame, and a customer payment cycle that often requires financing receivables until after Christmas. Investment economics and the risks of such a business are totally different than those of most manufacturers operating in stable markets. One big mistake can put a company out of business, but it has to make the bet to survive.

Certain "industries" represent little more than fads that rise and fall with amazing speed, as we all saw with the dot.com mania of overfunded, poorly managed startups from 1996 to 2000. Another example we are personally familiar with was the sports trading card business. Industry sales peaked at approximately $1.1 billion in 1991, but in the mid-90s commenced a steep and rapid decline to less than $400 million. On the way up the business was highly profitable. On the way down, after new competition had entered the market and very high fixed-cost commitments had been put into place, major losses were incurred as management refused to cut costs, believing the downturn was temporary.

Globalization of Product Sourcing

Dramatic impacts have been felt over time in a variety of consumer products industries, including textiles and apparel, consumer electronics, toys, footwear and many other volume products. At most troubled companies facing the potential of such threats, management have a series of arguments as to why the overall trends don't apply to their particular market niche. But, long term, they usually do. If there is no plan for getting ahead of the curve with advantages such as partial offshore sourcing or quick delivery cycles, the odds are that the business will not be viable long-term. It may take years, and good management may milk out considerable cash, but when faced with competition from continuing expansion of low-cost international production, odds of long-term survival are poor without an innovative change in business direction.

Investment Needs

Bruce D. Henderson of the Boston Consulting Group wrote extensively about "cash trap" industries, arguing: "The majority of products in most companies are cash traps. They will absorb more money forever than they will generate."[9] After investing in U.S. Air, Warren Buffett made similar comments about the airline industry. There are at least three different types of situations in which this becomes a major problem, resulting in well-established, historically profitable businesses that find themselves in situations where they are no longer viable:

1. Funds are either unavailable or expenditures are not financially justified to maintain required capital expenditure levels. Typically, this means the

---

[9] Bruce D. Henderson, "Cash Traps," *Perspectives on Strategy*, ed. Carl W. Stern and George Stalk Jr. (New York: John Wiley & Sons, 1998).

deferral of purchase of production equipment required to maintain cost competitiveness or to meet higher quality standards and the failure to replace obsolete, high-maintenance equipment that experiences significant production downtime. If a company can't keep its trucks on the road, production equipment operating or aircraft in the air, it is obviously at a serious competitive disadvantage.

2.   Leadership, or at least competitiveness, is not being maintained in product technology. Occasionally a small niche business may milk a product for years, but, more typically, constant development and redesign of products is required to maintain and grow sales volume. This is where the laggards in an industry face a significant disadvantage. The leader has market share; its higher volume and cost leadership generate high profits to reinvest as required. The follower may have the management and market coverage capability to continue an appearance of competitiveness, but cash flow cannot be generated to react to major investment requirements or the occasional business downturn. Gradual decline ultimately spells doom, but if the brutal facts of the situation are recognized, a high return on residual investment may be achieved for many years.

3.   In consumer branded products, production costs and related capital expenditures may be a rather limited competitiveness problem. However, advertising and sales promotion funding requirements become major issues as the leading companies build position. In branded consumer products, the market leaders have an overwhelming advantage in selling, distribution, advertising, sales promotion and general administrative expenses that grows from their volume leverage.

In evaluating business viability, the need for future capital expenditures must be carefully evaluated. Generating high levels of reported EBITDA while hemorrhaging cash is not the answer.

AUTHORS' CASEBOOK: Orderly Wind-Down of Operations

A Canadian-based distributor of computer industry products was unable to properly consolidate operations of two U.S. acquisitions, resulting in significant operating losses. A major infusion of additional capital by the parent company was being demanded by secured creditors as a precondition to continued revolving loan advances. The initial crisis management assignment was a due diligence evaluation for the parent company of viability and future potential of U.S. operations, to determine if an equity infusion was warranted based on potential future returns and risks of loss.

Critical Challenge: Review management's operational plans and related earnings forecasts, cash-flow projections and market penetration assumptions to determine if an operational turnaround could successfully be executed.

Evaluation of the industry environment with its established high-volume, low-cost competitors led to a conclusion that it was highly likely that ongoing negative cash flow would continue despite the proposed investment. An immediate liquidation was recommended.

Customer lists and fixed assets were sold to a competitor, a profitable subsidiary in the United Kingdom was sold as an ongoing business, receivables and inventory were liquidated by company employees and out-of-court settlements were negotiated with trade creditors.

Liquidation of the business was completed without a bankruptcy filing. Secured creditors were paid in full and trade creditors were satisfied by return of product and consensual out-of-court settlements. Although the parent company was forced to write off its large investment, it remained a viable entity without the overleverage and debt service obligations that would have been required had new cash infusions been provided.

Product and Technology Issues

Critical to evaluating whether a financially troubled company is viable is an understanding of its products and technology strength. Products or services do not have to be superior, but they must be competitive in terms of value provided to customers. This means satisfactory quality, prices generally in line with industry standards and technology that meets customer needs.

In our experience with financially troubled businesses, we saw fewer product and technology failings than might be expected. Those that occurred tended to be more related to quality problems than to lagging technology. However, in larger, financially stronger companies with the resources to continue support of selected product-line losers, lagging technology can be a drain of resources for many years.

In understanding the competitive environment and risks to long-term business viability, it is important to determine those risks that management has not yet addressed but that could prevent an operational turnaround. Companies with entrenched market positions rarely come up with the new technology or approaches to the market that will revolutionize an industry. It is the outsiders and new market entrants that most often accomplish this; vacuum tube manufacturers did not make a transition to transistors, Wal-Mart was not a new cost-competitive retail model started by a department store chain, and railroads did not start airlines.

Most mature troubled businesses are facing some major threat that management is doing its best to ignore or rationalize away. Part of the process of diagnosing the competitive environment of a troubled company is to identify such threats in order to understand the degree and timing of risk that may be involved.

Clayton M. Christensen in *The Innovator's Dilemma*[10] differentiates clearly between the sustaining technology advances of the existing firms and the disruptive technologies of the new entrants. He points out the reasons that managements are generally making rational short-term business decisions in taking actions that kill them in the long run – as we saw with mini-mills in the steel industry and midrange computer manufacturers that attacked the mainframe market and were themselves then undercut by the cheaper competition from personal computers.

AUTHORS' CASEBOOK: High-Tech Lease Portfolio Liquidation

A U.S. company with subsidiaries in five Western European countries had achieved rapid growth in leasing of computer peripherals and other office equipment. However, due to industry technology changes that resulted in rapidly falling prices, residual values assumed in leases were unrealistically high. The company began to incur major operating losses and defaulted on its bank loans. Working for the company's secured creditors, a crisis management team was assigned to establish control over receivable accounting and collection of lease payments as the basis for a liquidation.

Critical Challenge: Manage project in a manner best suited to achieving highest possible recoveries

It was concluded that the highest recoveries could be achieved by maintaining ongoing operations to wind down the portfolio while attempting a strategic sale. Using company employees, procedures were developed to clean up any missing documentation and collect all delinquencies. Potential strategic and financial buyers that had tax losses in the various European countries that could be used to offset leasing profits were identified and contacted. By focusing only on buyers that could take advantage of the unusual tax considerations involved and by demonstrating an ability to deliver an operating business with a clean, well-documented portfolio, the crisis management team was able to achieve proceeds greatly in excess of normal liquidation values.

Distribution Channels

What is the industry's leverage with regard to the distribution channel? In consumer products markets, the Big Box discount retailers such as Wal-Mart and Target often exert tremendous pricing pressure on their suppliers.

The revenue growth potential for suppliers to these large customers may be great and there is often no other practical customer alternative if revenue growth is to be achieved. But, over time, profitability tends to be squeezed down to minimal levels unless brand strength exists to offset pressure on pricing. Clearly, concentration of the customer base must be evaluated in all situations as a key risk factor.

---

[10] Clayton M. Christensen, *The Innovator's Dilemma: When New Technologies Cause Great Firms to Fail* (Boston: Harvard Business School Press, 1997).

Supplier Relationships

Supplier issues are often a major problem for financially troubled businesses (as was discussed in Chapter 8). Obtaining product supply can prove difficult if a company, because of financial weakness, is not viewed as a viable long-term partner in the suppliers' distribution channel. In addition to normal trade suppliers, other examples include potential loss of licensing rights to production of trademarked consumer goods and potential loss of rights to import high-volume consumer products.

Summarizing the Competitive Environment Review

Reports on the competitive environment are frequently arranged as a "SWOP analysis" of Strengths, Weaknesses, Opportunities, Problems. This simplified method often misses the strategic priorities of key issues. The first step, we've noted, is to understand the characteristics of the industry and how the characteristics of the company fit with requirements for success in the industry. The SWOP analysis then becomes a summary of certain key issues in terms of understanding sources of greatest leverage on business success or failure.

Conclusions from the completed competitive environment analysis provide a basis for comparison with conclusions derived from the operations evaluation (see Chapter 9) related to:

1. Details of changes in operating income trends
2. Analysis of where the company is making and losing money.

In the typical troubled business, it is likely that the competitive situation is driving many unfavorable operating trends of the company. To the extent that management is ignoring these unfavorable external factors, it is creating unrealistic expectations about the future and avoiding necessary change. Recognizing and defining details of the problems does not provide assurance of a solution but is a necessary prerequisite to attempting a solution.

Exhibit 10-1 is a risk-profile checklist of external market conditions that should be evaluated. There are no simple answers, but risk levels at the 4 to 5 rating for more than four to five of these questions are an indication of the potential for serious trouble.

Chapter Summary

To evaluate a company's competitive environment, these industry characteristics and issues should be considered:

- Market share position
- Profitability trends
- Product and technology trends
- Commodity pricing trends
- Globalization of production
- Industry capacity utilization
- Investment needs

- Market maturity/growth rate
- Industry business cycle
- Distribution channel strength
- Ease of entry and of exit
- Seasonality, fashion and fads
- Geographic location issues
- Supplier relationships

The objective of this evaluation, when coupled with an understanding of operations improvement potential, is to determine if a business is viable. Either of these two general areas may provide a reason that a financially troubled company is not viable.

However, operating problems that are internal are much easier to control and fix than the external environment over which management has little control. But with a good understanding of the competitive situation, management can either adapt its strengths to the greatest opportunities left open by competitors or plan for obtaining the highest possible proceeds from an exit strategy.

EXHIBIT 10-1
COMPETITIVE ENVIRONMENT RISK ASSESSMENT

Question	Risk Assessment					
	Low		Average		High	
	0	1	2	3	4	5
Industry Characteristics/Trends						
• Markets are mature, low unit volume growth?	N	N	??	??	Y	Y
• Industry return on investment is low?	N	N	??	??	Y	Y
• Principal products are commodities?	N	N	??	??	Y	Y
• Offshore production capacity is growing?	N	N	??	??	Y	Y
• Industry is down cyclically; excess capacity exists?	N	N	??	??	Y	Y
• Disruptive technology is changing markets?	N	N	??	??	Y	Y
• Industry has low barriers to entry?	N	N	??	??	Y	Y
• Products are seasonal or fashion oriented?	N	N	??	??	Y	Y
<u>**TOTAL SCORE**</u>						
Number of 4s and 5s						
Company Competitive Position						
• Low market share?	N	N	??	??	Y	Y
• Declining market share?	N	N	??	??	Y	Y
• Company lags in offshore sourcing?	N	N	??	??	Y	Y
• Product technology lags industry state-of-the-art?	N	N	??	??	Y	Y
• Latest industry show results were poor?	N	N	??	??	Y	Y
• Competitors have cost advantage?	N	N	??	??	Y	Y
• Suppliers exert heavy cost leverage?	N	N	??	??	Y	Y
• Significant new CAPEX required?	N	N	??	??	Y	Y
<u>**TOTAL SCORE**</u>						
Number of 4s and 5s						

KEY to scoring – Circle most accurate:

N = No	Y = Yes	?? = Uncertain; not clear-cut

0 = No. without exception   3 = Generally yes, with regular exceptions
1 = Generally no, minor exceptions   4 = Yes, but not a crisis
2 = Generally no, with regular exceptions   5 = Yes, creating a crisis

RECOMMENDED READING

Confronting Reality: Doing What Matters to Get Things Right (Crown Business, 2004) by Larry Bossidy and Ram Charan with Charles Burck.

These authors, whose *Execution* was published in 2002, here develop the theme of the need to identify and confront the total realities of any business situation, as the basis for adapting to both external and internal circumstances. Particular emphasis is placed on using a business model of "External Realities, Internal Activities and Financial Targets" to overcome denial and make sure that you understand the game you are playing.

Examples given are generally mature businesses faced with a need to adapt to changes in technology, international competition and retail distribution models. Specific case history examples clearly emphasize the need to fully diagnose problems and determine, as Part III is titled, "What to change and what not to change."

The Profit Zone: How Strategic Business Design Will Lead You to Tomorrow's Profits (Times Business, 1997) by Adrian J. Slywotzky and David J. Morrison.

One of a series authored or co-authored by Adrian Slywotzky of Mercer Management Consulting, this book is likely of greatest value after a turnaround is achieved and management is attempting to move on to business growth. However, it provides an unusually complete and innovative analysis of how to evaluate the competitive environment including providing extensive checklists.

The authors' focus on the "dimensions of business design," including how to determine which customers you want to serve and how you capture value in order to make a profit. Several case histories detailing the success of business "re-inventors" demonstrate opportunities available from alternative approaches to changing the focus of a business.

Taking Charge: A Management Guide to Troubled Companies and Turnarounds (Beard Books, 1999) by John O. Whitney.

Taking Charge, first published in 1987 by John Whitney, a professor at Columbia Business School with extensive consulting experience, is written from the perspective of the newly installed hands-on leader. In many ways it is a "what to do" and "how to do it" manual for such a leader.

Excellent insights are provided related to crisis management and control of cash. However, we found the sections of the book that touched on sales and marketing to be particularly useful in analyzing the competitive environment and identifying low-risk, low-investment segmentation and differentiation opportunities.

Chapter 11

REVIEWING MANAGEMENT AND ORGANIZATION STRUCTURE
Do Management Strengths and Business Processes Match Business Needs?

Problems of a troubled company are sometimes directly related to a mismatch between the organization's culture and the mission of the business. When a mismatch between approach and goals occurs, the resulting stumbles frequently get lumped into the generic category of "bad management." This often leads to a conclusion that all difficulties can be solved by getting in a new, "better" CEO or, even more frequently, a better, more experienced CFO.

In our opinion, owners, as represented by the board of directors, must define management's objectives. Hiring new management with an expectation that they will define the problem and set appropriate objectives sometimes works very well, if the strengths of the management hired coincide with the challenges of the business. But whether it is existing management or a new team is brought in, when the goals and strengths of management do not coincide with the best interests of the business, the result is generally unsatisfactory.

We generally concur with Warren Buffett's view that even the inept can run a good business and a bad business can easily be the downfall of a good executive. The diagnosis of management and organization structure in a troubled company needs to be addressed in the context of the business challenges, using information obtained from the evaluations of internal business operations and the competitive environment.

Understanding deterioration in operating results or shortfalls from plan provides a basis for addressing the actions taken that didn't work and actions that should have been taken and weren't. As we've noted, it must be determined if the problem is primarily:

1. "Unrealistic expectations" relating to a basically viable business;
2. Correctable internal problems that are negatively impacting operations;

3. A business that is not viable, with management thrashing around trying to find a way to reach an impossible objective.

As we've said repeatedly, in evaluating a financially troubled business, bad management is less often the key problem than is widely believed. The adage that "a fish rots from the head" may be accurate in some situations but not in many others.

One key difficulty in bringing in new management is that they are likely to define the company's problem as one they think they can fix. This can be a particular problem when the appropriate strategy is to exit with maximum proceeds, because it's rare that new management are hired with this objective – and rarer still for them to come to that conclusion on their own. If it is difficult for existing management to recognize a non-viable business, even after banging their heads against failure, it is doubly difficult for new management, after accepting the challenge of a turnaround assignment, to come back and say, "We can't get there from here."

Once again, we assert: *diagnosis must precede remediation,* and a full and open-minded diagnosis generally requires a different set of skills than those required for the operational turnaround or ongoing management of the business. Whether that diagnosis is undertaken by existing management, insiders on the board or an independent third party, we believe the broad scope, fact-based, disciplined approach outlined here will greatly improve the odds for a successful outcome.

Understanding the Organization

Problems of troubled companies are typically complex and arise from a number of sources. In addition to its business lifecycle position (discussed in Chapter 3), some key issues that must be considered in evaluating the company's organization and how well it fits the business mission include the following:

Corporate Culture and Management Style: Different businesses have different styles of management, ranging from autocratic centralized control to committee-oriented bureaucracies that run a group of independent fiefdoms with little integration of objectives among the various functions or divisions of the company. It is critical that the organization culture and management style be compatible with the corporate mission and strategy. As Michael Treacy and Fred Wiersema say in *The Discipline of Market Leaders*[11], if the objective is a strategy of operational excellence to obtain the industry's lowest costs, a highly dedicated culture like those of Federal Express or Wal-Mart, focused on getting standardized things done "by

---

[11] Michael Treacy and Fred Wiersema, *The Discipline of Market Lenders* (Boston: Addison-Wesley, 1995).

the book" as quickly and efficiently as possible, is the best choice. What such a company doesn't want is a lot of creative types doing their own thing in each function or geographic location of the company.

Core Competencies: As part of evaluating business operations and the competitive environment, it should have become clear what key competencies are needed for business success. After identifying the core competency requirements of the industry, it is essential to understand the company's effectiveness – or, in many financially troubled companies, lack of effectiveness – in acquiring and maintaining them. If clearly defined competencies have provided a past position of industry leadership, opportunities for a turnaround are good.

Business Processes: Business processes and administrative controls must be consistent with mission and strategy to be effective. At Federal Express and Wal-Mart, culture is consistent with mission and strategy. This is also true of the business administrative processes. Everything is focused on standardization, efficiency and low-cost operations that can be consistently replicated leading to profitable growth.

External Relationships: In every business, certain key external relationships are critical to success. The type and depth of these relationships will vary widely by industry. In evaluating both business processes and effectiveness of top management, these relationships and their importance to the business must be reviewed. These relationships are sometimes the limiting factor in making management changes. (The structured management interviews discussed in Chapter 8 should provide answers to many issues raised here.)

Corporate Culture and Management Style

In our experience, there are four key aspects of corporate culture and management style where weaknesses are likely to trigger the need for a management change:

1. Resistance to disciplined management of business risk and the establishment of administrative controls – particular problems in the early lifecycle phases of a business managed by an entrepreneurial founder.
2. Insulated executives and managers who have lost touch with requirements of the marketplace or continue with unreasonable expectations that past rapid growth rates will continue. These often result in businesses and managements carrying to excess what made them successful in the past.
3. Management deficiencies involving denial, arrogance, greed, complacency and lack of leadership (see Chapter 4).

4. Poor practices related to hiring, managing, measuring and developing the company's staff.

In all these areas, inappropriate or unplanned risk-taking must be evaluated. As we have noted, 40 of the 54 companies in our study with internal problems had difficulties with acquisitions or with other issues related to controlling growth.

Administrative Controls

Operational evaluations and competitive environment reviews described in previous chapters assess the company's key problems and opportunities. These evaluations will normally point out very clearly specific internal problems and management and organizational weaknesses that help explain profit trends and plan shortfalls.

Assuming that profit forecasts were not met, some key issues to be addressed during the evaluations, in addition to external market factors, include:

1. What is the planning or budgeting process and who controls it?
2. What were the key areas in which forecasts were missed? Sales volume? Cost improvement? Operating expenses?
3. Were misses the result of changes in the external environment, internal operations or generally unrealistic expectations?
4. If expectations were unrealistic, why? Who drove the process that resulted in lack of reality?
5. Were there specific, realistic plans to achieve improvement, or were improvements based on the wishful thinking that external forces would "lift all boats"?
6. Were the plan shortfalls specifically related to internal performance factors – such as unexpected manufacturing quality problems, loss of a major longstanding customer or delay in implementing well-defined product redesign cost-improvement programs?
7. Were clearly evident internal management problems, external customer relationship problems or other key issues allowed to fester without an attempt to resolve them as performance deteriorated?
8. Is management readily able to answer Questions 1–7? Are processes and disciplines in place to measure, evaluate and improve operational performance?

Results of such reviews often indicate that management either attempted to autocratically impose unrealistic top-down goals or liked to hear the optimistic message that significantly improved results are possible and allowed subordinates to establish unrealistic goals without the resources and or specific plans in place to achieve them. In either case, this clearly indicates that serious management and business process deficiencies exist.

Accounting Manipulations

In a few situations, the evaluation will indicate sharp discrepancies between P&L results and fundamental operating stability. Occasionally one finds a company facing competitive inroads and liquidity constraints that may have been obscured because profit forecasts have been achieved. In these situations, some questions to be asked are:

1. Have accounting policies been changed to improve results?
2. Does there appear to have been accounting manipulation to improve results, as indicated by unusual increases in asset balances due to factors such as:
   - Recording income from reversal of previous "non-recurring" writedowns;
   - Lack of adequate receivable reserves;
   - "Loading" of customers using extended receivable terms;
   - Recording systems-installation revenues for projects not completed and accepted by customers;
   - Improper calculation of progress billing revenues;
   - Failure to write off obsolete inventories;
   - Aggressive capitalization policies for research expenditures, software development or store opening expenses (or, as was the case at WorldCom, recording routine maintenance costs as capital expenditures);
3. Have advertising and sales promotion been reduced on key consumer brands to "milk the equity" at the expense of future results?

Despite these questions, the evaluation should not become an accounting audit. However, if there is a major gap between cash flow and reported profitability, a reconciliation is required. This reconciliation and a few judicious questions during management interviews after a review of balance sheet changes often quickly bring out issues that have a major effect on the potential for achieving future expected profitability. This process will also serve as a check on management credibility. Keep in mind that if something seems too good to be true, it probably is. Financial analysts could have used a great deal more healthy skepticism as they watched the growth of WorldCom and Enron.

If there appears to be a situation in which accounting is distorting results, immediately take up the question of whether this was careless, undisciplined accounting, wishful thinking or true fraud. Despite recent high-profile failures, in our experience true fraud is extremely rare. At many troubled companies, the classic denial syndrome results in attempts to postpone addressing problems by overly optimistic "judgments" relating to accounting assumptions. These often run right up to the edge of what is allowable or, in the worst case, over the edge into fraud. Although many regulators and others would like to believe differently, accounting involves many shades of gray and allows numerous opportunities both to "smooth out" earnings and to postpone the inevitable write-offs that a new management can take to excess when it arrives.

Unfortunately, it is easy for management to convince themselves that their fiduciary responsibility is simply to maintain technical compliance with loan covenants and regulatory requirements. Worse yet, when management are overly focused on putting the best spin on reported results, that is often symptomatic of their denial that problems exist. The Sarbanes-Oxley Act of 2002, with its expanded accountability, makes such actions harder to justify these days.

Effecting dramatic change is, of course, against human nature and the style of most managements. There is a strong tendency to rationalize the past and continue to deny the need for improvement. In addition to accounting maneuvers, efforts are often directed toward avoidance of the brutal facts of the situation by some combination of:

- Milking working capital asset values to provide cash to fund operating losses;
- Diverting attention to third parties as the source of problems;
- Attempting to grow via risky acquisitions or other diversification schemes;
- Making massive organizational restructurings or other ill-conceived changes in business structure and culture that do not address underlying problems.

Employee Development

Good organizations develop people and provide them with opportunities for both job satisfaction and personal growth. These are rare characteristics in most financially troubled companies, but to the extent that they exist it is a positive sign that the business may be viable and that current management may be the right people to effect a turnaround.

Results are best when everyone in the organization has a well-defined scorecard for measuring performance and an understanding of where the business stands in relation to its competition. This is accomplished by good internal communication and a focus on making best use of employees' abilities. The management interviews can provide strong evidence if this is the case.

Core Competencies

The concept and terminology of core competencies were developed by C. K. Prahalad and Gary Hamel in a series of *Harvard Business Review* articles preceding their book, *Competing for the Future*[12]. Core competencies can relate to a wide variety of areas such as product technology, manufacturing processes, marketing skills or low-cost processing of business transactions. The term is most appropriately used in the context of an expertise that provides competitive advantage and a leadership position. Standardized or easily available technology is not considered a core competency even though it may be essential to the effectiveness of a company's operations.

For this reason, many financially troubled companies in mature markets will have no bona fide core competencies that provide a competitive advantage. Rather, they are milking a previously established position in the marketplace as they lose ground. Identifying the closest approximation to a core competency and rebuilding the highest value-added portion of the business around it may be the best course of action for maximizing long-term value as position deterioration continues.

Business Processes

In proceeding from issues relating to characteristics of management to other questions about organizational effectiveness, the key question is whether the corporate culture and related business processes are consistent with the mission and the strategy of the business. Unless such consistency can be achieved, it is unlikely that long-term growth will occur even in what is inherently a viable business. As is often said, "to a man with a hammer, everything looks like a nail"; managers tend to do what they were familiar with doing in the past, not necessarily what the business needs.

---

[12] Gary Hamel and C.K. Prahalad, *Competing for the Future* (Boston: Harvard Business School Press, 1994).

Among the thinkers and writers we have found most insightful on this front (several of whom we cite elsewhere in this book) are:

Peter Drucker, in his many writings, but especially in *Managing for Results*, where he explained the need for constant renewal by understanding the need for management to focus on future opportunities rather than on solving yesterday's problems.

Ichak Adizes, on the effect of lifecycle position and the struggle to ensure appropriate administrative controls and types of management strengths required at each phase of the lifecycle. Entrepreneurs try to resist controls far beyond the point at which they become absolutely necessary for success of the growing business.

Danny Miller, on how business processes evolve to support (and later carry to excess) the successful management focus of the business. "Salesman"-type businesses have great marketing control processes, while "pioneers" tend to ignore marketing and focus on leading-edge research and development.

Clayton Christensen, on product technology and how the business processes and related decision-making involved in growing a business with a "sustaining technology" make it almost impossible for the same management group to compete against a disruptive technology.

A key factor in the well-known long-term success of Toyota has been its focus on continuous process improvement and elimination of waste from the manufacturing process. A prime example of "Lean Thinking," Toyota demonstrates that in mature businesses those with the best and lowest-cost processes are the most successful over time.

In evaluating a company's organization, culture and related business processes, recognize that if top management are focused primarily on reported results rather than details of the process by which those results were achieved, that is a major danger signal. The objective should be to improve businesses processes constantly in order to enhance long-term profit margin. If this is not the case and the business is not well-managed, results are more likely to be random. Our view is not shared by most investment analysts, who focus excessively on quarterly results and believe a company's objective is to make the numbers expected regardless of how such results are obtained. In worst-case scenarios, you end up with situations such as Lucent offering steep discounts and generous financing to artificially pull sales forward, Nortel booking revenues not yet earned and HealthSouth under-accruing its operating costs.

In addressing the integration and consistency of business processes used by the company, it is necessary to identify what the key processes are and how they evolved:

- How are the company's business units managed? Very decentralized or very centralized? Are lines of authority and accountability clearly established?
- How is management organized? Attempting to centralize management of a disparate group of business units can be a formula for disaster; time spent standardizing management reporting and accounting will often detract from a focus on running the business. Accounting must provide adequate information for the purposes of the Securities and Exchange Commission but management reporting for measurement and control needs to be designed to fit the needs of local management, not corporate analysts.
- Is the business organized on a functional basis? Is the structure appropriate and not based on perceived strengths of individual managers with long experience? Good management does build on strengths and doesn't try to fit everyone into the same mold, but the business must also be structured to minimize weakness and ensure constant improvement in value added.
- Are information systems and measurement tools effective for the circumstances? If they are generally recognized as having serious deficiencies (a typical and legitimate complaint in companies in the Go-Go Growth and Adolescence stages of their business lifecycles), this is generally expressed as "needing better computer systems." In many cases, however, management has not installed and does not insist on installing and enforcing *the disciplines required* to make such systems effective. In mature businesses, information technology may be excellent for providing centralized control, but far from "state of the art" in providing effective business operation tools to management.
- Is management generally capable of installing and enforcing the discipline required for effective administrative control systems? The typical entrepreneurial founder usually does not have the orientation to make this an objective and generally lacks such capability. He often resists installation of administrative controls because he might have to comply with the new rules. At many companies, this proves to be the classic battle between a highly qualified COO or CFO recruited from a well-managed larger company and the founder who doesn't want to lose personal control. Managers recruited from the outside often know exactly what needs to be done to fix the situation but haven't succeeded in getting required changes implemented. It is the rare founder-entrepreneur who can withstand the blows to his or her ego caused by

accepting the restrictions on their freedom of action that are required to effect an operational turnaround of a business in trouble due to over-aggressive expansion.

- Does an independent board of directors have control of the investment commitment process? Does the process require careful analysis of risks on major new projects or acquisitions? What has been the history of success of such investments? Why successful? Why unsuccessful?

- Does the measurement system clearly define success? "What gets measured gets managed" is a truism too often ignored.

Troubled businesses often hire operational consultants to address specific problems and frequently have a number of improvement projects in process. Such projects may have good objectives but typically are very narrowly focused in areas such as information technology, sales force training, lean manufacturing, improving employee motivation or some new consulting fad that promises to deliver miraculous results.

In attempting to reverse the tide of unfavorable operating trends, management will focus on a general re-engineering of existing internal processes without properly evaluating its total business situation. When such specific projects are in process and the CEO views them as the answer to the company's problems but is not personally driving the process with a full understanding of details of the current status, that constitutes *prima* facie evidence of a serious management deficiency.

Key Relationships

Sometimes cultivating and maintaining business relationships is more important to success than the actual execution of providing goods and services. Note that many such relationships are driven by the force of the leader's personality, and if top management are replaced, these relationships may be ruptured. This is a prime example of a situation that requires fixing internal problems by improving functional support for top management, rather than replacing them.

Among the examples of such relationships are:

- Customer relationships at the highest levels where a few Big Box retailers buy most of a company's output;

- In automotive manufacturing, tightly integrated supply contracts that require just-in-time delivery and immediate top-level attention to problems;

- In the aerospace industry, long-cycle technical design support and sub-contracting relationships where continuity of knowledge is important to both parties;
- In the financial printing industry, sales and customer service relationships are of vital importance to the quick turnaround of time-sensitive filings to the S.E.C.

Management Interview of CEO

Evaluation of the organization must include an understanding of the motivations and operating style of the CEO. The in-depth structured management interview (discussed in Chapter 8) is particularly useful in gaining knowledge about the CEO's understanding of the business, vision for the future and assessment of the competitive environment. Such information must be obtained both from the CEO and from other company management. Answers are often not the same, indicating weaknesses in implementing strategy and tactics of the business.

Sometimes this discussion will demonstrate that the CEO has an excellent grasp of the "brutal facts" and is aggressively searching for solutions. More often, the interview will illustrate a great deal of denial and wishful thinking in the CEO's approach to recognizing and resolving problems. Under these conditions, responses to questions will typically consist of blaming someone or something else for the problems, as though the solution of such problems were totally out of the CEO's control.

When a CEO is in denial about basic realities of the business, forecasts may be patently unrealistic on their face and destroy credibility with lenders, shareholders and employees. This loss of credibility often then leads to an insistence by lenders on a third-party assessment of the situation or the retention of a crisis manager. Such steps are a very negative signal about a company's prospects but don't necessarily mean the CEO has no hope of being retained.

Acting on Review Results

Results of the Management and Organization Structure Review discussed in this chapter should prove enlightening in the context of supplementing operational and competitive evaluations discussed in Chapters 8, 9 and 10. Those evaluations should have placed in perspective:

1) Whether the business is fundamentally viable;
2) What actions are deemed necessary to effect an operational turnaround or position the company's profitable core business for sale to a strategic buyer;

3) What the likelihood is of successfully implementing such changes;

4) What skills and approach are required to enhance the prospects of achieving that success.

Within the time frame available to fix a financially troubled business with external problems, it is unlikely that management changes, if they are necessary, are the key to success. Conversely, if the problems are internal, management changes are more likely to be required – but this does *not* necessarily mean top management changes. It may well be that shoring up functional management with specific expertise is what is needed. In particular it is imperative that a strong, mature CFO sitting on the board of directors be in place. If the CEO is to be given a chance to continue, his or her authority must be very clearly defined and restricted. But, as we've said, in many cases an entrepreneurial founder-CEO has become too rich and arrogant from past successes to put up with such restrictions for very long and will either have to be replaced or persuaded to leave.

It is important to evaluate management capability and continuation under two different scenarios:

1. If a conclusion has been reached from the evaluations detailed in Chapters 8, 9 and 10 that a company is viable and has potential for an operational turnaround, then resources, management and business processes must be in place to support this turnaround. If adequate management is not in place – and this means the CEO, CFO, VP Operations and Sales/Marketing executives – then changes must be made to get the right team in place as quickly as possible.

2. If it has been concluded that the business is not viable as a standalone entity in the long term, then an exit strategy must be devised that will maximize value to the company's owners. Such owners may be either equity holders or creditors where the company is effectively, if not legally, insolvent. After the exit strategy has been developed (discussed further in the next chapter), it is time to determine what management changes must be made. In many cases, existing management should be retained to assist with implementing the exit strategy, often under the direction of a chief restructuring officer (CRO). If the exit is a sale to a strategic buyer, the buyer is likely to want to select its own management team but will also want to ensure the availability of individuals with knowledge necessary for an orderly transition and operational integration.

Chapter Summary

Some key issues that must be considered in evaluating the organization of a business and how the organization fits the mission and strategy of the business include:

Position on the business lifecycle: financially troubled companies in growth phases are more likely to have internal problems, while companies in decline tend to have problems related to the external competitive environment.

Corporate culture and management issues: tend to vary based on position of the company in its lifecycle. During growth phases there are a lack of appropriate administrative controls and excessive risk-taking, while in decline bureaucracy and inflexibility restrict the ability and motivation to execute required changes necessary to reflect new marketplace conditions.

Core competencies of the business: if any, must be identified and used as a basis for an operational turnaround or debt restructuring that builds on strengths of the core business.

Business processes: must support the business strategy and focus on continual improvement in long-term operating results. If a troubled company has a history of being short-term results oriented, chances of a turnaround are less likely.

Key relationships with customers: are sometimes the major driver of business success. Retaining these relationships may be more important than other factors in executing a business turnaround. Any proposed change in management should fully consider the effect on these relationships.

EXHIBIT 11-1
ORGANIZATION AND BUSINESS PROCESSES RISK ASSESSMENT

Question	Risk Assessment					
	Low		Average		High	
	0	1	2	3	4	5
Organization						
• Management focuses on revenue growth not profits?	N	N	??	??	Y	Y
• Control over ROI has been a problem?	N	N	??	??	Y	Y
• Bureaucratic rules delay minor decisions?	N	N	??	??	Y	Y
• One person controls key customer relationships?	N	N	??	??	Y	Y
• Many long-service employees are resisting change?	N	N	??	??	Y	Y
• Decision-making is highly centralized?	N	N	??	??	Y	Y
• Long term business strategy is not well defined?	N	N	??	??	Y	Y
• Responsibility and accountability are not well defined?	N	N	??	??	Y	Y
TOTAL SCORE						
Number of 4s and 5s						
Business Processes						
• Above average quality complaints?	N	N	??	??	Y	Y
• Above average manufacturing costs?	N	N	??	??	Y	Y
• Operating reports are late or meaningless?	N	N	??	??	Y	Y
• Middle management is not provided operating data?	N	N	??	??	Y	Y
• Expenditures are not controlled with realistic budgets?	N	N	??	??	Y	Y
• Revenue budgets are dictated from management down?	N	N	??	??	Y	Y
• Quarterly result targets drive key decisions?	N	N	??	??	Y	Y
• High share of sales are at end of a quarter?	N	N	??	??	Y	Y
TOTAL SCORE						
Number of 4s and 5s						

KEY to scoring – Circle most accurate:

N = No   Y = Yes   ?? = Uncertain; not clear-cut

0 = No, without exception   3 = Generally yes, with regular exceptions
1 = Generally no, minor exceptions   4 = Yes, but not a crisis
2 = Generally no, with regular exceptions   5 = Yes, creating a crisis

RECOMMENDED READING

Corporate Lifecycles: How and Why Corporations Grow and Die and What to do About It (Prentice-Hall, 1988) by Ichak Adizes.

This book is about organizational characteristics, management talent requirements and effectiveness in accomplishing objectives of the business entity. It is *not* about how the organization reacts to a specific competitive environment or completes the operational and financial restructuring necessary for a troubled company. Adizes offers a detailed, professional body of theory about ensuring that the mix of management capabilities and business processes are best suited to achieving optimal results.

The Icarus Paradox: How Exceptional Companies Bring About Their Own Downfall (Harper Business, 1990) by Danny Miller.

Built on Miller's previous work, this book develops the theory that successful strategies carried to excess by mature companies are often the cause of major difficulties as the competitive environment changes. Miller focuses on the different types of cultures that developed over time as companies grew and became successful in their markets – he describes General Motors as having a "salesman" culture and Texas Instruments as a "craftsman" culture.

Miller discusses the deteriorating performance of successful companies operating within their own "closed system." He dissects in some detail the trajectories of decline likely to be taken by each of the cultures he identifies and the recommended actions to identify causes and achieve a turnaround.

Management: Tasks, Responsibilities, Practices (Harper & Row, 1973) by Peter F. Drucker.

This is a comprehensive reference guide, 840 pages long, to Drucker's views about management. Published in 1973, after Drucker had written 12 previous books, it incorporates and expands upon many ideas that he had presented elsewhere. Sections of the book are defined as: (1) The Tasks, (2) The Manager and (3) Top Management.

In particular, Part Two, "The Manager: Work, Jobs, Skills and Organization," provides a disciplined approach to developing business structure, processes, and staffing.

Part IV

ALTERNATIVES AND ACTION PLANS

INTRODUCTION

Building upon the factual knowledge and understanding obtained through the diagnostic process, we turn to developing and assessing realistic alternatives for maximizing the value of the business. Crafting a solution for a troubled business requires a detailed and practical assessment of opportunities, resources, risks and potential rewards, all in the context of the agendas, desires and relative leverage of the various constituencies.

In Part IV, we present recommendations for:

- Identifying, defining and assessing alternatives;
- Developing consensus and support for a chosen alternative;
- Selecting the right management to implement the plan;
- Maximizing the value of asset sales, whether they are going-concern businesses or underperforming or surplus assets.

Chapter 12

DEVELOPING AND EVALUATING ALTERNATIVES
Establishing Realistic Options

Simply stated, in all financially troubled business workouts, there are three basic options:

1. Cut your losses and exit now.
2. Reallocate the interests (i.e., restructure debt and equity) and move forward.
3. Change the course of operational results to increase the value.

Within each of these three options are various permutations and multiple choices that reflect more finely differentiated and detailed alternatives. But these three general options define the basic range of alternatives, and *each needs to be addressed.* We believe that a disciplined and complete factual evaluation and diagnosis of the troubled company's situation is critical both to fleshing out and documenting detailed alternative responses and to evaluating their relative merits. The end product and objective of the diagnosis process should be to obtain and document a clear understanding of:

- Challenges faced;
- Reasonable alternative courses of action;
- Relative risk/reward and probabilities of success and failure for each alternative.

This diagnostic end-product then becomes both a tool for the decision-making process and a factual basis for negotiations.

There is a natural tendency for the party in control, typically management and equity (at least in the early stages), to pursue its *desired* goal, regardless of how unlikely it may be to achieve, while consciously or unconsciously avoiding an evaluation or contemplation of the alternatives they find less palatable. This is a mistake. Failure to address the full range of alternatives can lead to dangerous blind spots in both decision-making and negotiations. It is important to develop a fair and balanced understanding of the full range of alternatives and their likely outcomes, in order to make rational and informed decisions in one's own best interests, and to be properly informed and prepared for negotiations with parties whose interests and desires may be adversarial. Particularly in stressed and adversarial situations, failure to understand and speak reliably to the alternatives can lead to unnecessary and unfortunate impasses in negotiations. Information is power. It is essential to develop a full and complete understanding of the situation from the viewpoints of all sides.

This process of evaluating alternative scenarios that require dramatic change, particularly the critical liquidation or breakup sale scenarios that are the most dramatic of all, will be threatening to management and employees. But, if handled properly, the process can become an intriguing intellectual exercise in "thinking outside the box" that can stimulate critical thinking and establish realistic expectations about the level of performance required to legitimately justify the firm's survival and success. Hopefully it will result in an innovative turnaround plan based on assumptions with a reasonable probability of occurring. If it does not, or if resources are not available to finance transition losses or investments needed, then an exit strategy to maximize proceeds should become the highest priority, and the work invested in understanding this alternative will be energy well spent.

This exercise is also likely to identify the members of the management team with the ability to accept the changes required, as well as those who cannot. When members of existing management can embrace the process and rise to the challenge, the experience and continuity they bring is generally invaluable. As we've noted, however, some management find it extremely difficult to:

1. Face the brutal facts of a situation;
2. Take the operational restructuring actions required for a viable ongoing business turnaround, or
3. Sell a profitable core business to a strategic buyer.

Obviously, difficult issues arise when management changes are required while a business is in a state of distress. But those who remain in denial will have to go. (Selecting the right management is discussed in detail in Chapter 14.)

Benchmarking Orderly Sale or Breakup Values

However unpalatable it may be for management or equity holders, as a company begins to falter a prompt exit via sale or breakup of the business must be evaluated. A fair and balanced assessment of the company's current value, reflecting its orderly sale or liquidation in as efficient a manner as possible, should be assembled to use as a benchmark for measuring all other operating scenarios. Painful it may be, but an orderly sale or liquidation often *does* represent a higher and better value than continued operations.

Too often, management seems to believe it can avoid this unpalatable truth by ignoring it, or, worse still, artificially "low-balling" the estimated values and measuring their plans against a "forced sale" scenario that reflects their active obstruction. Certainly, the liquidation or breakup analysis should include a range of variables in achievable recoveries, but it is generally imprudent to try to make the case for a cram-down or restructuring by artificially reducing the estimated current value. There are few better ways to permanently poison an already strained relationship with creditors than to low-ball the liquidation analysis and threaten, overtly or by implication, to damage the asset values upon which they are relying.

The benchmark evaluation of a current exit should not be either "best case" or "worst case," but rather should represent the fair and legitimate assessment of a real alternative. It should present credible analysis of the best reasonable course of action designed to maximize current value. (This will be discussed more fully in Chapter 15.)

The use of third-party professionals to assist in preparation of the asset liquidation and market value analyses is highly recommended. They can provide specific technical expertise and active knowledge of the current marketplace, increasing the credibility of the analysis. The calming influence of a reputable, independent third party can also defuse the tensions that may be released if, as is often the case, the results of the analysis are regarded as bad news.

Identifying Operational Alternatives

The process of developing alternatives should draw on the diagnostic work discussed in previous chapters. These diagnoses (and where they were first discussed) include:

- A first-pass understanding of the company's financial situation in terms of (1) near-term cash flow, including potential for a liquidity crisis; (2) borrowing availability potential, and (3) asset values around which either to attempt a standalone turnaround or to maximize proceeds via business sale or liquidation (Chapter 6).

- An understanding of reasons for unfavorable operating trends or missed projections that created the current financial stress and a functioning understanding of where the company is making and losing money (Chapter 9).
- An evaluation of the competitive environment in which the company operates, including an overview of the industry, current market trends and the company's relative position in its industry and markets (Chapter 10).
- Information relating to the management and organization structure of the business, including an evaluation of its key business processes. These should produce an overview of the extent to which they are consistent with the company's past and current strategy and its lifecycle position, as well as an evaluation of the likelihood of achieving an operational turnaround with existing organization and business processes (Chapter 11).
- Results of structured management interviews that verify, modify or supplement conclusions from other work (Chapter 8).

Facts of the situation should now be pretty clearly in focus. Assessment of current value, whether in liquidation or via an orderly sale or breakup, is available as a benchmark against which to measure the viability of operations.

Now, the challenge is to develop appropriate responses. Presumably, since by definition this is a "troubled business," the status quo is not an option. What are the reasonable alternatives for changing the course of events? That depends primarily upon the nature of the challenges faced. Chapter 3 discussed at some length our view that there are three basic categories of problem company situations, with a very high overlap between the nature of the problems and the lifecycle of the business. We defined those three categories as:

- **Undisciplined Racehorses:** Good, developing businesses that have seen growth and profitability suddenly compress, typically as a result of specific internal operating problems or mistakes;
- **Overburdened Workhorses:** Profitable, stable, established businesses that are saddled with an unrealistic debt structure;
- **Aging Mules:** Businesses in decline, generally plagued by external challenges in their competitive marketplace.

No situation is totally black and white and there will always be overlap and a mix of major and minor problems. But conceptually placing the business in one of these categories, determining if problems are largely internal or external and whether the business has continued growth potential, is mature or declining should be relatively straightforward and can provide insights helpful to identifying realistic alternatives. At this stage the major issues and forces at play upon the business must be addressed in conceptualizing potential solutions.

Likely Alternatives

In many cases few reasonable alternatives may be available, in others a wide range. In undertaking operational improvements, the principal tools will be variations and combinations of the following tasks:

1. Fix functional problems
2. Downsize to core competencies/Shed loss operations
3. Divest surplus or nonproductive assets
4. Rationalize overhead and expense structure

While each situation is unique, we believe that if you've accurately and objectively identified the driving issues and categorized the problems, it becomes much easier to see what potential courses of action promise to bear fruit and which bear risks in excess of potential rewards.

Exhibit 12-1 provides a summary of the actions most often required for a turnaround in each of the three different business classifications.

EXHIBIT 12-1

EXPECTED ACTIONS REQUIRED FOR TURNAROUND

	Undisciplined Racehorses	Overburdened Workhorses	Aging Mules
Likely Key Threats	Internal	External/Internal	External
Common Causes	• Excess risk/unrelated expansion • Dysfunctional organization created by CEO/Founder • Loss of internal control/business process problems • Acquisition integration	• Cyclical demand • Commodity pricing • Global competition • Disruptive competitive technology • Acquisition integration	• Lack of marketing focus • High cost structure • Lagging technology • Loss of market share • Poorly performing management and organization
Key Analysis Required	• Where making and losing money • Details of functional problems • Organization structure • Management and controls	• Where making and losing money • Expectations vs. historical trends • Plan shortfall detail • Competitive environment	• Where making and losing money • Competitive environment • Product line strengths/weaknesses • Organizational culture • Business process costs
Expected Actions Required	• Fix functional problems • "Dump the losers" • Assign responsibility and authority • Install administrative controls • Cut back to core growth business	• Wait out cycle • Establish realistic expectations • Reduce costs • Consolidate operations • Restructure debt	• Reduce expense structure • Cut back to profitable core • Exit loss operations • Merge with/sell to strategic buyer • Sell business assets

Undisciplined Racehorses

The most likely priority in these situations is to fix major operational problems. Handled properly, the fix has a high probability of success and is most appropriate where internal execution problems are causing a viable business to incur operating losses. Under favorable circumstances, this approach may even be fully self-funded by short-term operating profit improvements. It will likely require improving administrative controls and properly assigning responsibility and authority. In most situations where operational difficulties are confined to specific functional areas, external resources can be used to achieve a fix without new top management. (The branded personal care products manufacturer discussed in Chapter 2 was such a situation.)

In situations created by overly aggressive expansion into low-margin businesses or overpriced acquisitions, the formula for a turnaround is often to dump the losers and refocus attention on the company's core – and hopefully growth – business.

Overburdened Workhorses

In developing solution options, the first questions involve why and how the business became overburdened with debt.

1. Were earnings growth expectations too high?
2. Has there been a loss of earnings power due to cyclical conditions?
3. Have internal problems reduced earnings power?

Depending on the answers, and in connection with a financial restructuring or forbearance agreement to alleviate the debt-service burden, one of these actions is appropriate:

1. *Business as usual*: This is, of course, the preferred alternative of management in denial, yet occasionally it is the correct thing to do. However, even then, such inaction is usually precluded by a lack of internal financial resources and uncertainty of the extent to which additional financial resources are required to ride out the storm. Business as usual does not mean that no cost-reduction actions are taken; it means no change in the basic operations of the business. (The tempered glass manufacturer case history is a good example of where recommending this approach was the correct diagnosis; see Chapter 2.)

2. *Cost-reduce existing business operations*: initiate cost-reductions consistent with drops in volume and implement other cost-improvement programs, while deferring capital expenditures and reducing working capital investments. This

is the second most-popular management approach and often works if a work-horse business facing a cyclical downturn has significant financial resources. There are two major problems with this approach. First, when revenue declines reduce working capital needs, cash flow provided may be used to offset operating losses, weakening long-term business value. Second, it defers taking the operational restructuring actions necessary to fix long-term problems. Lenders particularly object to a deteriorating loan-to-value ratio resulting from using working capital reduction proceeds to fund operating losses.

3. *Asset sales to reduce debt*: this approach assumes some operational restructuring in order to release assets for sale. In some cases, the most valuable assets of the business or the preponderance of working capital investments are contained in a portion of the business that is generating losses. These assets can be sold or liquidated with the objective of obtaining the funding to reduce debt to levels that can be serviced by the residual portion of the business, which has better long-term value growth potential. Such asset sales may not necessarily represent sale of product lines or business segments but could represent assets such as real estate made available by consolidation of plants or other facilities or receivables and inventory balances liquidated by exiting low-margin segments of the business.

(The specialty chemical business case history in Chapter 10 was an illustration of how a company serving mature markets can be restructured to exit historical core markets to focus on more profitable growing product lines.)

Aging Mules

Turnarounds are much less likely for businesses in this category. When they succeed, it is usually a result of an operational restructuring to refocus on the core business or other viable business segments. If the core business is profitable and not in a declining volume trend, this is the ideal platform for a turnaround scenario: Stop the bleeding by getting rid of the poorly performing product lines or money-losing diversification attempts and return to the company's roots. The key questions with this approach are:

1. Is a Chapter 11 filing needed to allow elimination of contractual commitments such as store leases or to allow debt restructuring?
2. Are potential management replacements needed to implement restructuring actions?
3. Does management have the ability to develop a realistic business plan, including overhead reductions, that allows an appropriate capital structure to be put in place?

Sale or merger of the entire business may be the only logical solution for maximizing value. Even if the business is not viable on a standalone basis, the result for a buyer could be a valuable franchise involving certain product lines that generate significant margin. Under these circumstances, the buyer provides the expertise to reduce costs and eliminates low-margin products while integrating the business into its existing operations.

Developing Alternative Scenarios

As noted above, the initial categorization of problems is primarily conceptual. It should be quite helpful in identifying promising avenues for review and focus. But once the conceptual approach is identified, it becomes necessary to dig deeper and flesh out a more detailed understanding of the alternatives. At this stage, no matter what the category of problem faced, three major assessments should be considered when developing and documenting alternative scenarios.

First, review the evaluation of industry trends and the company's position in its competitive environment. Be certain not to attempt to evaluate turnaround potential in a vacuum, without consideration for the external forces and changes in the market. This may provide useful insight into ways in which the competition has thrived, pointing to specific courses of action that need to be pursued in order to regain a position in the market. Or it may indicate that there is no hope for long-term viability due to the company's weak position and lack of resources, financial or human, to effect needed improvements. These weaknesses may involve product technology, market share, capital expenditure funding needs or business process. This analysis may point to the need for a synergistic merger, manufacturing outsourcing or vertical integration to have any chance of success. In any event, if the business is not viable, a rapid exit strategy must be devised that provides maximum proceeds to owners whether debtholders or equity. In these situations, it is necessary to be mindful that operating losses are a major drag on developing maximum proceeds and must be reduced as quickly as possible. (The sound equipment manufacturer discussed in Chapter 2 illustrates this point. Costs were cut dramatically almost immediately after the problem diagnosis was completed, leaving a marginally profitable core business that could be integrated into the operations of a strategic buyer.)

Second, determine the conceptual actions necessary to return to some satisfactory level of past operations. These can be reconstructed from the operational analysis that clearly defines the changes that have occurred as profits decline (discussed in Chapter 9), which often provides an excellent guide to actions that are necessary, particularly where internal operational problems are the key issue. Such situations often involve product quality or loss of a major customer. Sometimes the biggest single problem is that costs were increased in anticipation of volume growth that did not occur. Eliminating these costs may be the most important operational restructuring that is required. (The agricultural products company discussed in Chapter 2 is an example of such a turnaround. Profit declines occurred as a result of specific problems relating to a new plant startup, and business improvement came from fixing these problems.)

Third, identify where the company is making and losing money and construct operational restructuring alternatives around the operations with the highest profit potential. This may point the way to a satisfactory turnaround by divesting losing operations. Overhead structure should be planned on a zero-based budget basis using only what is necessary for the profitable operations that will remain. Administrative and support personnel not required by the residual operations must go; the biggest danger in constructing the plan is trying to retain unnecessary support staff. (The specialty chemical manufacturer discussed in Chapter 10 and mentioned above is an example of such a turnaround. Money-losing product lines were divested, and corporate overhead cut by 90%.)

Developing Insights

Referring back to the qualities we advocate in the KUIL concept of management (see Chapter 4):

Knowledge has now been assembled through the diagnosis process and related analysis work.

Understanding has been developed of the business model and what specifically caused problems leading to failure to meet expectations.

Developing and documenting data required to define, describe, and evaluate the reasonable alternative scenarios available to the company will help provide the **Insight** necessary to arrive at the best possible solution.

The term "scenario" is used advisedly. Management in denial is usually looking for any excuse not to face the brutal facts. Communications to management, lenders, and shareholders need to be extremely clear if they are intended to motivate people to action. A clear, concise description of each scenario and related necessary actions is usually more important than detailed accuracy of the forecast numbers attached to it. Many forecast numbers will be highly subjective and can be evaluated only in terms of a written description of key assumptions and a discussion of the nature and magnitude of risks and costs.

Principal advantages and disadvantages for each scenario should be clearly identified and analyzed. To the greatest extent possible the likelihood of success and the potential for implementation difficulties should be quantified and incorporated into the forecast in terms of a range of results. To restate the obvious, time and money are commodities in very short supply in a financially troubled business. Adequate provision for investment costs of the options and any anticipated continuing operating losses must be acknowledged and budgeted into forecast results.

Scenarios selected as viable alternatives *must focus on correction of the characteristic or category that causes the business to be considered as troubled.* For example:

- For the **Undisciplined Racehorse**, the scenario description must ref erence specific identification of the problem and illuminate the spe cific actions to be taken to fix it, along with the management and organization changes required to ensure execution.
- One obvious scenario for the cyclically depressed **Overburdened Workhorse** is a return to "normal" conditions – but it must be pre sented in conjunction with a rational and credible discussion of the factors impacting the cycle – and evaluated with sub-scenarios repre senting alternative periods of time required for an industry turnaround.
- The **Aging Mule** with a weak competitive position must have a sce nario that credibly reverses the declining trends or milks cash while servicing a restructured debt load.

In all cases the scenario and its associated financial projections should identify and evaluate the costs and benefits of implementing the corrective actions as well as the key obstacles and risks of failure.

- Where commodity pricing changes are required to effect the turn around, those changes that will drive the market improvement must be clearly demonstrated on a more-than-wishful-thinking basis. Knowledge that the cycles have always reversed themselves and re verted to the mean in the past may not be a true guide if either supply or demand conditions have changed permanently, as they often do in a world of increasing globalization.
- Details of the scenario and the operating results forecast should in clude the effect of unusual delays in returning to "normal" conditions and a recognition that "temporary" poor market conditions some times continue for years.
- If a manufacturing cost-reduction turnaround is contemplated, the

scenario description must be clearly defined in terms of the competitive environment and market-share position of the specific product lines involved. Cost-reducing obsolete manufacturing processes of a market leader by installing proper management and new equipment has a relatively high probability of success, and expected results can likely be estimated within relatively narrow parameters. However, cost-reducing the processes of a market follower expecting to im prove its relative position in order to return to profitability is a much more speculative endeavor. In all cases, there should be a benchmark evaluation against outsourcing costs and full consideration of global ization trends.

- It must be recognized that competitors will not be standing still. If the company can get a rapid investment payback from new equipment, so can its competitors, and industry pricing tends to spiral down to continue previous unsatisfactory margins.

Strategic Business Redesign Options

Strategic business redesign leading to an operational restructuring can produce dramatic operating improvements over time. *The Profit Zone*[13] by Adam J. Slywotzky and David J. Morrison evaluates the potential for such change and includes extensive detail about identifying customers, focusing on their true needs and priorities, evaluating alternative business designs and developing a model for maximizing profit from the business design and markets selected.

Understanding both the concepts and the detailed material in *The Profit Zone* is an excellent base for someone diagnosing operational and strategic problems of a troubled company. However, implementation of a major strategic business redesign is usually a much longer-term process than the crisis circumstances of the typical financially troubled company allows. Generally, this is Step 3 of the process shown below:

Step 1   Manage crisis/React to immediate needs
Step 2   Diagnose problems; Implement solutions
Step 3   Long-term growth in profitability of operationally restructured company

While identification of potential long-term strategic-redesign opportunities may emerge from the initial troubled company analysis, such options can seldom

---

[13]Adrian J. Slywotzky and David J. Morrison, *The Profit Zone: How Strategic Business Design Will Lead You to Tomorrow's Profits* (New York: Times Business, 1997).

be considered as viable alternatives for a cash-strapped troubled company unless a very confident investor is prepared to step in to fund them..

The Bankruptcy Option

It can be tempting to think that a bankruptcy filing is a full-blown and distinct option or alternative to explore, a unique, free-standing scenario. It is not. As described briefly in Chapter 5, bankruptcy law provides a set of rules and principles for dealing with the resolution of competing rights relating to a distressed company. It is a tool that may be used to facilitate a variety of different strategies and objectives, including, in different circumstances, any or all of the three general objectives set forward at the start of this chapter.

In certain situations, provisions of the Chapter 11 bankruptcy code provide specific benefits that are not readily available outside of a proceeding:

1. The company has contractual obligations such as closed store leases that it needs to terminate in order to restructure operations into a viable ongoing entity. Employment agreements, union contracts, and take or pay supply contracts fall into the same general category. The code has provisions that limit and control the allowable claims for cancellation of long-term contractual commitments.

2. Sale of a major asset of the business has been negotiated but cannot be closed due to buyer concerns relating to its ability to obtain clear title or its exposure to potential fraudulent conveyance claims. In the bankruptcy court process, such title can be conveyed free and clear of all liens.

3. It is perceived that certain creditor actions are resulting in deteriorating value for other stakeholders of the company. In addition to equity shareholders, such stakeholders may be creditors with either conflicting objectives or out-of-the-money debtholders pursuing a "scorched earth" policy to enhance their position vis-à-vis other creditor groups.

4. A "prepackaged financial restructuring" has been negotiated among key senior creditor groups but needs the blessing of the bankruptcy court to force the cooperation of unwilling minority participants and eliminate potential for future litigation.

There are also certain situations in which a bankruptcy filing becomes almost inevitable, including situations where:

1. Companies are facing massive class-action litigation such as that related to asbestos or silicone-implant claims.

2. Multiple, complex liabilities exist with conflicting claims relating to creditors' security interests in various classes of assets.
3. Trade vendors have discontinued shipments to the company, threatening to cause a "meltdown" of operations.
4. Creditors have obtained judgments against bank accounts or other essential company assets that limit flexibility of operation.
5. State court litigation has resulted in an order to appoint a receiver.
6. Default or expiration of revolving working capital facilities leave the company unable to fund its day-to-day operations.

As we have previously observed, the "protection of the court" provided by a bankruptcy filing is far more effective with regard to managing liabilities and claims than it is in maximizing value. Although bankruptcy filings no longer have the highly negative stigma attached that used to accompany them, the bankruptcy process is extremely expensive and can be highly disruptive to business operations. Less than 20% of the bankruptcies with which we have been associated resulted in a successful turnaround or restructuring in which the business emerged as a standalone entity. Arguably, this low emergence rate is at least partly a result of our success in guiding the stronger companies toward out-of-court restructurings accomplished through consensual negotiations.

In our experience, real operational turnarounds and successful standalone restructurings were usually accomplished without a bankruptcy filing. Where bankruptcies were filed in support of turnarounds or restructurings, they were generally prepackaged filings with agreement from controlling parties negotiated in advance. The filings were used to accomplish specific goals, such as shedding long-term lease obligations on unprofitable locations.

As shown in Exhibit 12-2, based on our 100-project sample, bankruptcy filings occurred in only 8 of 52 turnarounds and restructurings.

EXHIBIT 12-2

BANKRUPTCY FILINGS COMPARED WITH PROJECT RESULTS

Project Results	*No. of Projects*	*No. of Bankruptcy Filings*	*Percent Bankruptcies*
Turnarounds	31	7	23 %
Restructurings	21	1	5 %
Business Sales	26	12	46 %
Liquidations	22	19	86 %
Total	**100**	**39**	**39 %**

Liquidations are almost exclusively managed through bankruptcy filings unless claims are highly concentrated to facilitate out-of-court settlement. If general unsecured creditors are going to receive less than full-value payment of their claims following a sale or liquidation, a bankruptcy filing is almost legally essential. However, when the sale will pay off all creditors or where a buyer assumes the liability for payment of trade creditors, a bankruptcy filing can often be avoided. Evaluating the strategy for maximizing net proceeds from business sales requires careful consideration of the trade-offs between the uncertainties, timing and costs of a potential bankruptcy filing, the quantum and concentration of claims, and the flexibility of the various parties of interest.

In evaluating results of electing the bankruptcy option, the "chicken or egg" question always exists. Did the bankruptcy force the sale or liquidation, or was a reorganization never feasible? As a subjective commentary on this conundrum, we observe that in many of the successful turnarounds or restructurings with which we were involved, we are inclined to believe that had a filing been triggered before an agreement was reached, the company might not have emerged intact.

In any event, it is crucial to understand both the business challenges and the exit strategy before rushing into a bankruptcy filing. The bankruptcy process is most effective when used as a tool to quickly pursue specific objectives.

Comparing Alternative Scenarios

After the detailed scenarios have been developed, described in detail and financial modeling completed, all scenarios should be put on a comparable basis using a discounted cash-flow model covering a relatively short time-frame, no more than two or three years. Five-year forecasts are interesting, but in a troubled business any forecast improvements beyond three years are so speculative as to be meaningless.

As indicated previously, each scenario should define key downside risks and upside potential. Evaluation should include attempting to identify the most likely unexpected events or unintended consequences of changes proposed. Some of the more perceptive strategic thinkers identified in the management interview process will be helpful in developing more fully the pros and cons of each individual scenario. In evaluating risks, the time factor is critical. If a logical, high-probability-of-success action takes six months to implement and the company only has three months' cash left, something has to give.

After cash-flow needs of the business are calculated, they must be evaluated in the context of availability of financing. Even if the average ongoing company could raise the financing necessary, this is not the average company.

It is a company with a troubled past, a history of not meeting forecasts and, presumably, a weakened competitive position. Without some enhancements or the leverage of a Chapter 11 Bankruptcy Plan of Reorganization, it is not an easy sell to obtain adequate financing for what many lenders will consider as a new venture.

Communicating Recommendations

Communication of the results of the problem diagnosis process and proposed alternative scenarios needs to be something more than a written report distributed to interested parties. Even in a crisis, such reports tend to go on shelves and are not acted upon. What is needed to drive home the message is a detailed advance review of findings, with verbal presentations and extensive discussion of the material detailing company operations and the logic of conclusions reached. As is well known, some people absorb and understand written material best and others much prefer verbal input. For the greatest impact, use both types of presentations. The goal should be to bring out the objections of management, valid and invalid, related to conclusions reached and to focus attention on inconsistencies that always exist in analysis work in order that they can be reconciled.

Additionally, this step gives management in denial an opportunity to "seize the moment" and take responsibility for implementing necessary changes. Ideally, management has endorsed conclusions of the problem diagnosis and is leading the discussion and advocating required changes to its board of directors, lenders and other third parties.

Financial modeling used to project business results is often treated as if it were an exact science when, if assumptions are wrong or not well defined, the results of such modeling may be of little more usefulness in making good business decisions than throwing darts at the wall would be. In evaluating, forecasting and communicating expected results, it must always be understood that the expected result is really a range, not a specific number, and that the related execution plan must provide for flexibility to react to changing circumstances – and this means including contingency funds for unexpected events. "Stretch goals" may productively be used to improve performance of stable businesses at the prime phase of their lifecycle, but they tend to be high-risk and a recipe for disaster in a financially troubled company where time frames for execution are short and "Murphy's Law" is always at work. This is particularly true where the stretch is a top-down imposed objective of a management that does not address the realities of the situation, but insists on results without an understanding of what is required to achieve them or how low the probabilities of success actually are.

Chapter Summary

The objective of the diagnosis process is an even-handed evaluation of the risks and opportunities from the full range of alternative available options. It becomes a reliable tool for both the decision-making process and for fact-based negotiations regarding debt restructuring and required operational and financial support.

The time available, resources applied and complexity of the business situation will all have major impacts on accuracy and completeness of the problem diagnosis. In some cases, critical decisions must be made within days. Evaluating potential actions is heavily dependent on assessments of risks involved. In many situations, a quick exit is the only practical alternative.

Strategic business redesign and long-term change management are not a near-term option for the usual financially troubled business. They are Step 3 to achieving growth in profitability of an operationally restructured business, after diagnosing problems (Step 1) and implementing short-term corrective actions (Step 2).

Alternative scenarios are usually developed using a combination of the three following approaches:

- Identifying and responding to changes required by the external competitive environment.
- Returning to a past level of satisfactory operations by correcting problems.
- Restructuring around operations with the highest profit potential while eliminating the losers.

Alternative scenarios are plans with meaningful differences, not just high, medium and low results of the same plan. As a baseline comparison, alternative scenarios should include the results both of business as usual and of sale or liquidation of the business.

In the process of addressing troubled company problems, communication is of major importance. Alternative scenarios and related key assumptions need to be described in detail. Financial modeling of results of these key assumptions is a secondary exercise.

Comparative evaluation of alternative scenarios should be done based on discounted cash flow over a relatively short period of time. Forecast improvements over more than three years are so speculative as to be meaningless in a financially troubled company.

RECOMMENDED READING

The Essays of Warren Buffett: Lessons for Corporate America, first revised edition (Carolina Academic Press, 2001). Selected, arranged, and introduced by Lawrence A. Cunningham.

This book consists primarily of excerpts from Warren Buffett's essays in the annual reports of Berkshire Hathaway, Inc. They are organized into seven sectors covering subjects ranging from corporate governance to accounting policy and tax matters.

It's a delight to read anything Buffett writes, and we are particularly interested in his insights into the stock market. As for troubled companies, he makes it very clear he wants nothing to do with them. However, for purposes of evaluating alternatives, his views of what constitutes value and inherent good or bad businesses are quite helpful. These are contained primarily in Section V on mergers and acquisitions and Section VI on accounting and valuation. In addition, his essay "Aesop and Inefficient Bush Theory" is a classic discussion of valuation and the use of capital.

Distressed Investment Banking: To the Abyss and Back (Beard Books, 2005) by Henry F. Owsley and Peter S. Kaufman.

As its title indicates, this book offers the investment bankers' perspective, with a focus on financial restructuring negotiations and the various options that may be available. Troubled company restructuring examples are heavily oriented toward bankruptcy court resolutions.

In evaluating alternatives for the troubled company requiring a financial restructuring, bankruptcy must be considered, and this book provides an excellent guide to the players who will be involved and the key legal and technical issues that must be addressed. Particular emphasis is placed on valuation issues that must be analyzed and resolved in all financial restructuring negotiations.

Don't Jump to Solutions: Thirteen Delusions That Undermine Strategic Thinking (Jossey-Bass Publishers, 1998) by William B. Rouse.

Rouse is CEO of a company that produces software systems and tools, and, as a consultant, helps companies develop and implement strategic plans. This book focuses on "the perils of acting first and thinking later." Rouse documents in some detail why you should avoid the "Ready, Fire, Aim" approach to business turnarounds. Each of the book's 13 chapters discusses a "management delusion" (or excuse for denial of the need for change, to use another term).

In developing alternative solutions for troubled companies, it is easy to fall into the trap of making assumptions that are either wrong or much higher risk than is justified. Rouse's Chapter 6, "We Just Need One Big Win: Avoiding Chasing Purple Rhinos" is an excellent discussion of how management often attempt to solve their problems by devoting resources to potential solutions that have a low probability of success.

Chapter 13

REACHING CONSENSUS
Negotiating Support for Realignment of Risk and Reward

The disciplined process of diagnosis and evaluation is designed to illuminate the issues and challenges that have created the distressed situation and continue to threaten the business, and more importantly, to identify the reasonable options and alternatives that may be available to change the course of events and maximize the value of the enterprise for the benefit of its various stakeholders.

In some cases, the diagnosis may result in a recommended solution so clear and irrefutable that all the parties promptly come to a congenial agreement, amend their contracts, modify their expectations, commit to provide required incremental resources and collectively support the new plan under continuing control of existing management. Occasionally, this does happen. If the new path is clear and obvious...if it requires mainly patience and forbearance...if it is self-sustaining and doesn't require new money or external resources...if management have retained their credibility, then...maybe.

But in most situations, the end-product of the diagnosis and evaluation is the beginning of a complex dance of negotiations. There is likely to be more than one choice. All the alternatives are likely to entail risks and disappointments for some, if not all, of the parties at interest. Those overseeing the descent into distress remain in control. And the conflicting agendas and objectives remain to be addressed.

In a rational negotiation, while all the parties may seem to have conflicting desires and objectives, it is safe to assume that they are driven by one common goal: *the desire to maximize their potential returns while limiting their perceived risk to an acceptable level.* But just what constitutes an acceptable level of risk is a highly subjective determination that varies widely depending upon the criteria of the investor, be it an individual or an institution.

All potential participants in the capital structure must become convinced that they will be adequately compensated for the risks being assumed. They assess the materials presented for evaluation of the company's new business plan, perform whatever independent due diligence they determine necessary and make their judgments, all generally in reliance upon and trust of the information provided by management and advisors of the borrower. They then negotiate "acceptable" terms for their investments.

The art of deal-making revolves around carefully defining, isolating and structuring tiers of risk and reward; identifying and creating a balance between potential returns and perceived risks. Restructuring a distressed investment is deal-making under duress: Disappointment is in the air. Promises have been broken. Expectations shattered. Trust breached. The honeymoon is over.

If an acquisition or merger can be likened to a marriage, a restructuring negotiation often feels like a mediated reconciliation that threatens at any moment to degenerate into divorce. Too often the baggage and recriminations obstruct rational analysis. Too often the management or equity holders of a troubled company think that because a lender or investor is already captive, it can be "forced" to act in ways detrimental to its own perceived best interests or in violation of banking regulations.

Do not expect any party to act against its own best interests to protect the interests of others. The sole exception to the guiding principle of self-interest is that parties may occasionally be so eager to punish the guilty that they become unable to discern or acknowledge an alternative path to their own best interest.

Conflicting Objectives

In implementing whatever strategy is selected for maximizing the value of a business, three conflicting objectives related to the agendas of parties at interest must be considered and balanced:

1. Enhancing long-term ownership value of the business: recognizing that ownership value may reside with either existing equity holders or one of the creditor classes.

    *   To the extent that potential exists for generating future equity value, shareholders will push to focus on this objective.
    *   Within the various creditor classes, a great deal of time, effort and expense are likely to be devoted to attempting to jockey for an enhanced position.

2. Providing an exit strategy or prompt stabilization for lenders: either a quick exit with cash or a properly collateralized performing loan, which, if it has been discounted, will probably need to be supplemented with some future upside potential in the form of warrants or other equity participation. As we've noted, lender workout groups generally have a very short time horizon. In a regulated bank environment, upside value potential of a business is typically considered as zero and has little attraction as an inducement to postponing receipt of cash without allowing final and complete exit from the credit.

3. Maintaining job security and future opportunity for company management and employees. These groups almost always resist major asset sales while pushing for a debt restructuring and survival of the business entity, to preserve both employment and their perceived future equity-increase opportunity.

Dealing with these conflicting objectives, which are most in evidence in a Chapter 11 bankruptcy proceeding, is critical to selecting an alternative that can be effectively implemented.

Keys to Success

One key benefit of the fact-based, disciplined diagnosis process we advocate is that it tends to promote calmer, more rational negotiations. The biggest challenges in a restructuring negotiation are often re-establishing at least some level of credibility and trust while eliminating as many as possible of the emotional responses that lead to irrational negotiating positions.

Disciplined and comprehensive factual analysis is a valuable tool with which to tackle these challenges. The facts and analysis developed from the diagnosis process address both internal operational issues and the external competitive environment. Reasons for the company's problem have been well defined, the brutal facts and grim realities well documented. The base case "do nothing" scenario (outlined in Chapter 12) should have clearly demonstrated that aggressive action to effect change is required and that, otherwise, failure is inevitable.

Accepting and documenting that the "do nothing" scenario is unacceptable is a major step toward building credibility and trust, particularly when there has been a history of denial and wishful thinking. The analysis should clearly demonstrate an understanding of the challenges the business faces. Both internal errors and external challenges must be identified and confronted. In order to be viable, the plan must include credible remediation responses to the

company's key problems. Creating forecasts for the alternative scenarios selected, supported by clearly documented and conservative estimates of likely
results, will generate credibility and trust – provided that specific implementation plans for necessary remedial actions are realistic and have been or are in the
process of being executed. This is the point at which risks should be clearly
acknowledged.

By definition, the process of developing and selecting alternative scenarios
should have eliminated the irrational and insupportable options while addressing
misconceptions about the business situation. This does not mean that certain parties may not have irrational and insupportable demands, but, at least, projected
outcomes should be supported by reasonable, rational expectations and by documented requirements for additional capital funding or projected deterioration in
loan-to-value ratios required to achieve these results.

Put another way, negotiations should either start from the same set of facts
or illuminate clearly where, over what and why there is a disagreement over the
facts. A disagreement over facts is often relatively minor in significance and can
be built into the starting point of negotiations with a variance in assumptions.
In many cases, at the end of the day, despite some parties' highly emotional
attachment to Assumption B (such as the projected volume growth rate), rather
than the recommended, slightly lower Assumption A, there may be little impact on the sharing of the valuation pie among the parties to the negotiation.
Use of alternative assumptions and range of results for valuation purposes can
apply both to downside risks and upside opportunities.

If variances in assumptions regarding the facts can be understood, documented and incorporated in alternative projections, there is a basis for negotiations
about allocation of risk and reward. Under these conditions unreasonable demands based on assumptions about unreasonable outcomes can be avoided.

Reaching Agreement

Despite everything that we've said about how thorough and disciplined problem diagnosis can identify the optimum path to maximizing enterprise value,
reaching agreement in a distressed restructuring negotiation is not easy. Working with disappointed and disillusioned constituents requires patience, prag-
matism and flexibility to strike the balance between perceived risks and potential rewards. A structure must be found that addresses the conflicting goals of
the parties, balancing their appetite for, and perception of, risk with the potential rewards.

In our experience, when a potentially viable alternative must be aban-
doned due to failure to reach agreement, the failure often has less to do with a

disagreement as to the viability of the plan and its related assumptions than with a failure *to balance new or continuing risk with future rewards*. Parties act as though the regular rules of deal-making have been repealed; they are unwilling or unable to realign and balance potential returns with perceived and acceptable risks for the parties. In many cases, failure to reach such agreement may actually represent evidence that the plan is indeed not truly viable. Among the examples we've seen of this are situations in which:

- Equity puts forth an operational restructuring plan that requires new investment or near-term negative cash flow to implement, but is flatly unwilling or unable either to fund the new investment or to share the expected benefits.
- The Senior Secured Lenders' debt is currently marginally covered by tangible collateral, but in order to pursue the restructuring plan without incremental third-party investment, the lenders' collateral coverage will be compressed over time.
- Parties cannot agree on the risk profile of the proposed new course of action.

Unless the company can credibly put forward a plan that will allow it to grow out of its problems without requiring significant modification of its debt or new investment, negotiations will require all the parties to confront the realignment of risks and rewards among their respective interests.

Valuing Contributions of the Parties

As we noted in our discussion of liquidity (see Chapter 6), a liquidation analysis is needed to establish the baseline for value. The three prime goals of workout groups for secured lenders are:

1. No new money
2. No deterioration of loan-to-value ratios
3. An adjustment of fees and interest income upward to compensate for increased real or perceived risk of continuing the lending relationship

Understanding that business liquidation is the baseline alternative from which contributions of the parties must be measured is a key starting point in the process. All parties to the process should understand that from the perspective of the secured lender, any actions of the company that reduce this liquidation value or otherwise impair the collateral will be viewed as a contribution to the recovery process for which they should be rewarded. This reward relates both to recovering the loss of value that may occur and to the increased risk of greater exposure.

Often the secured lender is helpless to avoid the loss of existing value but is not helpless in avoiding the incremental new money. Such new money will be considered "venture capital" and will be offered at a high price, even if it is helpful in recovering the lenders' temporary loss of value during a period of forbearance from initiating actions that could result in liquidation. The price of forbearance will be more onerous terms, higher interest rates and loan amendment fees.

Equity and management are at the other end of the spectrum from secured lenders. They are the key to improvement by operational turnaround or enhancement of value by sale of assets at more than estimated liquidation value. This can be a major contribution, totally for the benefit of creditors when debt is greater than value. Logically, incentives to management and equity should come in the form of future incentive payments based on achieving specific objectives related to value enhancement.

First Impaired Party

Between the extremes of the secured lenders – which, assuming they have evaluated the collateral accurately, can often expect to receive a full recovery of principal plus some incremental interest and fees – and equity – which, if it loses control in a truly distressed situation, can expect to have zero recovery – sit the other groups of creditors. These include subordinated or unsecured debtholders, landlords, suppliers, contract and joint venture partners, employees and retirees, and so on (discussed in detail in Chapter 7). Within this continuum of liabilities it is critical to understand which is the "first impaired party," the party that is most directly affected, for better or worse, by incremental changes in value of the business and which, by virtue of this position, may hold a weighted influence upon the decision-making process.

In general, secured creditors, particularly to the extent they are unimpaired, are risk-averse and motivated primarily by a desire to facilitate an exit from the situation prior to further deterioration. Conversely, unsecured creditors typically have a vested interest in seeing a continuation of ongoing business in the hope that the situation may improve. Anything that causes a liquidation with proceeds going first to secured creditors is likely to represent an extremely unattractive result for unsecured creditors. Identifying the likely first impaired party and understanding both the motivations and the leverage they may have regarding approval of any restructuring or forbearance deal is a key to effective negotiations.

Within the bankruptcy process, if the workout is so unfortunate as to reach that point, issues relating to the impairment of secured parties become critical. Without attempting to address the intricacies of bankruptcy law, let us lay out two key concepts:

First, even in bankruptcy, a secured lender cannot be forced to provide forbearance and waive its enforcement rights unless the debtor can provide "adequate protection," *i.e.*, assurances and guarantees against deterioration in the value of the lender's collateral.

Second, the court cannot approve a Plan of Reorganization that provides value to a subordinated class unless each senior class of creditors either receives 100% recovery on its claim or approves the terms. The single exception to this rule is when a subordinate party (generally equity) provides "new value" in return for which it may receive a distributed interest in the emerging entity that does not follow the strict priority rule.

For obvious reasons, these concepts of "adequate protection" and the "priority of interests," which are judicially enforceable within a bankruptcy proceeding, are important considerations in out-of-court negotiations as well. At each tier in the capital structure, the company's lenders and creditors have various and sundry enforceable rights that provide them specific recourse in the event of default. So long as a company maintains full compliance with its loan covenants, its lenders' only rights and controls over the company are those defined in the original loan documentation. Even as a company starts to falter, so long as the owners are prepared to absorb increasing risks and infuse more equity to maintain adequate loan-to-value ratios, the lenders will generally sit happily still, after extracting what they can in interest and fees.

The same applies to the other creditor classes. So long as the company meets its obligations as they come due, the creditors have no say in its operations. But when equity is no longer able or prepared to continue refilling the coffers, the real and perceived risks begin to rise and shift, and each of the various constituents can be expected to apply whatever leverage it has available in order to realign its risk and reward.

As general rules:

1. Parties that perceive they are being adequately protected and compensated can be expected to participate in a plan;

2. Parties that are deeply out of the money are likely to allow the company to swing for the bleachers and try to hit a home run, so long as they retain an interest in the outcome and don't have to increase their risk;

3. "Wiping out" parties that are deeply out of the money is not as easy as it might seem. There is typically a significant incremental value obtainable from an orderly restructuring or workout, as opposed to a liquidation. Despite any strict rules of priority, a legitimate value must be considered as the "price of cooperation" from subordinate interests;

4. The "first impaired party" (particularly if it holds secured interests) generally sits in a position of relative power, as it evaluates the trade-offs between its current situation, the plan(s) being proposed, and the demands of the other constituents.

AUTHORS' CASEBOOK: Restructuring and Merging Operations

The Cerplex Group, Inc. was a leading provider of repair services, spare parts sourcing and service management for manufacturers of computer, communications and electronic office equipment in the U.S., France and the United Kingdom. Based on a series of acquisitions, the company experienced rapid revenue growth in the mid-1990s to a revenue level of approximately $200 million. As a result of acquisition integration difficulties, writedowns of acquired inventory and corporate overhead expenses added to handle anticipated growth, the company reported losses of $65 million over a two-year period. However, due to the nature of high-value inventories required for its business, liquidation was not a viable option for secured creditors. The secured lenders had stopped advancing funds under revolving credit agreements and the company was in default of payment schedules on unsecured debt. In connection with a debt forbearance agreement, the company retained co-author Steve Hopkins as interim CEO.

Critical Challenges: Survive the liquidity crisis while making strategic changes in business operations to focus only in areas with immediate potential for positive cash flow. Simultaneously, reduce the very high corporate overhead established in anticipation of future growth.

Due to the severe liquidity crisis that the company was suffering, operations were managed on a very short-term cash-flow basis. Cash was managed through semiweekly telephone conference calls participated in by all senior management and plant managers before releasing any payments. This process and the extended discussions involved quickly provided the information for a good understanding of where the business was making and losing money and why. Analysis of the situation quickly disclosed that the company's rapid growth plans had no possibility of being achieved with the financial constraints imposed by the company's history of operating losses.

Actions taken within the first six months included:

- Sale of a non-strategic subsidiary to provide working capital during the operational transition;
- Consolidation of U.S. repair and parts sales activities from seven locations to four;
- Reduction of corporate overhead by 60%, including major cost savings from outsourcing information technology and network telecommunications services.

As a result of these actions, the company returned to profitable operations but had no ability to service or reduce the $50 million of debt that remained outstanding. Merger negotiations were begun with another public company in the industry that was continuing to experience the same operating difficulties that had been corrected by Cerplex. A private equity firm provided the capital required to recapitalize the merged firms. Secured debt was paid in full, the merged companies assumed liabilities for trade payable and unsecured notes were repurchased by the company at a significant discount.

Chapter Summary

The path to agreement is easy to identify but hard to follow:

1. Establish a common and credible fact base: identify and address misperceptions and factual disagreements.
2. Demonstrate understanding of the challenges.
3. Acknowledge and address risks.
4. Define opportunities.
5. Realign risks with rewards
   - Respect existing rights and interests.
   - Compensate new or continuing risks and contributions toward success.

Chapter 14

SELECTING THE RIGHT MANAGEMENT
Different Horses for Different Courses

A key part of planning for rescuing a troubled business is to take a fresh and careful look at whether existing management have the ability to implement whatever revised strategy is developed. As we've noted repeatedly, management changes should be made when circumstances require them, but such a step should be deferred pending a careful consideration of business objectives and the type of management background, experience and temperament needed to go forward in the specific situation.

In previous chapters, the diagnosis and evaluation process has been described in detail. Presumably, this process will lead to decisions about what needs to be done and, in general, how to go about doing it, what will work and what will not. Risks relating to liquidity, operational restructuring requirements and the competitive environment have been considered. The standalone future value of the business on a discounted cash-flow basis, assuming realistic probabilities of expected success, has been compared with the current sale or asset liquidation value. In addition, the engaged parties have negotiated how to realign business risks and rewards as the process moves forward. All this sets the stage for resolving who should manage the execution of the agreed-upon plan.

Pros and Cons of Changing Management

Management implementation risk is a key factor in deciding to go with either a long-term standalone turnaround plan or a quick fix using highest potential return actions to prepare the company for sale. Exhibit 14-1, below, lists recommended management characteristics under selected scenarios and key assumptions. This rough guide must be viewed in the context of specific individuals and circumstances.

EXHIBIT 14-1

LIKELY ALTERNATIVE SCENARIOS AND ASSOCIATED MANAGEMENT CHARACTERISTICS

Selected Operational Scenario	Key Assumptions	Recommended Management Characteristics
Undisciplined Racehorses		
1. Fix internal problems	• Problems are execution-related • External resources can be added for a fix	Present CEO if there is commitment to use external assistance
2. Dump defined losers/Resume core business growth	• Strong core business • Losers are clearly defined • Management was key to prior growth • Adequate resources available	Experienced insider with good customer relationships who has overcome denial about problems; add CRO to provide credibility and manage dispositions
Overburdened Workhorses		
3. Cut costs; wait out the cycle	• Company has strong market position • Management drives cost-reduction • Debt can be restructured	Industry veteran who understands the cycle, has credibility with lenders and is willing to reduce costs
4. Restructure debt	• Excessive debt due to unrealistic expectations • Operation of business has not deteriorated from historical trends	Current experienced management – absent other operational weaknesses
Aging Mules		
5. Re-focus on core profitability	• Business lacks leadership • Acceptable competitive position in core • Surplus assets to reduce debt	Replacement CEO to abandon unprofitable business segments, reduce costs, divest non-core assets and pay down debt
6. Business/product-line sale	• Management accepts need for sale • Proper sale incentives are in place • Buyer integration continuity important	Experienced insider with vested interest in business and good employee motivation skills
7. Liquidate assets	• Management too emotionally involved in business continuation to be effective	Experienced specialist in divesting assets

The key organizational functions that management must perform, using the terminology of Ichak Adizes, are:

Performance: the "Doer" focusing on specifically what to do now.

Administration: the "Controller" focusing on how to do it.

Entrepreneurship: the "Planner" focusing on when and why something should be done.

Integration: the "Integrator" who organizes the bringing to bear of resources on solving a problem.

All managers have a responsibility to do all of these functions if they are to be successful. However, the needs and job focus will require vastly different strengths in each situation.

Managers brought into crisis situations have to be "Doers": They have no time to contemplate their navels while figuring out what to do. And to the extent that the "Planner" function of focusing on a longer-term future is required, the typical crisis manager is not particularly well-suited to do it. What the crisis manager wants is discipline, control and lower costs as the chips fall where they may.

These circumstances support our premise that the problem diagnosis function is separately definable work that needs to be done as early in the process as possible – before commitments to the future are made. Earlier (see Chapter 4), the characteristics of problem management were discussed. Presumably, managers unsuited for their positions were either removed as part of the crisis control process or have been identified for replacement as part of the organization review (discussed in Chapter 11). Where necessary, replacement should happen as quickly as possible in order to get on with the business of effecting a turnaround, debt restructuring or exit.

In our opinion, an internal candidate with an understanding of what is needed and who can be supported with turnaround management consultants or individuals with specific functional expertise offers an ideal solution, particularly if the strategy is a return to past core business growth or to fix an identified major internal problem.

Effecting dramatic business change in the form of operational restructuring or entering new markets is a skill that requires experience on the part of both top management and key employees. In certain businesses, such changes have been required regularly in the past and can be expected to be needed again in the future. In these circumstances, the likelihood of planning and implementing major business change has a greater chance of success than in a more stable, mature environment.

General Arguments Supporting CEO Change

- The current CEO is unable to overcome denial of the "brutal facts" of the company's problems;
- Credibility has been lost with lenders and other stakeholders during liquidity crisis;
- The CEO refuses to recognize fiduciary responsibility to creditors in managing an insolvent company;
- The brute force of a "crisis manager" is required to effect major cost reductions;
- Standalone turnaround potential is good and time is available to effect major change, but the new focus is dramatically different than what built the company; e.g., marketing skills are needed rather than R&D expertise;
- Management needs unique skills to deal with a liquidity crisis and financial restructuring; this may argue for a Chief Restructuring Officer with CEO-level authority;
- Cynically, replacing the CEO shows investors or other stakeholders that the board is willing to take action when it doesn't understand what else to do.

General Arguments Against CEO Change

- The CEO has control over key relationships of the business that represent a major portion of its "franchise value";
- The CEO has overcome denial and accepts the need for dramatic action to effect defined strategy;
- External resources can be added to effect required changes, i.e., fix internal problems or sell non-core assets, while CEO manages a viable core business;
- The financial problems relate to cyclical issues of industry, and the market position is improving.

Actions required and likely management changes for various categories of troubled companies are shown in Exhibit 14-2.

All changes in management involve trade-offs, which we discuss below:

Undisciplined Racehorses: If possible, the best solution is to continue the existing management, which achieved rapid growth in the past and have the relationships that built the business. The key need is tight control by the board of directors over new investments and risk, supplemented by highly ex-

EXHIBIT 14-2

LIKELY ACTIONS/MANAGEMENT CHANGES NEEDED FOR TURNAROUND

	Undisciplined Racehorses	Overburdened Workhorses	Aging Mules
Likely Key Threats	Internal	External/Internal	External
Expected Actions Required	• Fix functional problems • Dump defined losers • Assign responsibility and authority • Install administrative controls	• Wait out cycle • Restructure debt • Reduce overhead structure • Shut down high-cost operations • Offshore manufacturing and/or sourcing	• Overcome cultural inertia • Restructure around historical core • Sell surplus business assets • Exit loss operations • Refocus on customers • Reduce expense structure • Merge with/sell to stronger strategic buyer
Management Change	• Bring in functional expertise to fix specific problems • Use CRO/crisis manager for credibility • Overcome CEO arrogance/denial • Improve controls with new CFO and outside Board • Ensure continuity of business relationships	• Least likely to need CEO change if CEO retains credibility • CEO must be willing to face facts of situation and act	• CEO usually can't overcome denial and must go • Best long-term alternative is internal candidate with specific action plans • May need interim crisis manager to manage liquidity crisis, cut costs, and enhance business and asset sale proceeds

perienced second-line management. The big questions are the extent to which the crisis has caused the CEO to overcome the arrogance engendered by past successes and whether a founder-entrepreneur will submit to appropriate administrative controls.

The turnaround of Undisciplined Racehorses generally involves action relating either to installing administrative controls while bringing in functional expertise to fix specific problems or curtailing aggressive risk-taking behaviors of the entrepreneurial founder and pruning the business back to its profitable core. In some cases, the classic "take no prisoners" turnaround manager can really shine, at least in the short term. In most situations, he doesn't have to change the culture of the business too much. The culture is based on doing what the CEO says to do. Middle management and employees now have a different CEO to tell them what to do and to the extent they can't do it, he or she can replace the laggards. However, it has been our experience that a specific internal functional problem caused by lack of resources and attention can most effectively be fixed with new functional management to help the existing CEO with that particular problem – rather than by replacing the CEO. This is a different situation than dealing with entrepreneurial risk-takers who have let prior success drive them to focus totally on growth. In these latter cases, there must be willingness to dump the losers and low margin non-strategic operations in order to focus on the core business.

AUTHORS' CASEBOOK: Selecting New Management

A privately held company that had acquired several small electronics assembly operations lost market position and began to generate operating losses. As a recovery strategy, equity investors developed and obtained financing commitments for a program of expanding into molded plastic product manufacturing. A new CEO, whose primary experience was as CFO of significantly larger companies in unrelated industries, was recruited to implement the new acquisition program. He completed two acquisitions of mature operating companies at reasonably attractive prices, but specific markets served were impacted by loss of production volume to East Asian sourcing. In addition, significantly increased marketing and administrative overhead costs were being incurred. Rather than the new strategy providing funds to meet debt service on what were now much larger borrowings, operating losses had increased. At the request of the secured lenders, co-author Steve Hopkins was retained as chief restructuring officer to control cash and develop a debt restructuring plan.

    Critical Challenge: Evaluate the company's growth plans, which included continued entry into new markets, and determine if operational restructuring could return the business to profitability.

    It was concluded that by abandoning plans for new acquisitions, consolidating certain plant operations and sharply reducing overhead, the company could remain viable. This change in strategy did not fit either the skill sets or career objectives of the CEO and a consensual termination agreement was reached. An interim CEO with strong manufacturing experience was retained to begin immediately effecting cost reductions, while a new perma-

nent CEO was recruited with directly related molded plastic products marketing and manufacturing expertise.

Within 90 days, new permanent management with more appropriate experience and
expertise were in place and a debt restructuring had been concluded. A major turnaround in
business operating results was achieved and reduced debt service payments were made
as scheduled.

Overburdened Workhorses: These companies may have either internal or
external problems, but decision-making related to change of management incorporates consideration of the same general issues. By definition, debt is excessive
and must be restructured. In a situation of unrealistic expectations, a credible,
conservative new plan must be in place that acknowledges and explains the bridge
from past expectations. If earnings have declined sharply due to cyclical factors,
dramatic cost-reduction actions required to ride out the cycle must be in place with
a realistic assessment of risks involved in effecting these actions. The CEO will
be responsible for maintaining credibility in future planning. If the CEO was
the driving force establishing the unrealistic expectations that led to previous
problems, it is critical to ensure that he or she understands and embraces the
new perspective. Otherwise a change will be required.

Aging Mules: For Aging Mule businesses with a good core, the focus will
be on eliminating the losers and pushing the winners, so replacing the existing
CEO with a strong internal candidate with the motivation to manage operational change is probably the best choice. This replacement CEO will understand the company culture and know the players but must have a clearly defined plan for immediate action.

More frequently, an Aging Mule will have a generally weakened financial
and competitive position and the likely end objective will be sale of the business to a strategic buyer that can make required investments and assume responsibility for long-term management decisions relating to consolidation.

Retaining Management

Whatever the category of business, the future role of management and its
willingness to support the process should not be overlooked when attempting
to sell a business to a strategic buyer. Allowing management with conflicting
objectives to control a sale process can become a serious obstacle to consummat-
ing an attractive transaction. Conversely, management can be a great aid in
facilitating such a transaction and their potential contributions should not be
undervalued, particularly in the circumstance where they are effectively working themselves out of a job.

With an understanding of the people, skills, and financial resources required and a decision that current management will be retained, appropriate reward systems and incentives can be put in place. These should be relatively generous to keep in place those employees, including existing management, who are needed currently but have no long-term future with the company. A mix of long-term and short-term incentives is appropriate when the objective is cutting back to the core business while sharply reducing losses in other segments of the company. With proper communication, people understand the objectives. Failure to treat properly those being terminated, either at once or in the future, is likely to come back to hurt the business by weakening its credibility with individuals expected to be retained for the long term.

Temporary retention agreements for both management and employees who are being terminated should be structured around providing the greatest motivation consistent with allowing them to get on with their lives in an orderly way as quickly as possible. These agreements typically offer a certain number of weeks' pay for staying through a certain date or bonuses yielding a higher pay rate for additional time worked, i.e., a bonus of one week's pay after each four weeks time worked. Concurrently, it is often possible to provide these employees additional security by guaranteeing a short notice period (one to four weeks, perhaps) to provide some certainty about when the transition will be completed, as well as improving net proceeds realized by providing a group incentive bonus to all employees based either on period of time required to complete assigned tasks or the gross proceeds from an inventory liquidation or other asset disposition.

Management bonuses for employees retained will vary greatly depending on scenario objectives and specific needs of the situation. Stock options may be the best long-term program for a true turnaround, but a cash payment is needed for the individual who manages integration of the business being sold into a strategic buyer's operations and then goes on to other things. The extent to which such bonuses can be offered or guaranteed for a company in bankruptcy has been severely restricted by the Bankruptcy Act of 2005.

Replacing Management

When the decision has been made to change management, the objective should be as orderly and effective a transition as possible. Although difficult to pull off, the ideal situation is one in which the primary focus is on the needs of the business rather than the ego requirements of the outgoing or incoming CEO. In most cases, this requires treating the outgoing CEO with dignity and respect for accomplishments over the years. Failing to provide such respect often migrates into a money dispute, which is the only basis on which to do battle in the courts.

Dignity and respect are more likely to be achieved if it is acknowledged that circumstances rather than competence drive the need for management change. Applying hindsight bias and retaliating for perceived bad decisions should not drive the decision-making process. In general, the arguments in favor of management change listed above have little to do with management competence.

As we noted earlier, it seems to be human nature for new management to place an exaggerated amount of blame for problems on their predecessors, in order to look better when these problems get fixed or a change in the economy raises all boats. The less of this game-playing in the transition process, the better for future company results.

In some circumstances, it may be appropriate to try to retain the old CEO as chairman of the board or some other ongoing role with the company. Often, the CEO is the technology leader of the company, an industry guru or has important external relationships. Retaining the CEO's talents should be a primary objective. And, frequently, what the CEO wants is to be released from the stress of day-to-day administrative problems. At the same time, a clear segregation of responsibilities between the chairman and the CEO must be established, and the old CEO must refrain from second-guessing the new one.

Whatever the new arrangement is to be, it must be clearly defined and quickly communicated to employees and third parties. There must be no ambiguity about who is in charge going forward and what the responsibilities are of those reporting to management. If there is an interim management team, duties of each member should be spelled out at the time it is announced.

In selecting new management, it is essential to identify strengths that can be focused on the problems at hand. We have seen a number of instances where an outstanding candidate was hired whose credentials were established by growing profitable businesses rather than fixing ailing ones. Often these CEOs failed in their new positions. In two very similar situations in our first-hand experience, standalone profitability turnarounds were engineered by interim managers, restructuring debt without bankruptcy filings and leaving the businesses stable although thinly capitalized. Both businesses subsequently filed Chapter 11, after private equity firm owners brought in highly capable new permanent management who promptly attempted to implement unrealistic, high-risk growth strategies.

AUTHORS' CASEBOOK: Closing an Acquisition

A private equity firm purchased a large family-owned retail automotive services chain and installed a new CEO. As a result of underperformance of operations, unresolved issues relating to strategic direction of the business and a deteriorating relationship with other members of management, the CEO resigned within two years. With no CEO at the helm, the company was offered for sale. Then, during the sale process, the CFO resigned to accept another position. On behalf of a potential purchaser, co-author Steve Hopkins directed a due diligence team that extensively evaluated the business, including providing opinions on management and organization structure. Although the business was basically strong and had many highly experienced operating managers, lack of good reporting systems and a poorly defined organization structure were resulting in operational disruptions and a great deal of finger-pointing about responsibility for problems.

    Critical Challenge: To determine where the company was making and losing money, both by line of business and by location. Then evaluate the situation in terms of competitive environment and organization changes that were necessary, to determine the likely potential for future success.

    Results of the investigation, together with a recommendation strongly supporting the acquisition, were provided to potential lenders. In addition, as part of closing the transaction, an interim CFO was provided to assist with installation of improved information-technology systems and better management reporting. The acquisition was closed, new top management more attuned to the culture were selected from within the company and a permanent, highly experienced CFO was recruited from the outside. With only minor modifications to its operations, the business proved highly successful for its new owners.

Elements of Managing Change

In most cases, the time frame available to make the essential changes at a troubled company is weeks or months, not years, and so a short-term approach is essential. Gary S. Topchik laid out an excellent short-term approach in "Attacking the Negativity Virus,"[14] an article published in September 1998 by the American Management Association. Topchik's format for thinking about the elements of managing complex change was:

- **Vision:** *The better people understand the reason for change, the more they will remain positive about it.*
- **Incentives:** *If individuals believe a change will benefit them or the organization, negativity subsides.*
- **Skills:** *People become anxious — and anxious people become negative — when they feel they lack the skills needed to perform.*

---

[14] Gary S. Topchik, "Attacking the Negativity Virus," *Management Review*, (87(8) September 1998), 61-64.

- **Action plan:** *Individuals like to know the specific steps involved in a change. The more they know about how it will be implemented, the more positive they remain.*
- **Resources***: Employees need time, tools, money and other resources to implement change in a positive manner.*

To Topchik's outline we would add the element of communication – to ensure that everyone understands both the vision and action plan.

Compensating Management

We hold a general view that most management are overcompensated for the results they achieve. This is partially a result of the bias of our sample, which is heavily skewed toward the unsuccessful. However, many problems we see result from arrogance and greed, and we believe that an inverse relationship exists between the level of current compensation and the likelihood that the incumbent CEO can effect a business turnaround. Some of the most successful turnarounds we have seen have been accomplished by the lowest-paid CEOs. This reflects their understanding of the value that others bring to the management team, as well as a lack of ego that allows them to make the best use of the talent reporting to them.

Lucrative compensation and bonuses may be justified if a high degree of success is achieved, but such bonuses should be based on achieving specific objectives, not just spending a specific length of time presiding over continued deterioration in value.

We note, too, that CEOs who focus a great deal of time and attention on compensation in the form of stay bonuses or retention agreements before committing to fixing problems that developed on their watch are exactly the CEOs who should not be retained.

Aging Mule Management

Aging Mule companies are often no longer viable as standalone entities due to the external competitive environment. Technology, product innovations and markets are passing them by and management has become focused on internal processes rather than on customers and external markets.

Although they don't use our definitions, most business literature about managing change seems to assume that an Aging Mule is involved. In general, such literature assumes a turnaround is possible but does not provide a conceptual lifecycle context to help understand how the businesses got where they are. Management and culture of these companies is very difficult to change and, unless there is a core business with good profit potential, they may very well not be worth the investment of resources. In any event, turnaround would be a long process, and even if probabilities of success are reasonably good, obtaining adequate financial support will be difficult.

The specific business processes of the Aging Mule business were likely, in an earlier day, to be very good and suitable to the business. Now, the company's external environment and competitive conditions have changed, and the company's historically successful business and administrative processes have been carried to excess. If anything, as revenues and profits decline, rules and procedures get tightened to prevent policy deviations resulting in increasing ratios of general and administration expense to revenues. Such companies often suffer from "silo management": Each function has its own bureaucratic agenda with decreasing effectiveness in focusing on customers and the overall strategic direction of the business. If a turnaround is to be effected, management has the difficult task of overturning the culture of internally focused second-tier management and employees.

Financial plans and budgets may well be very conservative – except when it comes to increasing expenses for the latest management fad that is expected to be the "magic elixir" that will solve the company's latest "temporary problem." Such companies are fertile ground for the installation of high-cost enterprise software systems, and the talent is probably available to make such systems work. But what is the point of standardizing procedures and developing reams of new data about customers and products if these declining businesses will not survive as independent standalone entities? Management need to objectively evaluate the competitive environment and future opportunities before assuming that better data and business processes will fix their problems.

Chapter Summary

CEOs who are arrogant and greedy (the two seem to go together) are unlikely to change and must be replaced, despite their strong protests and their often high level of technical competence. Unqualified management also must be replaced. They almost always recognize themselves that this is necessary and are relieved to put their suffering behind them.

The outlook and attitude of managements that are in denial or just complacent can be changed; they may not need to be replaced. However, they will change only under crisis conditions, often a crisis created by extreme pressure from third parties.

The best new CEO for a financially troubled company with a strong core business is often an insider who understands the culture, recognizes the problems and has a specific detailed plan to effect change.

The big questions in a troubled company are:

- What drives the need for business change?
- Who will make the decision about future direction?
- When will the changes be made?
- How are the changes to be implemented?

These questions should be answered before deciding on what management will execute the changes.

The board of directors must make the final decision, but outside parties such as secured creditors, customers or minority shareholders may have an effective veto on results of the process.

RECOMMENDED READING

Corporate Turnaround: How Managers Turn Losers Into Winners
(McGraw-Hill, 1982) by Donald B. Bibeault.

Published in 1982 with analysis dating from the 1970s, *Corporate Turnaround* remains the most comprehensive book available on leadership and management strategies in turnaround situations. It includes extensive discussion of actions required at each stage of the turnaround cycle.

In addition to his personal experience, Bibeault drew on exhaustive research of published material, interviews with 16 turnaround management professionals and questionnaires completed by 81 other chief executives of companies that had achieved a successful turnaround.

Although we disagree with Bibeault's general premise that the first step in working with a troubled company is a change in management, the book provides invaluable guidance regarding management characteristics and actions necessary to achieve a turnaround.

Winning (Harper Collins, 2005) by Jack Welch with Suzy Welch.

Shortly after his retirement, Welch wrote *Jack*, which was primarily a history of his years at General Electric. *Winning* is a more general view of his management philosophy and how to make things happen in business. Sections Two, "Your Company," and Three, "Your Competition," provide excellent guidance about selecting business leadership and adopting the right strategies.

This is a very practical book written by someone of demonstrated expertise and a great ability to get his ideas across. His chapters on leadership, crisis management and change are particularly useful to anyone involved with troubled businesses.

Barbarians to Bureaucrats: Corporate Life Cycle Strategies (Fawcett Columbine, 1989) by Lawrence M. Miller.

In this thought-provoking comparison of corporate lifecycles and the rise and fall of civilizations, Miller uses interesting terminology to emphasize stages of development and the managers most likely to be involved in each, starting with the visionary "Prophet;... who creates the breakthrough and the human energy to propel the company forward."

Miller's very readable work uses many examples from business history to make his points. He introduced his description of the "Barbarian" who drove the growth of McDonald's as "Ray Kroc was his name, expanding territory was his game."

Chapter 15

MAXIMIZING VALUE FROM ASSET SALES
The Parts May Be Worth More Than the Whole

Frequently, only those scenarios with a low probability of success yield business values in the future that are greater than an immediate sale to a strategic buyer. That is because the existing business requires (or at least management assumes that it does) a significant level of selling, general and administrative overhead to maintain and potentially grow its competitive position. A strategic buyer, on the other hand, will assume that very little of this overhead is needed once the business is integrated into the buyer's operations. Thus, the strategic buyer can forecast significantly improved profit margins related to expense synergies. Of course, the buyer find out that those synergies did not materialize and that the acquired business did, in fact, need more of the overhead than expected. But that reality does not usually intrude on purchase price negotiations.

In addition to the expected expense synergies, a strategic buyer may find additional value in the opportunity to take a competitor out of the marketplace, reducing pressures on industry pricing, while blocking other competitors from acquiring the property, thereby enhancing the buyer's competitive position. In a competitive bidding environment that produces high prices, these factors, along with acquisition implementation delays, are why buyers often have difficulty realizing an attractive return on investment.

Inherent in valuing the discounted cash-flow values of the restructured business is a series of cash-flow assumptions. Not only must operating cash flow be estimated but also working capital needs for growth, capital expenditures for asset replacement and advertising and promotion investments required to correct a deteriorating market position.

When all this is said and done, and despite all the potential problems, a strategic acquisition is often a wise long-term decision for the buyer.

Sale of a Troubled Business

The sale of a troubled business is much different than the sale, to either a financial or a strategic buyer, of a business with a historical stream of cash flow that can be valued at a multiple of earnings. As we've noted, the strategic buyer is likely to pay a higher price because of the synergies it expects, but buyers make that determination based on their due diligence assessment of the situation and the potential for future cost reduction.

In the sale of a troubled business, either in its entirety or as a series of product-line units, there is no historical earnings stream to value. Sellers must consider two key factors in making the business or product lines attractive:

Pro forma projections using a baseline of normal operations, adjusted for specifically planned operational restructuring and integration cost reductions. A well-defined "bridge analysis" should clearly communicate what the expected changes are and the reasons for projecting that they will happen.

Detailed assumptions regarding plans for integrating the business being sold into the operations of a strategic buyer. This, of course, requires making assumptions that may be incorrect when all facts become known, but as long as assumptions are clearly defined, they become a basis for logical, objective discussions with a potential purchaser.

The steel foundry business case history (see Chapter 17) is a good example of the turnaround and sale of a cyclical business.

Often the best value increases can be obtained by the most complex and innovative transactions. This may mean soliciting and beginning negotiations with a potential buyer that does not readily perceive the potential synergy involved in two very different businesses, such as the vertical integration of supply sources for a manufacturer or other moves up or down the supply chain.

AUTHORS' CASEBOOK: Maximizing Value Through Asset Sales

A wire and tube manufacturer owned and held for sale by an estate faced numerous problems, including:

1. A long strike at the company's two manufacturing plants;
2. A history of operating losses in key product lines;
3. Industry overcapacity in a major segment of the business;
4. A poor general economic climate.

Because the business was not operating as a result of the strike, its sale as a going business at a reasonable price appeared highly unlikely and a liquidation was planned.

Critical Challenge: Developing a plan to yield the estate maximum value from surplus inventories and money-losing plants in a high-cost area of the country.

Detailed financial projections of potential future earnings for various segments of the business if machinery and equipment were moved to new locations were developed. Negotiations were conducted with a number of potential purchasers and within six months:

1. Copper-tube manufacturing equipment was sold to a major air-conditioning manufacturer to implement a vertical integration project conceived and developed conceptually by representatives of the seller.
2. Aluminum-tube manufacturing equipment was sold to a foreign buyer.
3. Brazing alloy manufacturing equipment, inventories and customer lists were sold to a competitor.
4. Excess raw materials and in-process metal inventories were sold to companies using these metals in their operations.
5. Manufacturing and warehousing space totaling more than 450,000 square feet was sold to an industrial real estate developer and local users.

Proceeds obtained were much greater than could have been realized by outright sale of the company in its entirety or by normal liquidation auctions.

Segregating Asset Values

In developing a plan of action for maximizing value, it is important to have an objective view of both tangible asset values and the intangible values created by generating positive cash flow from ongoing transactions with customers. The tangible asset values evaluation will have been clearly identified in the "baseline" liquidation analysis, but understanding the intangible values generated by gross margin from a company's ongoing business transactions is more difficult.

The total projected value of the business will have been forecast as part of selecting alternative scenarios. Now that it is time to implement the selected scenario, the segregation of tangible asset values should be re-evaluated with an objective of eliminating (for separate sale or liquidation) as many tangible assets from the ongoing business requirements as possible, while retaining the intangible cash flow from operations values as the basis for maximizing the business sale price.

Remove from the transaction for separate sale all surplus assets that do not add value to the transaction. In negotiating a sale to a specific strategic buyer, agreements will need to be reached on what to add or drop from this excluded assets list. Some potential exclusions from the sale might include:

1. Fixed assets such as a manufacturing plant that a buyer with excess capacity would not need;
2. Receivables of questionable collectibility. Typically, if seller's personnel who are knowledgeable about the background of questionable receivables can be retained to handle these collections as a full-time, short-term

job, the proceeds will be significantly higher than the heavily discounted valuation of a skeptical buyer;

3. Inventories of both finished goods and raw material that are no longer
   sold or used in the business on a day-to-day basis.

Such assets may be perfectly saleable over time or may be attractive to a
liquidator, but in most instances the purchaser of a going-concern business, which
needs to focus all its attention on assimilating the acquired operations, will view
these surplus assets as a liability to the transaction and price them accordingly.

In general, if the seller excludes such assets from the transaction and handles
the "nut-and-bolts" dirty work of making integration of operating units easy for
a purchaser, total proceeds of the transaction will be enhanced and knowledgeable employees of the seller will have a much-appreciated opportunity for income
before making the transition to work with another employer.

In this evaluation, we again come to the 80/20 Rule. Something on the order
of 80% of the tangible assets are required to generate the last incremental 20% of
the cash flow that creates the total value of a business. In a scenario designed to cut
back to core operations, this will have been considered to some degree, but now
needs to be reviewed in depth to ensure that all possible assets – be they fixed
assets, inventories or receivables – are liquidated separately from implementing
the new operational strategy. In general, working capital assets will fall out naturally as low-profit customers or product lines are eliminated. However, the need
for fixed assets should be studied in detail. Does projected concentration on high-
margin customers eliminate the need for a manufacturing plant? Is surplus equipment available? Can high-cost corporate headquarters real estate be sold or subleased? Can selected manufacturing or overhead functions be outsourced, eliminating the need for related investment? Other such assets might include product
lines that no longer fit the business strategy, surplus real estate held for future
expansions, trademarks no longer used, investments in joint ventures and so on.
Such assets should be carefully evaluated by knowledgeable individuals with the
objective of concluding an advantageous sale without diversion of management
attention, which needs to be focused on improving business operations.

In extreme cases, this evaluation could lead to a conclusion that the entire
value of the business is represented by its brand name, which can be licensed for a
future royalty with all internal operations discontinued and working capital liquidated.

To the extent that these surplus assets can be identified and sold without
impacting the cash flow and related value of the selected scenario, significant
additional value can be created. This value, when converted to cash, can be a

potential source of new capital for debt retirement and for growing residual retained operations. Typically, such surplus cash would be expected to go to pay down debt, but in a true turnaround involving revenue growth in the core business, this cash might be available for redeployment to finance such growth. Lenders are much more receptive to allowing redeployment of existing assets to improve future returns and security of their loans than they are to incremental new borrowings that make them "venture capital investors."

For greatest effectiveness, the responsibilities for the asset sale or liquidation process and the applicable reporting should be clearly segregated from those involving management of the operational turnaround of the ongoing business.

AUTHORS' CASEBOOK: Valuing and Selling a Brand Name

A well-known designer and marketer of kitchen products (manufacturing was outsourced) was sold by its founders to a private equity group. As a result of the company's failure to achieve its marketing goals and excessive debt-service requirements, the company entered bankruptcy proceedings within 18 months and was placed under the control of a court-appointed trustee. The situation was complicated by contentious relationships with and damage claims by suppliers who had possession of product tooling, massive operational disruptions created by the Chapter 11 filing and lack of inventory for the coming Christmas season.

Critical Challenge: Preserving value of the brand name to the estate while minimizing liabilities and obtaining highest possible value from liquidation of receivables, inventories and other assets.

Negotiations with buyers focused on both the price to be paid for the brand and details of assumption of liabilities to suppliers to ensure access to high-value tooling. In slightly more than four months from the time the assignment was begun, the sale of the business to a strategic buyer was closed at a net price far in excess of initial expectations. Secured lenders were paid off in full, and a substantial return was generated for unsecured creditors.

Financial Buyers

Although the logical purchaser of a troubled company is usually a strategic buyer, in a few, relatively rare situations a financial buyer might be interested. This would typically involve a niche product with good long-term growth potential requiring a separate overhead structure. A financial buyer might be attracted if the acquisition could be viewed as a platform for future acquisitions. Standalone turnaround prospects may be good, but current owners, particularly creditor groups, may not be prepared to wait for a long-term exit. With such a financial buyer, it becomes easy to develop a plan for compensating management with stock options or other valuation incentives based on future profit growth so that they will stay with the business.

The turnaround buyer will also be interested in specific recommendations regarding management and organization structure, including the ability to deliver the existing management to the new owner as required.

Liability Settlements and Other Exit Barriers

Maximizing the value of a business with a good saleable operating cash flow is often complicated by contingent or uncertain liabilities that must be resolved, such as workmen's compensation liabilities, environmental claims, pension liabilities, product liability claims, real estate upgrading requirements and potential future warranty claims.

Although it is typically debt and excessive trade liabilities that result in a bankruptcy filing, other liabilities of the type listed above may be a major barrier to a quick, logical exit from a business. To the extent practical, these liabilities need to be separated from assets and settled separately. Even more than with the valuations of questionable surplus assets, uncertainty about liabilities can dramatically reduce the value of a business or make a transaction very difficult, even impossible, to close. Negotiating the reduction or elimination of liabilities can often be as important or even more important to enhancing the value of a troubled company than the price received for the core assets. Where significant uncertain liabilities are involved, outside advisors with specific knowledge can often enhance the net proceeds received. The key is to understand the situation fully and come to the negotiations armed with the necessary facts.

The ability to define and settle liabilities, including leases on surplus real estate, is often the most important reason that a Chapter 11 bankruptcy filing becomes necessary. The buyer faces considerable risks in closing a sale outside the bankruptcy process if the company from which assets are purchased may be insolvent.

"Cash trap" industries (discussed in Chapter 10), in particular, often have very high exit costs for items such as pension liabilities, environmental liabilities and plant-closing expenses. Three key sources of leverage are available for reducing these payments:

1. Disputed unsecured claims will be tried before a bankruptcy judge who has little patience with inflated claims and usually makes quick, objective decisions based on the facts.

2. Major liabilities such as environmental claims can be set for trial at a future date, while assets can be sold immediately with a clear title to the buyer.

3. Trade creditors in a liquidation outside bankruptcy would usually prefer a cash settlement that gets them out quickly to facing the ill-defined and

uncertain results of the bankruptcy process with large potential unsecured wind-down liabilities.

The publishing industry rollup (see Chapter 2) was concluded with a cash settlement of trade payables rather than a bankruptcy filing.

Finding the Best Deal

The traditional investment banker auction approach, when applied to selling marginal or loss companies and operating units, often results in a bottom-dollar price and the lowest recovery. Potential buyers discount the purchase price, based on past and current unsatisfactory operating results and balance sheet, and they assume a continued deterioration in operating results going forward before a turnaround to positive cash flow is achieved.

The auction approach also tends to attract low-ball bidders and bottom-fishers.

And a wide dissemination of knowledge about the availability for sale of a troubled company, over time, makes the company seem "shopworn" – much more so than when a profitable company with a consistent trend of earnings is up for sale. Potential buyers tend to assume that if the opportunity were a good deal, the company would have already been sold. And yet another issue is the so-called "FUD Factor" (Fear, Uncertainty and Doubt), which can make it hard for a buyer to pull the trigger on the decision-making process and to get financing for the acquisition.

To offset these negative tendencies, the key to maximizing recoveries from the sale of marginal or money-losing companies is to determine and document how profitability can be dramatically improved and to establish a selling price based on restructured future earnings potential as part of a strategic buyer's organization. These steps are essential:

- Determine how cash flow and profitability can be improved based on new strategies, tactics and operating configurations;
- Describe and document the new strategies and operating configurations in a detailed business plan with three- to five-year pro forma financial projections;
- Analyze and document key assumptions going forward, justifying the asking price for the company;

- Don't prematurely start the sale process without doing the required homework; that would just confuse the marketplace and the best potential buyers;
- Identify, target, and contact, on a worldwide basis, the logical potential strategic buyers of the company.

The best and most likely potential buyers will be highly knowledgeable about the business and the industry of the company being sold. The potential buyers can and will quickly use their background knowledge to evaluate the new business strategy, proposed business plan and financial projections. They will make a judgment about whether the plans and projections are reasonable and feasible. If so, they will recognize the potential for value added from proposed restructuring and market synergies and will, accordingly, compete for the right to buy, paying a higher price. (Potential buyers lacking this familiarity will often be turned off by the high price being asked for a business without historical earnings.)

Potential buyers in the same or related business generally have all or most of the SG&A functions and expense in place. By eliminating duplication of overhead expenses, they may be able to make an acquired troubled company profitable almost immediately. In the age of globalization, Western European and Asian companies may represent very promising prospects because of their desire to establish an operating base in U.S. markets.

Substantive meetings and discussions with the most promising potential buyers expressing initial interest should be held to explain and "sell" the proposed business strategy, operating plan and financial projections for the company being sold. Personal contacts and detailed discussions explaining assumptions and rationale in the business strategy and plan can often reduce or eliminate doubts or concerns held by potential buyers.

In order to create and maintain a competitive environment, avoid, if possible, allowing one potential buyer exclusive rights for due diligence or negotiating. Because many troubled companies are essentially wasting assets in their current configuration, granting exclusivity to a potential buyer early on puts the seller at a tremendous disadvantage. The longer negotiations drag on, the more the value of the company is reduced, giving additional leverage to the potential buyer that has been granted exclusivity.

Conversely, it is in the seller's best interest to make it as easy as possible for a buyer to do the deal, by reducing the real and perceived risks. In addition to excluding surplus assets and settling liabilities, these steps may facilitate a closing at an attractive price:

- Resolving all outstanding licensing issues;
- Extending or reaffirming customer contracts;
- Renegotiating unfavorable leases;
- Wrapping approval of restructured, more favorable union contracts into the process;
- Settling environmental liabilities before transfer of title;
- Renegotiating supply contracts.

Establish a good data room where potential buyers can work and have access to knowledgeable seller personnel. Prepare in advance good answers to the inevitable tough questions. Resolve messy accounting issues and provide documentation related to valuations of working capital, to clear up such murky situations as:

- Poorly organized or out of date details of receivables;
- Inadequate, badly documented inventory reserve calculations;
- Disputed or inaccurate payables;
- Liability for excessive potential warranty claims;
- Inaccurate royalty and licensing accruals.

Develop a deal structure and asset details that will simplify a buyer's ability to finance a transaction. Consistent with this development of financing capacity, there should be an understanding of equity requirements involved in order to quickly eliminate from the process those buyers who lack adequate resources.

Structuring the Business Sale

In structuring and financing a business sale, there is an opportunity to make use of trade payables and normal ongoing business accrued liabilities as a source of financing. This financing can provide much of the "equity" for a purchase and must be considered in structuring the purchase and sale agreement. Shown below is the highly simplified conceptual effect for a $200 million company with 5% free cash flow and net income ($10 million each). A sale price of $55 million plus $5 million in fees and expenses is assumed.

EXHIBIT 15-1
HYPOTHETICAL DEAL STRUCTURE

	Balance Sheet at Closing (in Millions)	Balance Sheet After 90 Days (in Millions)
Cash	$ 2.0	$ 2.0
Receivables (45 days sales)	25.0	25.0
Inventories (75 days C/S)	25.0	25.0
Capitalized Fees and Expenses	5.0	5.0
All Other Assets	3.0	3.0
Total	60.0	60.0
Payables and Accrued Expenses (not assumed at closing)	0.0	13.2**
Working Capital Loan	30.0*	14.3
Mezzanine Term Loan	20.0	20.0
Total Liabilities	50.0	47.5
Net Equity	$10.0	$12.5

*At 80% of receivables and 40% of inventories availability, fully drawn at closing.
**40 days C/S

The normal levels of accounts payable and accrued expenses, plus 90 days of profits, reduce the working capital loan from $30 million at closing to $14.3 million at the end of 90 days.

Integration Assistance

Most buyers have a tendency to think that they have superior knowledge simply because they are the buyer. This may or may not be true in any individual case, but it is not generally demonstrated by the long-term results of most acquisitions. The problem is usually not so much one of conceptual strategy, but rather of excessive price and problems integrating the acquisition with the buyer's business. Some large companies that make multiple acquisitions as a growth strategy have excellent, experienced staffs to manage planning for the integration of acquisitions. General Electric, Bank of America and Illinois Tool, for example, have had successes on this front, but these are the exception rather than the rule.

Maximizing value for the buyer and, by inference for the seller, requires a good integration plan and the availability of adequate management expertise. This knowledge will typically reside with seller personnel and is a key reason for retention bonuses and other incentives. These employees of the seller are also often the best "deal closers," so long as they have no conflicting agendas with the objectives of the sale. Our experience over the years has generally demonstrated that seller personnel, if treated with respect and compensated fairly, do a good job. These people have a psychic investment in the business, want to show off their abilities to outsiders and often hope a good job will be available with the buyer.

Chapter Summary

Frequently, only ongoing standalone business scenarios with a low probability of success yield higher value than immediate sale or liquidation of a business. The best price for a business usually comes from a strategic buyer. Carefully prepared pro forma projections and bridge analyses to document profitability improvements are a key to justifying a good price. It is also generally advantageous to liquidate separately all surplus assets to improve total value received.

Liabilities may be a major barrier to a quick, logical exit from a business. Resolving such liabilities in advance will enhance total sale proceeds. This may require a bankruptcy filing.

Simplify the entire process for potential buyers to the greatest extent possible, by having good information available, resolving as many financial and operational uncertainties as possible and developing plans for integration assistance after the sale closes.

Part V

LESSONS LEARNED

INTRODUCTION

As we noted at the outset of this book, the observations and recommendations we present are the fundamentally subjective views of the authors. Be that as it may, our views are built upon our broad base of experience, accumulated over two and a half decades as consultants to troubled companies.

In the admittedly unscientific experience sample we have assembled and quantified, we have found trends and patterns. From time to time in preceding chapters, we have referred to this experience base, which we divide into three distinct categories:

- Undisciplined Racehorses
- Overburdened Workhorses
- Aging Mules

The likely courses of action and outcomes are predictably quite different among these three groups. In the following three chapters, we discuss the nature of the cases and the experiences that we have drawn upon in developing these categorizations and our conclusions about them.

We find this pattern recognition quite useful in diagnosing and evaluating the troubled businesses with which we work. It may be even more beneficial to those seeking investment or turnaround situations in the universe of distressed companies.

Chapter 16

TRAINING UNDISCIPLINED RACEHORSES

What we have labeled "Undisciplined Racehorses" are dynamic businesses, typically in the earlier stages of their lifecycle. They are not standing still; they are not trotting gently down a path. By definition, they are continuously in a state of flux, managing and actively seeking growth and change. It should therefore not be at all surprising that those that stumble often do so because they have not developed adequate controls and administrative procedures with which to manage change. Although there are exceptions, these businesses tend to be susceptible to internal, self-inflicted wounds.

Indeed, approximately 85% of our projects involving Undisciplined Racehorses were the result of internal problems. The good news is that these internal problems are much more responsive to corrective actions than external problems. Real operational turnarounds were achieved in almost 50% of these companies we were involved with – more than twice the rate with other categories of troubled businesses.

Investors seeking to profit from distressed opportunities may do well to focus on this segment of the marketplace and to understand how to deal with such companies once acquired. Likewise, management and investors who find themselves confronted with Undisciplined Racehorses should gain confidence, knowing that if the specific challenges are approached in a timely manner and appropriate functional experience is deployed, the prospects of engineering an operational turnaround tend to be well above average.

Exhibit 16-1 provides a summary of the types of problems encountered by Undisciplined Racehorses in our 100-project sample, and the resulting outcomes.

EXHIBIT 16-1
UNDISCIPLINED RACEHORSE BUSINESSES
PROJECT RESULTS

	Turn-arounds	Restruc-turings	Sales	Liqui-dations	Total	% of Total
External Problems						
Weak competitive position	–	–	1	–	1	3%
Permanent market change	1	–	–	3	4	11%
Total External	1	–	1	3	5	14%
Internal Problems						
Growth management	7	1	2	1	11	33%
Project management	3	–	1	1	5	14%
Acquisition problems	6	1	2	3	12	31%
Fraud	–	–	–	3	3	8%
Total Internal	16	2	5	8	31	86%
TOTAL	17	2	6	11	36	100%
Percentage of Total	47%	6%	17%	31%	100%*	

*Total of percentages exceeds 100 because of rounding.

External Problem Projects

Just because a business was recently healthy and growing and can be classified as an "Undisciplined Racehorse" doesn't mean that it can return to its previous path and glory. Where external problems existed among our Undisciplined Racehorses, the outcome was fatal to its standalone existence in four of five instances. This is quite logical. When immature and developing organizations become financially weak while faced with strong competitive pressure or external market changes, they seldom have the resources and experience to confront those challenges effectively.

Indeed, it may well be that the reason we saw so few Undisciplined Race-horses with external problems was because of the high and rapid fatality rate in those situations. In the mid- and late 90s, for example, hundreds of dotcom companies were flying high, often with exceptionally high market valuations. When the market shifted and the bubble burst, many, if not most, folded their tents and disappeared with no serious consideration of a restructuring, simply because their fundamental business model was so weak. Even companies that appeared to be investing in tangible assets were subject to the same fate. In 2001, Metricom filed for bankruptcy after investing more than $1.5 billion dollars in a high-speed wire-less communications network that it had rolled out successfully (at least in terms of technical performance) in 13 major cities. But when Metricom offered its network for sale at auction, it initially attracted no bids. Its subscriber base was small, maintenance and operating costs high, and continuing capital requirements so daunting that no one wanted it at any price. Its tangible assets were eventually liquidated, yielding less than 10 cents on the dollar.

Among the serious external challenges that we found Undisciplined Racehorses had to face were these:

Weak Competitive Position: Situations are rare in which companies with weak competitive positions enjoy rapid growth, but we did see one, a small sporting goods manufacturer whose growth was being financed by a "deep pockets" investor who personally guaranteed high-cost advertising and sales promotion expenses in the belief that they could drive revenues high enough to gain critical economies of scale. Unfortunately, the business did not have any compelling differentiating competitive presence and was simply growing unprofitably. After the investor tired of the losses, the secured lender forced a sale to a strategic buyer.

Permanent Market Change: On occasion, rapid-growth businesses are faced with sudden, major changes in the industry or market served. In the four situations in our project base, these changes all had a significant negative effect on the company. In each case, the problems seemed unlikely to be temporary or correctable in the near-term future. In effect, the market had moved away from the company, rather than the company's position in the same market deteriorating. In the one turnaround that was accomplished, the profitability of a plastic molded products manufacturer was dramatically improved by cost reduction and facility consolidation. But even here, the results would have been only marginal had not favorable external market changes reversed past trends. The restructured cost base gave the company time and allowed it to capitalize on the cyclical shift. But the underlying turnaround relied greatly upon external forces over which the company had little influence.

Other examples of dynamic growing businesses forced to deal with abrupt external market changes, all of which resulted in business liquidations, include:

- An electronics product-leasing business during a period of rapid technological change that eliminated residual values of leased equipment;
- A sports trading-card publisher faced with a 70% drop in industry sales that turned the industry business model unfavorable;
- A kerosene space-heater importer faced with product safety concerns.

AUTHORS' CASEBOOK: Consumer Fear Decimates a Niche Product

After spotting a kerosene space heater in Japan, an enterprising businessman struck an exclusive agreement to import the heaters using a high-cost distribution channel to specialty retail stores. The annual rate of sales exceeded $200 million, profits skyrocketed and, building for the expected rosy future, the entrepreneurial owner put a high-cost corporate overhead structure in place. However, after unfavorable publicity relating to safety concerns, retail sales dropped sharply at the beginning of the following heating season, leading to excess inventories at all levels of the existing distribution channel and a liquidity crisis when the distributors did not pay outstanding receivables. Based on nonpayment of receivables by the importer and failure to comply with "take or pay" contracts, the sole Japanese supplier of the product began to ship directly to U.S. retailers. The entire specialty retailer channel and related importer headquarters costs became unnecessary and the original importer was forced into liquidation.

Survival Alternatives: Recognize the likely temporary nature of rapid growth of hot products as market saturation occurs. Carefully control both inventory and receivable investment and keep overhead low while developing alternative product sources. Be prepared to move to lower-cost distribution channels when the market expands and competition develops.

Internal Problem Projects

It has often been observed that even the best companies must continuously reinvent themselves. Fashion and technology companies that let design or research and development languish invariably fall by the wayside. Manufacturing operations that fail to measure productivity and strive for continuous incremental process improvements become ripe for competitive incursions. Service businesses that fail to monitor their customers' needs, their competitors' innovations and their own performance are inviting the market to pass them by. Dynamic growth and change do indeed increase the risks of implementation failures. However, the alternative of standing still is not an option.

Dealing with dynamic growth is a nice problem to have. When vibrant and healthy companies stumble from self-inflicted wounds, they usually have a reasonable chance of prompt recovery, so long as they respond quickly.

Internal problems are fundamentally failures of execution. They encompass both functional performance failures and judgmental faux pas, manufacturing process and operational execution breakdowns as well as misguided, mistimed or mispriced acquisitions. Most companies deal with execution failures of one kind or another on a continuous basis without falling into our universe of "troubled businesses." But when a company is operating with a narrow liquidity reserve or fails to identify and respond to problems promptly, internal problems can threaten the survival of the business.

In evaluating our experience base we found that the nature of the problems encountered fell into three distinct categories: Project and Growth Management, Acquisition Problems and Fraud.

Project and Growth Management: Nearly half of the problems among our Undisciplined Racehorses resulted from failures in internal administrative and management control systems. Two general categories are involved:

Management of rapid revenue growth: Profitability can deteriorate precipitously when revenue growth outpaces functional capabilities and internal execution problems develop in areas such as manufacturing, servicing customers or collecting receivables. Problems in these situations tend to involve the individual entrepreneur who has hit the market right and is moving his business into a stage in the corporate lifecycle in which rapid revenue growth is achieved. Businesses become harder to control, administrative systems need to be enhanced in order to keep pace with revenue growth and new, more experienced personnel need to be hired. In some situations, the execution failures are allowed to persist and result in failure to deliver products and services, which can destroy critical customer relationships, erode accumulated good will and inflict serious fundamental damage on the business. In other situations, the customers' interests may be carefully protected, but the company's efficiency and profitability erode rapidly as a result.

Management of projects requiring internal change: A company embarks on a major change in its operations, usually a project involving process changes, new physical facilities or entry into new markets, and finds that a lack of planning or failure to deploy adequate resources results in poor execution, unforeseen cost overruns, disruptive schedule delays and occasionally an outright project failure.

For the most part, implementation failures related to both growth and project management are functional problems that are responsive to operational turnarounds. They require proper identification of the problem and appropriate corrective actions, typically including guidance and prioritization combined with deployment of additional resources. They generally also require some level of forbearance support and patience from the lenders. The turnaround success rate is high. True operational turnarounds of growth and project management problems among our Undisciplined Racehorses have been achieved in almost 70% of the situations.

However, when the conceived projects are massive or strategic in nature, they sometimes are "bet-the-business" initiatives in which failures may be irreversible:

- A subsea contractor operating in the Gulf of Mexico quadrupled its debt and went bankrupt attempting to build a high-tech vessel to move into deepwater construction.
- A leading consulting engineering company expanded into project contracting and encountered devastating cost overruns after acquiring major, complex construction projects with fixed-cost bids.

The key lessons to learn when evaluating implementation failures are that the objective is not to avoid change and risk but to manage it, and that when healthy companies stumble, prompt recognition and response can generally set them right.   Clearly, accepting bet-the-business risks is not for the squeamish and generally should be avoided.   But perfection is not a realistic goal.   The shame is not in stumbling, but in allowing denial or ego to postpone corrective actions.

AUTHORS' CASEBOOK: Health-Care Company Restructuring

A publicly held health-care company had been aggressively growing its business by making a number of acquisitions of small service businesses.   However, its historical core manufacturing operations were incurring large operating losses.   Turnaround consultants were retained by the company to evaluate its business strategy and recommend operational restructuring actions that would be a condition of a debt restructuring agreement.   The viability review focused on the competitive environment of each of the company's several businesses, where each was making and losing money, potential for future growth and the operational restructuring needed to maximize future value of the business.

Critical Challenge: Develop a plan for generating sufficient cash from working capital reductions and sale of operating businesses to reduce bank debt to acceptable levels.

As a result of the detailed strategic review, plans were developed and implemented by existing management to:

- Sell a valuable but low-growth manufacturing business;
- Exit certain other product lines where the company had relatively small revenues and limited market share;
- Achieve major cost reductions through consolidation and restructuring of remaining manufacturing operations;
- Reverse a tentative decision to liquidate a subsidiary with disappointing results; instead a highly successful fix for its operational problems was developed and implemented.

Debt was restructured and within three years equity value of the company increased almost 20-fold.

Acquisition Plan Shortfalls: In these situations, post-acquisition operations fail to produce the earnings expected at the time the applicable debt was incurred.   In some cases, these shortfalls can be the result of operating declines. More frequently, they result from failure to achieve cost reductions, growth and synergies anticipated at the time of the acquisition.   Here again, the simple failure to meet expectations does not create a distressed company.   Distressed companies arise only when the magnitude of such failures exceeds the margin of error provided in the capital structure.   When this occurs, some combination of management greed, arrogance and ignorance of the marketplace is often involved in the acquisition decision-making process.

We found two general categories of acquisition problems encountered by Undisciplined Racehorses:

Failed Industry Rollups: In the 1990s, it became fashionable to attempt the rollup of a series of a small entrepreneurial businesses into an "industry leader" that could be taken public. One presumes there were some successes with this strategy, but it also resulted in many spectacular failures, so much so that in certain lender circles "rollup" became almost synonymous with "debacle." Logically, the grouping together of similar, generally successful businesses, then benchmarking operations and imposing best practices upon each of them should generate strong synergies. But certain types of businesses have proven extremely resistant to such consolidation. Businesses that were built upon and require close personal service relationships more than the standardized delivery of goods and services did not transition well into rollups. It proved extremely difficult to control, properly motivate and develop group synergy among a series of entrepreneurial former owners who now had enough readily available cash that they no longer need to work. While they may have achieved their own successes by ruling with an iron hand, they particularly dislike autocratic changes implemented by a new owner that demonstrate a lack of respect for their abilities or past judgments.

These businesses are often highly dependent on their owners' longtime business relationships, integrity and ability to make good service trade-offs. When a good customer sees "Joe the Owner" at a party or on the golf course and complains, he expects action and usually gets it. This is not necessarily the case with a complaint to "Joe the New General Manager," who now works for a private equity firm in Manhattan.

We found that, in many cases, the former owners were so difficult to control that administrative corporate-level overhead increases more than offset functional consolidation savings theoretically available as a result of the rollup. (The overhead costs ended up as a reverse synergy.) Worse still, extracting value from a failed services rollup is very difficult, because low current earnings and lack of management don't justify a strategic sale. Business buybacks by the former owners may offer the only viable path and ability for new owners (or creditors) to exit the investment, but such buybacks generally occur only at low prices, because the former owners control the customer base due to their past relationships and have all the leverage in the sale negotiations.

Other acquisition-related problems: The bulk of the other acquisition problems tended to arise from integration and implementation failures, which become most pronounced when the business being acquired is of meaningful size compared with the acquirer. Undisciplined Racehorses tend to be young, administratively weak and inexperienced in systems and operational integrations. Furthermore, most managers underestimate the challenges of executing operational and cultural change within an organization. The integration of disparate corporate cultures, often from former competitors, adds significantly to the operational challenges, not infrequently triggering subtle (and not so subtle) political posturing and infighting as middle management seeks to carve out their position in the new entity.

In summary, distressed situations resulting from acquisition-plan shortfalls present three fundamental issues and challenges:

1. The ultimate strategic reasonableness of the acquisition;
2. The immediate and continuing ability to service debt incurred to finance the transaction;
3. Implementation performance in execution of integration tasks and the post-acquisition business plan.

As we've observed, implementation failures can generally be corrected and operating performance improved. But the degree to which a true turnaround can be achieved is, in many cases, dependent upon how sound the strategy was and how severely leveraged the transaction. While profitability may never reach the levels originally conceived of in the glow of the acquisition due diligence, if an acceptable basic level of operating performance is achievable and the company remains viable, forbearance or restructuring of the debt can generally be negotiated. If the fundamental strategy of the business combination is flawed, however, the business may have to be disassembled.

Fraud: In situations involving fraud, all the rules change. Deliberate factual misrepresentations lead to false conclusions. Once the existence of fraud is revealed, even legitimate facts become suspect, further clouding the decision-making process. The testosterone levels among the damaged parties spike and a desire to punish the guilty can overwhelm efforts to mitigate the damage.

The good news is that the incidence of fraud, at least in our experience, is far less than is popularly perceived. Unfortunately, there are two painful reasons why the incidence of fraud seems to be popularly viewed as so much more frequent than our experience suggests. One is that some of the most publicized cases (Enron, WorldCom) have involved truly massive fraud; the other is that when fraud occurs, the recoveries are often counted in pennies to the dollar.

Our Undisciplined Racehorse category includes three projects in which it was credibly believed that fraud was involved:

- The oceangoing tanker fleet described below that was financed using grossly inflated appraisals. Poorly maintained vessels continued to receive satisfactory seaworthiness ratings based on apparently fraudulent inspection reporting.
- A rapidly expanding, publicly held cheese manufacturer that overstated both inventory and receivable values to report increasing profitability and support market valuation as a growth business. Less than 15% of the reported borrowing base assets were legitimate.
- A finance company that hid client loan defaults by rewriting poor credit loans. Operating losses were understated and remedial actions postponed as excessive borrowings were drawn against the inflated borrowing base.

All three situations turned into asset liquidations.

AUTHORS' CASEBOOK: Adrift on the High Seas

After 24 months of rapid expansion, an owner-operator of more than 80 oceangoing vessels missed a scheduled interest payment on nearly $250 million in privately placed notes. The payment default occurred only 15 days after drawing new funds from a debt restructuring.

Working on behalf of senior secured lenders holding mortgages on 49 vessels, a three-man team that included co-author Doug Hopkins was dispatched to Greece to confirm immediate cash requirements and undertake an accelerated viability assessment of the business. Within seven days the team documented major operating and administrative deficiencies and a rapid collapse of trading operations and revenue-producing capability. The key problems included:

- Operational misrepresentations and gross overstatement of loan collateral values;
- Poor vessel maintenance of an aging fleet leading to loss of seaworthiness certifications;
- Admiralty seizures of vessels for nonpayment of crew and provisioning expenses, some in very unfavorable legal venues;
- Inability to obtain cargoes due to lack of credibility with shippers.

Critical Challenge: Working — against the active obstruction and interference of the owner — to develop a forced recovery program that would yield maximum possible proceeds from assets dispersed across 33 different international legal jurisdictions.

Establishing an operational base in London and using the resources of a London-based commercial shipping manager and four different worldwide technical managers, an asset recovery program was developed that included:

- Evaluating fair market values and future earnings potential for each vessel;

- Identifying and evaluating outstanding maritime claims and priorities related to the mortgages, including variations in jurisdictional legal requirements;
- Developing, prioritizing and implementing individual vessel recovery plans based upon estimated potential net recoveries from alternative actions;
- Exercising rights under mortgage documents and seizing or relocating 19 vessels from the owner's control or unfavorable jurisdictions to mortgagee-friendly legal venues;
- Establishing minimum-value thresholds and bidding at admiralty auctions to protect asset values;
- Repurchasing, repairing, reactivating and trading a fleet of 26 vessels to re-establish their serviceability and maximize recovery values before managing their subsequent orderly disposition.

Actions and Outcomes

Turnarounds: As observed repeatedly, operational turnarounds are much more likely when internal problems are involved than when the problem is the external competitive environment, where, in many cases, the business model no longer works. Nowhere is this more clearly apparent than among Undisciplined Racehorses. What actions deliver these results? Each situation is unique, but major themes recur:

- Where implementation performance failures occurred, the situation required evaluating processes and practices, sourcing and deploying experienced functional resources, fixing specific operational control problems and, in some cases, orchestrating plant consolidations.
- Where strategic misjudgments were made, the situation required resetting reasonable expectations and, in many cases, exiting from failed initiatives and retreating to core competencies.
- Where unrealistic growth expectations led to expansion of fixed costs and overhead, disciplined forecasting procedures were installed and fixed costs were cut back to more reasonable expectations.

Management Changes: As we've noted throughout this book, management change should be resorted to only after fully diagnosing the nature of the problem and the potential solutions. This summary of CEO changes at Undisciplined Racehorses and actual project results supports that view:

EXHIBIT 16-2

CEO CHANGES AT UNDISCIPLINED RACEHORSES

	No. of Companies	CEO Changes	Percent
Turnarounds	17	6	35 %
Restructuring	2	–	0 %
Sales	6	2	33 %
Liquidations	11	6	55 %
Total	36	14	39 %

In almost two-thirds of the situations where turnarounds were accomplished, they were achieved without a CEO change.

In the six turnarounds in which CEOs were replaced, each CEO had previously demonstrated successful management ability. None suffered from the disqualifying characteristics of excessive arrogance or greed (a little arrogance and greed seems to serve as a motivating force for most CEOs). The common characteristic of all six was that they were not motivated or temperamentally suited to reversing their growth plans, downsizing the business and cutting costs, even when initial denial had been overcome and the need was recognized. Their recent objectives and past background experience had been in business growth, and they did not envision themselves in any other role. The turnaround required a CEO more suited to the changed role.

Of the eight changes of CEO where sale or liquidation of the business occurred, two involved fraud situations discussed earlier and the balance followed the pattern of inability to manage in other than a growth mode.

Bankruptcy Filings

Only 2 of the 19 cases resulting in turnarounds or restructurings required bankruptcy filings:

- Creditors of a furniture manufacturer that had filed Chapter 11 brought in crisis managers who were effective in achieving a turnaround during the bankruptcy process.
- After putting in place actions needed for a turnaround, an electronics manufacturer filed Chapter 11 in order to complete the restructuring of its debt.

Of the 11 liquidations in this category, only two avoided a bankruptcy filing. One case involved foreclosure by creditors on specific assets and the other involved consensual settlements with creditors relating to the sharing of liquidation proceeds.

Chapter Summary

Businesses in the earlier, rapid growth phases of their lifecycle typically do not have adequate controls and administrative procedures in place. This can cause problems in the form of poor control of operations, acceptance of high risk to expedite or continue growth in volume, or both.

Since, by definition, these Undisciplined Racehorses are fast-growing businesses, whether organically or via acquisition, external problems are relatively rare as the source of financial trouble. However, in some cases a sudden, permanent market change caused operational difficulties. When such changes occur, the business model often no longer works and a liquidation can quickly result

The highest potential for turnaround exists where internal problems related to management of growth or new projects have caused the company to incur large negative shortfalls from expectations. Such problems can normally be fixed using appropriate external resources or installation of improved operational controls. In certain circumstances, in fact, nothing is wrong with the business – only the expectations are unsound.

In some cases, a new CEO is needed, but often the existing CEO is the best person to fix the situation if denial can be overcome. The common reason for making CEO changes was not lack of basic competence. Rather, it was the inability of the individual CEO to accept the new responsibilities of business downsizing and cost-cutting.

Failed industry rollups and other acquisition difficulties are relatively frequent occurrences when companies are unprepared to provide adequate administrative controls or their entrepreneurial founders cannot be controlled.

Fraud, in our project sample, was a rare source of financial problems. The three fraud situations all led to liquidation, due to loss of management credibility at businesses that arguably had a viable core operation.

RECOMMENDED READING

Only the Paranoid Survive: How to Exploit the Crisis Points That Challenge Every Company and Career (Currency-Doubleday, 1996) by Andrew S. Grove.

This well-written best-seller focuses on both high-growth technology companies like Intel and other businesses undergoing what Grove calls the "10X Factor" of change. He brings his long experience as a CEO to bear on avoiding denial and staying ahead of the curve in a rapidly changing competitive environment.

Grove makes a major point of the need to recognize "strategic inflection points" when major changes are occurring in an industry. Breaking the barriers between what he terms knowledge power and organization power requires that management solicit and accept bad news about the "six forces" he defines as impacting the competitive environment, rather than indulging in the normal management reaction of killing the messenger.

The Unnatural Act of Management: When the Great Leader's Work Is Done the People Say, 'We Did It Ourselves' (Harper Business, 1992) by Everett T. Suters.

Written as what might be termed a fable, this book is a fictional account of a 90-day turnaround. The company involved has been attempting to grow with high-cost manufacturing investment. Suters describes a series of lessons that the interim president teaches his management team as he forces them to make the decisions that solve the company's internally oriented problems and put it on the road to recovery.

Of particular usefulness to the process of turning around a troubled company is a series of checklists for planning, decision-making and managing people. Lessons of the book are most useful for the hands-on entrepreneur attempting a transition to business leader while solving internal administration problems.

Direct From Dell: Strategies That Revolutionized an Industry (Harper Collins, 1999) by Michael Dell with Catherine Fredman.

An interesting first-hand account of the development and growth of the low-cost Dell model for manufacturing and distributing computers, this book is heavily oriented toward executing a business growth strategy. Chapters 3, 4 and 5 discuss in detail the missteps that caused crises, which in Dell's case were quickly recognized and acted upon, but that could have resulted in the company's downfall.

From the viewpoint of the turnaround of an Undisciplined Racehorse business, conditions leading to a need for major operational and organizational changes are discussed in detail. As the book emphasizes, "Facts are your friend," an argument in favor of a detailed problem diagnosis when a business becomes troubled.

Chapter 17

LIGHTENING THE LOAD OF
OVERBURDENED WORKHORSES

Overburdened Workhorses are mature, relatively stable businesses with historically positive operating cash flow that find themselves unable to support their debt service obligations. Their core product lines – the solid cash-flow generating businesses that Peter Drucker called "Today's Breadwinners" – seldom stumble badly from operational challenges if they remain adequately capitalized. But as management, the board of directors and shareholders seek ways to enhance investment returns through acquisitions, capital structure changes or aggressive growth strategies, they occasionally make misjudgments.

Even sound businesses can become financially troubled when overburdened with debt. This can result either from unreasonable future expectations of cash-flow growth (often associated with over-aggressive or ill-conceived initiatives aimed at stimulating growth in a mature environment), or from a downturn of the industry business cycle, which leads to reduced earnings. These businesses were not considered overleveraged at the time debt was incurred, but the business is struggling and, in hindsight, it is clear that the risks assumed were greater than anticipated. The company has become unable to meet the debt service obligations with which it has been saddled.

In our experience, Overburdened Workhorses present a broad array of problem types and ultimate resolutions, split equally between internal and external causes. Exhibit 17-1 summarizes the problems encountered and the resulting outcomes for the 34 Overburdened Workhorses we identified in our 100-project sample.

EXHIBIT 17-1
OVERBURDENED WORKHORSE BUSINESSES
PROJECT RESULTS

	Turnaround	Restructuring	Sales	Liquidation	Total
EXTERNAL PROBLEMS					
Permanent market change	–	2	1	–	3
Business cycle	5	4	1	–	10
Commodity prices	–	2	1	1	4
Total External	5	8	3	1	17
INTERNAL PROBLEMS					
Growth/Project management	1	2	2	–	5
Acquisitions implementation	1	2	3	1	7
Inept management	1	1	5	–	7
Total Internal	3	5	10	1	19
TOTAL	8	13	13	2	36

The characteristics of these internal and external problems are similar to those in the other two general categories of financially troubled businesses (Undisciplined Racehorses and Aging Mules), as are the likely solutions. The key difference is that these Workhorses have mature and established management processes and controls. They have been generating satisfactory cash flow in the recent past and are not losing market share – or at least they weren't until their inability to service their debts began to impose liquidity constraints.

The operational characteristics of the stable Overburdened Workhorses are:

1. Profitable earnings history and potential
2. Minimal change in position in the external competitive market
3. Reasonably strong niche in the industry
4. Competitive products and technology
5. Effective operational management structure

The company is financially troubled because of its debt level, not its operating results compared with historical trends or its competitors in the current economic environment. Among the causes of such problems are:

1. Although EBITDA has been used as a basis for projecting debt-service capacity, recurring capital expenditures use most or all of the cash generated.

2. The company has been recently acquired, often in a LBO by a financial buyer. Overly optimistic assumptions have been made about earnings growth by anticipating expense-reduction synergies; the acquisition debt levels were justified by unrealistic earnings expectations.

3. The company has increased its borrowing to finance expansion or capital expenditures based on expected increases in core business earnings, which didn't materialize.

4. Due to general economic conditions, credit has tightened and credit lines are not being renewed or extended as expected. Earnings may have remained constant, but a liquidity crisis is looming due to inability to roll over debt.

5. Earnings declined significantly after a downturn in volume related to the business cycle.

6. An acquisition outside the company's area of historical core strength has failed or faltered.

Excepting the business-cycle situations, Overburdened Workhorses are typically not strong turnaround candidates. Certainly, every organization has room for incremental – even continuous and perpetual – process improvement. But the common characteristic of the Overburdened Workhorses is that the company's core operations and its competitive position have not deteriorated materially but debt-service capacity is running well below what turned out to be unrealistic expectations. In these circumstances, the best strategy for all concerned parties is a debt restructuring that allows the company to dig out from its overleveraged situation.

Depending upon the severity of the mistake, the equity holders may find their value diluted and, in extreme cases, wiped out. But if the debt burden is reduced, a company in this category can generally rebound from the other challenges it may face. Many debt restructurings leave the company with excessive debt, and if it is too severely hobbled the company may continue to struggle and ultimately fail. But if a company has a reasonable core business that generates reliable cash operating earnings, a debt restructuring is generally the most appropriate solution for all concerned.

Agreement on a restructuring does not come easily, however. It's instructive to remember that, from the creditors' perspective, debt restructuring means they are being coerced into becoming unwilling venture capital partners of an overextended management. In many situations where a business might be viable with properly restructured debt, the lenders will not agree to a longer-term debt restructuring. This most often occurs when holders of the company's secured debt have lost confidence in management's credibility; the lenders will usually insist upon maintaining the leverage of their collateralized position, put a short-term forbearance agreement in place and make it clear that they desire a quick exit. If the exit is not forthcoming through a third-party refinancing, the next time the company trips a covenant, pressure will be applied to force a sale.

> **AUTHORS' CASEBOOK: Achieving Acquisition Synergies**
>
> Doskocil, Inc., a publicly held specialty-meat products manufacturer, acquired much larger Wilson Foods in an unfriendly tender offer. Subsequently, the company was unable to complete planned asset sales and to retire acquisition debt, and it filed for Chapter 11 bankruptcy. Consolidated liabilities approached $500 million. Although post-acquisition disruptions relating to the Chapter 11 filing and integration difficulties were significant, each business had inherent strength and viability on a standalone basis. Investment bankers were strongly recommending an unwinding of the merger.
>
> **Critical Challenge:** Develop a Plan of Reorganization that provided the greatest value for unsecured and subordinated creditors; secured creditors were clearly adequately collateralized and there was no residual equity.
>
> An evaluation of the situation on behalf of the acquirer's subordinated debtholders led to the conclusion that logical potential market synergies expected from the consolidation of the two companies remained a reasonable objective. Unwinding of the merger would have adversely impacted value for this creditor group and was rejected as an option.
>
> Management obtained approval of a Plan of Reorganization involving retention of the total business. Under the Reorganization Plan, bank debt was restructured to be paid in full over a seven-year period, with other creditors receiving substantially all of the company's common stock. Under a new CEO, recruited from within the acquired company, and new outside directors, the company prospered. It was acquired by a strategic buyer at three times the bankruptcy exit valuation within two years.

Through our experience with Overburdened Workhorses, we have identified typical types of problems, the key issues they raise, considerations, responses and likely outcomes:

External Problems

Permanent Market Change: Significant changes in the industry or market served cause deteriorating operating results, and the best information available indicates that the situation is not temporary and will not correct itself in the near term. In effect, the market has begun to move away from the company, rather than the company experiencing a competitive deterioration of its position. We have seen such changes in the industrywide moves to offshore production facilities and, in one situation, charges of price-fixing against industry leaders that resulted in a collapse of operating margins.

Cyclical Market Demand Downturn: Total industry demand declines in response to overall business cycles but is expected to revert to normal revenue growth patterns in the reasonably near future. Suppliers of heavy equipment, raw materials, construction supplies and certain service providers tend to be particularly susceptible to such cycles.

Commodity Price Changes: Companies face severe price reductions in the commodities they produce or large price increases for the commodities they purchase as raw materials. We have seen such changes in the fertilizer industry; as natural gas prices spiked, and at plastic molders that rely on petrochemical-based resins.

Internal Problems

Management of revenue growth: Profitability deteriorates when internal execution problems develop as volume exceeds production capacity or administrative capabilities. Although it is unusual among Workhorse companies, two examples in our project sample involved inventory increases that outstripped borrowing capacity, resulting in a liquidity crisis.

Management of projects requiring internal change: Implementation failures (poor quality, cost overruns, schedule delays) stem from major changes in operations, usually projects involving new physical facilities or entry into new markets.

Acquisition Plan Shortfalls: In these situations, acquisitions fail to provide the earnings increases expected.

Inept Management: Unqualified or inattentive management either didn't have the ability to manage the business properly or for some reason lost interest in effective management, withdrawing from day-to-day influence in the business.

These problems are essentially the same as those faced by Undisciplined Racehorses but, in our experience, the mix with which they are encountered shifts fairly dramatically in the more mature and stable Overburdened Workhorses category. We find these challenges to be broadly dispersed within the Overburdened Workhorses, split evenly between internal and external challenges. We note, too, that absent their leveraged financial structure, most mature Workhorse-type businesses are not likely to have entered our universe of troubled companies. Without the drain on resources of their debt-service burden, most of these companies would address and solve their normal business challenges, internal or external, as though they were just slight bumps in the road.

Operational Responses and Improvements

It would be a gross mistake, yet typical of what can occur at troubled businesses, to conclude that because the primary problem faced by Overburdened Workhorses is overleverage, these companies have no need for operational changes. One problem with overleverage is that it reduces a company's flexibility and hinders its ability to address operating challenges that might otherwise be taken in stride.

In our experience, one key difference between the Overburdened Workhorses and our other categories of troubled companies is that the functional management team at a Workhorse company is much more likely to have both a clear understanding of the problems it confronts and the skills required to respond to them. But lack of resources and the day-to-day difficulties of dealing with liquidity pressures result in delay, deferral, distraction and eventually, if unchecked, decline.

Among the short-sighted approaches to problems we have seen are companies that:

- Defer technology upgrades, productivity improvements and other capital projects while their competitors gain ground or move ahead;
- Maintain excess capacity and superfluous staffing levels because they can't fund the one-time cash expenditures associated with restructuring operations or won't take the hit to reported earnings of accounting write-offs;
- Complicate their operations and compress their margins by seeking low value-added incremental volume to fill their excess capacity and maintain the fiction of continued revenue growth or stability.

Even in those situations where the primary operational challenge is the impact of external business cycles – the one area where patience is the greatest virtue – the greatest successes come at companies that use the impetus of the cycle to restructure operations and processes, improving efficiency and profitability and emerging more competitive and poised to take advantage of the next boom cycle.

Successful businesses do not stand still; they continuously evolve and change. In many cases it's an ebb and flow, as business up-cycles or internal initiatives lead to periods of growth, which are followed by periods of retrenchment as the company consolidates from business down-cycles or missteps. While robustly capitalized companies may take advantage of downturns or problems to reinvest in new growth strategies, troubled businesses very seldom have that option. Typical options and alternatives available to improve profitability are heavily focused on retrenchment to core strengths and remediation of functional errors. These can include:

- Shedding non-core or underperforming assets and operations;
- Culling low-margin products and business lines;
- Consolidating facilities and adjusting capacity to meet changing demand requirements;
- Examining opportunities to convert fixed costs to variable costs;
- Sourcing functional expertise to solve specific implementation problems.

AUTHORS' CASEBOOK: Plant Consolidation to Eliminate Excess Capacity

A high-quality steel foundry sold its products to the construction and mining industries. Although producing excellent products, it operated two separate plants and had significant overcapacity. During a cyclical downturn, large operating losses soon occurred. Attempts to sell the business were hampered by environmental cleanup liabilities at the older plant.

Critical Challenge: Eliminate operating losses caused by excess capacity in order to restore viability.

Cost structure and market conditions were reviewed in detail. Based on this analysis, a profit turnaround plan was developed based on consolidating all production into the more modern of the two plants. The modern plant and all working capital assets were then sold to a joint venture of two major steel companies. An excellent price was obtained due to the projected higher profitability of the consolidated, one-plant operation. The remaining plant was sold to a real estate developer for a price that more than covered close-down and environmental cleanup costs.

Financial Restructurings and Business Sales

When a stable business with significant earning power gets into financial difficulties due to internal problems, it most typically ends up with either a financial restructuring to reduce debt service or a sale of the business. As we've noted, these businesses do face real challenges and require active operational management and change. However, major operational profitability improvements in these businesses generally are driven by improvements in the external business cycle. Occasionally, Overburdened Workhorses can work out of their distressed situation without concurrent financial restructuring. We have seen that occur at businesses where a lack of attention to working capital management has built an accumulated asset reserve that can be tapped to fund the actions required for the company to be responsive to its challenges without losing its competitive edge.

In our experience, liquidation of Overburdened Workhorses almost never happens because sale of these viable businesses as going concerns yields much better results than asset liquidation. In the two cases noted in Exhibit 17-1 as liquidations, both were bankruptcy filings where management had lost credibility and real estate assets were arguably at least as valuable as the ongoing business.

Two primary factors can push a business toward a sale rather than a restructuring. The first, noted above, is deterioration of management credibility. The second is the broader market-driven benefits of consolidation. By its nature, the Overburdened Workhorse is almost certainly in a mature industry. These industries tend toward consolidation over time, with the strong devouring the weak. When the results of a restructuring proposal from the company is not perceived as offering greater benefits and significantly less risk than a prompt sale could provide, a sale becomes the more attractive course of action. When management credibility is low, the risk-adjusted expectations of anything they put forward are correspondingly low.

The natural conclusion to be drawn from this is that establishing credibility for planned operational change and related operating income projections are the most critical prerequisites to constructing and executing a financial restructuring transaction. If the competing parties have widely divergent views of the likely future performance of the company, if they distrust the intention or the competence of management, or if they believe they are being treated unfairly relative to other parties, negotiations on a financial restructuring are likely to fail. Conversely, if the various parties can come to share a relatively common view of the challenges faced and the risks and probabilities of future performance, if their relative rights and interests are treated with respect, and if the anticipated outcome from the treatment they receive can be demonstrated to exceed the outcome from other likely options, a restructuring agreement should be achievable.

AUTHORS' CASEBOOK: Using Bankruptcy to Close a Sale

A leveraged buyout firm had purchased the metal buildings manufacturing business of a major steel company. The business was evaluated as having a strong brand name and good market position in the geographic areas it served. However, for various reasons including industry overcapacity in a highly cyclical industry, assumption of excessive employee retirement liabilities and the burdens of excessive debt, the company was in default on secured loans and, in addition, was on C.O.D. terms with most of its vendors.

Critical Challenges: Achieving a profitability turnaround to enhance business value and effecting an orderly sale to provide maximum recoveries to creditors.

Actions taken by management related principally to major cost reductions, including closing two of the company's three manufacturing plants.

Although the company returned to profitability, it was necessary to file for Chapter 11 bankruptcy to settle outstanding liabilities. During the Chapter 11 proceedings, the business was sold to a Japanese buyer wishing to enter U.S. markets. The business then continued successful ongoing operations under new ownership with adequate reserves to survive in a cyclical business.

Management Changes

The 34 Overburdened Workhorses in our 100-project sample provide the basis for several observations about the role of management and considerations for initiating management change. The following table summarizes CEO changes and project results at our Overburdened Workhorse companies:

EXHIBIT 17-2
CEO CHANGES AT OVERBURDENED WORKHORSES

Project Results	Number of Companies	CEO Changes	Percent
Turnarounds	8	2	25 %
Restructurings	13	1	8 %
Sales	13	5	38 %
Liquidations	2	1	50 %
Total	36	9	25 %

As might be expected in businesses that we have defined as having mature and established management processes and controls, in most cases where the business survived through turnaround or restructuring, existing management were retained. Overall, CEOs were replaced in only 9 of 36 cases. In more than half of the cases where senior management was removed, the business was sold.

Bankruptcy Filings

Of 21 cases resulting in turnarounds or restructurings, only three required a bankruptcy filing. These filings were all helpful to the process:

- The metal-buildings manufacturer in the case history above closed plants and reduced retirement liabilities during bankruptcy proceedings;
- Doskocil, Inc., also discussed earlier in this chapter, restructured its excessive acquisition debt and completed integration of two profitable businesses;
- Fairfield Communities, Inc., reduced debt by sale of selected assets with a Plan of Reorganization that resulted in highly successful future growth. (This case was reviewed in Chapter 10.)

Chapter Summary

Overburdened Workhorses are mature and relatively stable businesses. They are normally cash-flow generators, are not losing share in their core markets and have good operational controls and administrative systems in place. Their primary problems can result from either internal or external factors. In our experience, external problems will usually be related to the industry business cycle or to sharp changes in commodity prices. Internal problems are likely to be acquisition-related, or, in a relatively few cases, due to inept management that has not yet had the opportunity to destroy market position and move the business into the Aging Mule category.

Working capital control sometimes becomes a problem because, in the normal course of business, these companies tend to be cash-rich and to focus on reported profitability, not return on investment. Where this situation exists, working capital improvements can offer a relatively prompt source of liquidity relief.

Turnarounds of Overburdened Workhorses with external problems usually occur as a result of a favorable upturn in the business cycle together with classic cost reduction, operational restructuring and a refocus on the most successful business segments.

The most common outcome if problems are external is a debt restructuring, which brings debt service requirements in line with reduced cash flow. But if management is inept or creditors cannot be persuaded to share a consistent and reliable view of the company's future operating performance, a sale of the business becomes highly likely.

Liquidations of Overburdened Workhorses are very rare. Value is usually much greater as an ongoing business entity.

RECOMMENDED READING

Good to Great: Why Some Companies Make the Leap...and Others Don't (Harper Business, 2001) by Jim Collins.

This heavily researched book, deservedly on best-seller lists for several years, is a follow-up to *Built to Last*, written by Collins and Jerry Ponas in the 1990s. *Good to Great* examines in detail and draws lessons from the successful turn-around of 11 mature workhorse businesses that have subsequently achieved major financial successes over a period of at least 15 years.

As the title suggests, in general these were not financially troubled companies. The turnaround came when good leadership confronted the brutal facts of each company's situation, focused on specific business strengths, and maintained the discipline to avoid diffusion of effort into other areas.

A finding of Collins' research that defies conventional wisdom is that 95% of the CEOs who accomplished or extended the great companies' leap forward came from within the organization. We believe that this further supports our thesis that turnarounds are most likely to be achieved by either existing management or an internal candidate.

Control Your Destiny or Someone Else Will: How Jack Welch Is Making General Electric the World's Most Competitive Corporation (Currency Doubleday, 1993) by Noel M. Tichy and Stratford Sherman.

This book was written by individuals with insider exposure to the change process that occurred during the first decade of the Welch regime at GE. Tichy, a business professor at the University of Michigan, was both a business organizational consultant to GE and manager of GE's Crotonville Management Training Institute for two years while on leave from the University. His details of how Welch accomplished his dramatic early changes in the entrenched GE culture are of value in dealing with any mature business in need of revitalization.

From Worst to First: Behind the Scenes of Continental's Remarkable Comeback (John Wiley & Sons, 1998) by Gordon Bethune with Scott Huler.

This well-written, first-hand account by its CEO describes Continental Airlines' 1994 to 1997 operational turnaround and financial restructuring. The book is heavily spiced with anecdotes by someone who knew how to change a culture by his focus on "defining success right and measuring the right stuff."

We define Continental as an Overloaded Workhorse business because it held a position in the marketplace that filled a growing need while it carried excessive debt. However, the airline's prior management was moving it quickly into the Aging Mule classification. Bethune describes in detail his involvement in providing leadership, dumping the money-losing routes and establishing the nuts-and-bolts measurements that change an organization.

Chapter 18

REHABILITATING AGING MULES

An exceptionally large body of business literature discusses the pitfalls faced by companies that become complacent. Many, many voices offer variations of the same advice – that management must remain engaged and forward-thinking, must seek out change and embrace it and must continually reinvent and re-engineer their businesses. These are not easy challenges. But those companies that succeed in attaining these goals can remain strong and profitable for decades, perhaps even moving from "good to great" (an evolution that Jim Collins describes in his book of that name, cited as recommended reading in Chapter 17).

Those that fail in these tasks are destined to be overtaken, if not by the competition than by changes in the markets in which they operate. Lead, follow or get out of the way: in business, standing still does not seem to be an option. Once forward motion stops, deterioration seems to be inevitable.

Aging Mules are businesses whose forward motion has stopped, businesses that are past their prime and have become, or are becoming, subject to stagnation and decline. Administrative functions have become bureaucratic and inflexible, and the organization seems be infected with a tendency to look inward or backward, rather than outward and ahead. Typically, these businesses are losing touch with customers' needs. Sometimes quickly, more often slowly and steadily, they find themselves facing declining unit sales, loss of market share and increasing levels of financial problems.

The best turnaround stories and the most difficult management feats involve revitalizing such companies.

In general, the problems of Aging Mules stem from external sources rather than a loss of internal control over operational details. Management may well be at fault, but their sins are likely of omission, not commission. The company is in an aging part of its lifecycle, and the management mules are too stubborn, limited in vision or complacent either to understand that a change of direction is required or to perceive what that new direction should be. This leads to a tendency to do more of what was successful in the past, using more bureaucratic centralization and stricter policies and procedures to ensure compliance by the troops in the trenches.

Alternatively, and perhaps simultaneously, managers of Aging Mules may be faced with the dilemma laid out so well by Clayton M. Christiansen in *The Innovator's Dilemma:* lower-cost competitors take away pieces of the lowest-margin business until ultimately nothing is left for the Aging Mule, whose management have made rational economic decisions every step of the way to bankruptcy court.

The problems and challenges that confront these Aging Mules generally develop well before the company becomes financially troubled. If they are addressed appropriately while the company still has the financial strength to finance major initiatives from internal resources, the company may have the option of formulating a new strategic direction to drive continued growth. However, our experience has been exclusively restricted to situations in which the company allowed itself to become financially weak, as well as operationally challenged. Once that happens, it becomes exceptionally difficult to use an Aging Mule as the platform from which to launch a new strategic initiative. None of the turnarounds of Aging Mules with which we have been involved resulted from a significant new strategy or change of direction for the core business. They all concentrated on refocusing upon the successful, profitable parts of what had existed in the past. This may not mean that it is impossible to achieve a turnaround to a successful new growth strategy involving a significant change in direction by a financially troubled company in the face of external problems, but we have never seen it happen.

In our experience, when you're dealing with an Aging Mule, the challenge is to determine whether some configuration of the pieces is worth more than the whole. Is there any profitable core competency and strength that still resides within the organization and operations? And, once identified, can its value be best maximized as a standalone operation or through a strategic sale?

Exhibit 18-1 provides information on the sources of problems and the ultimate results of our projects involving Aging Mule businesses.

EXHIBIT 18-1
AGING MULE BUSINESSES
PROJECT RESULTS

	Turnarounds	Restructurings	Sales	Liquidation	Total
EXTERNAL PROBLEMS					
Weak competitive position	5	3	2	4	14
Permanent market change		3	2	2	7
Business cycle /Commodity prices			2	1	3
Total External	5	6	6	7	24
INTERNAL PROBLEMS					
Inept management.	1	–	1	2	4
Total Internal	1	–	1	2	4
TOTAL	6	6	7	9	28

Inept Management

In our experience, the problems that beset Aging Mules are overwhelmingly external in nature. Only 4 of the 28 within our sample experience base were classified as having internal problems, and all four were plagued by certifiably inept management:

- An agricultural food products company that stubbornly kept operating large, unprofitable plants in marginal locations. This was the only turnaround achieved within this group, the result of closing certain plants and focusing on its most profitable product lines, which were workhorse cash generators.

- An auto parts supplier, where management bemoaned the industry imperative to provide continuous and progressive price reductions over the life of its contracts but failed to implement productivity measurements or acknowledge that continuous productivity improvement was a critical requirement for success. The business was sold to a strategic buyer that better understood realities of the market.

- A trucking company that focused on increasing the real estate values of its many terminals while attempting to operate its business without implementing information systems and productivity measurements that were becoming standard among the competition. Loss of credibility with creditors resulted in the disorderly liquidation of what was, arguably, a saleable business entity.

- A privately owned manufacturer of nonferrous tube, wire and solder products that lost its focus on operations as its owner initiated large, speculative investments in raw material stockpiles. Liquidation of the company's valuable assets occurred after union employees went on strike.

Outside of these situations, the problems confronting the Aging Mules with which we dealt were consistently the result of external forces.

Let us re-emphasize that Aging Mules are not companies that tend to make big, active mistakes. They are not companies that launch innovative products that fail. They are often companies that manufacture different, progressively more costly and complex models of the same thing, year after year, and see their customers slowly move to the competition – which manufactures new, lower-cost, innovative products that succeed.

Aging Mules also tend to be businesses that, even when no specific disruptive technology is affecting them, have taken the lower-risk road, over time, in making individual decisions. In hindsight, the cumulative effect may be disastrous, but at the time, each decision was generally rational and probably had the highest short-term benefit. It involved the type of decision-making applauded by investment analysts who believe that management's primary objective should be achieving uninterrupted quarterly earnings growth. Looking back, we can say that General Motors should have taken a more aggressive negotiating stance with the United Auto Workers starting in the 1950s, but at the time of each negotiation there was little appetite for taking a harder line.

AUTHORS' CASEBOOK: Unwinding a Conglomerate

Evans Products, a conglomerate with operating subsidiaries in several industries, had revenues of more than $1.5 billion and debt exceeding $1 billion prior to filing Chapter 11 bankruptcy. A creditor-proposed Reorganization Plan provided for Grossman's Inc., a home-materials store chain subsidiary, to be the surviving public company entity. Ownership of all other businesses and assets was to be transferred to a newly formed holding company owned by the financial institutions that had been lenders to the company. On the plan confirmation date, as a part a new interim management team, co-author Steve Hopkins became a director of Evans and its chief financial officer. The team's objective was to make the reorganization plan effective while disposing of surplus assets and businesses.

Rolling eight-week cash-flow forecasting and control systems were installed immediately at each operating unit, with the management of each business assigned responsibility for becoming cash-flow positive. By discontinuing the commingling of corporate, operating division and subsidiary funds while requiring each business unit to immediately settle in cash for payroll and other payments made at corporate headquarters on its behalf, details of negative cash-flow quickly surfaced. Priorities were then established for operational restructuring actions required to maximize proceeds from sales of these businesses.

Critical Challenge: As a prerequisite to making the Plan of Reorganization effective, it was necessary to maintain positive cash flow while developing a plan for disengaging the company and its various businesses from a conglomerate ownership that provided most administrative services on a high-cost centralized basis.

Grossman's Inc. became the surviving entity as scheduled. During the wind-down process, other operating divisions and subsidiaries were sold as ongoing individual business entities in a series of 14 separate transactions. Simultaneously, a complex series of liability and close-down projects were completed, including sale of surplus real estate, environmental remediation and termination of pension plans. Creditors received significantly higher net proceeds than had been initially projected, with the incremental proceeds largely achieved by returning operating businesses to profitability and negotiating favorable settlement of the multiple known liabilities and other potential claims that existed.

Identifying the Profitable Core

It is perhaps unfair to imply that Aging Mules are primarily the product of complacent management. Try as they might, not every business can be No. 1 or No. 2 in its industry, as Jack Welch famously challenged GE's operating units to be. As businesses and markets mature, a natural and appropriate trend toward consolidation takes place. As growth and innovation slow, efficiencies of scale and execution begin to be more dominant factors of success and profitability. As Exhibit 18-1 shows, 75% of the Aging Mules (21 of 28) with which we have direct experience were confronted by the external factors of either dominant competitors or permanent market changes in their industries.

It is instructive, and even a bit surprising, to note that despite the apparent benefits of consolidation in these mature industry situations, fewer than half of these competitively weak businesses were promptly sold or liquidated. More than half the time, it was possible to turn around or restructure these businesses as smaller, continuing concerns with greater value than had existed previously or could be realized from a sale. This was achieved by refocusing on the successful core components, restructuring operations, reducing operating costs and overhead expenses and shedding underperforming or money-losing operations.

It is also instructive to note that the differences among a turnaround, a restructuring and a sale (as we define these terms in our sample experience base) are a lot smaller than they look. Without exception, all the Aging Mules we've worked with required operational restructurings, disposition of underperforming assets and identification of a profitable core business. As we've defined a turnaround and a restructuring, the difference between them is basically whether, after implementing operational changes, the profitability rebounded sufficiently that the business could service its original debt (a turnaround) or some level of debt forgiveness, conversion to equity or extended payout was required in order to reach stability (a restructuring).

Typically the standalone restructured operations remained at a competitive disadvantage but, at least for the present, offered greater value than was believed to be attainable in a prompt sale. Many such survivors continue to be candidates for sale or consolidation in the future. Some, once refocused, may become reinvigorated and find renewed growth; others may enjoy an extended lifecycle of profitability, but without growth.

There is, of course, a logic at play here. Often it is management's dissatisfaction with the status quo, their unwillingness to relinquish dreams of being No. 1 or No. 2, their resistance to becoming a consolidation target, their ambition, that leads them to increase debt in order to expand into or stubbornly hold onto unprofitable business segments.

Real operational turnarounds from which an Aging Mule can emerge as a strong growing entity are indeed few and far between. But unless the situation has been allowed to deteriorate to extremes, buried within the operations are generally valuable components. The analytical challenge, therefore, is identifying those valuable components. Careful attention to the tasks outlined in Chapter 9 – evaluating operating costs and contribution margins by product line, function, geography, facilities and so on to determine where and why the company is losing money or conversely generating the greatest profits – becomes the path to understanding the value of an Aging Mule.

AUTHORS' CASEBOOK: Shrinking Retail Geography

A long-established Southeastern home products retail chain with approximately 50 stores and good gross margins was struggling to survive after two consecutive years of unprofitable operations. On behalf of the owners, a team of consultants worked with management to develop a turnaround plan. Individual store profitability and potential was reviewed in detail with particular emphasis on location, competitive environment, sales mix, and advertising and distribution coverage alternatives. To ensure continuity and objectivity, retention agreements were provided to management employees in advance of developing a detailed operational restructuring plan.

Critical Challenge: Develop a chain configuration consisting of residual stores with the lowest possible advertising and distribution costs, while maintaining sales volume and gross margin ratios. Simultaneously, release maximum possible real estate assets for separate sale.

Plans were developed to close stores that could not be included in centralized advertising campaigns or serviced at reasonable cost from centralized warehousing. Existing management conducted going-out-of-business sales at these stores, owned real estate was put up for sale and, as appropriate, excess leases were terminated or subleased. Overhead was reduced by moving headquarters to a new location, warehousing was consolidated into one location and product selections and advertising and promotional practices were refocused. A return to profitable operations was achieved within six months of initiating the project.

Other examples of the turnaround of Aging Mules have been detailed earlier in the book:

- A Midwestern retail chain that closed a third of its stores and concentrated on smaller markets (Chapter 3);
- A branded consumer products manufacturer that closed high-cost manufacturing plants (Chapter 9);
- A specialty chemical and pharmaceutical manufacturer that exited its historical core warehousing and distribution business to concentrate on higher profit manufacturing (Chapter 10).

Liquidations and Sales

Liquidations – situations in which operations have been allowed to deteriorate so extensively that the only value left is that obtainable from the tangible assets – represent the true failures among these Aging Mules. In most cases, a more timely resolution would likely have presented an opportunity to exit with greater value, but denial, delay and wishful thinking conspired to erode any and all going-concern value that may have been accumulated in the business.

The "success" or desirability of going-concern business sales is somewhat more difficult to evaluate. Assuming there has been success in identifying and operationally restructuring around a profitable core, the challenge now shifts to identifying whether its value can be maximized through continuing operations or through consolidation with another entity. In some cases, once the operational restructuring has been completed, the business can return to profitable growth from its smaller, more focused base. But this is more often the exception than the rule.

Far more frequently, the restructured entity remains a relatively weak player in its marketplace and the evaluation process should then turn to examining potential exit strategies and timing. The baseline evaluation is, of course, how much cash the business can be anticipated to generate over time as a standalone entity. Even with flat or declining revenues, some aging businesses can be expected to generate long steady streams of cash – particularly if management recognizes the company's trajectory and does not persist in reinvesting cash flow in high-risk diversification efforts.

More commonly, particularly if there is recognition that long-term prospects continue to be flat or negative, it becomes apparent that the restructured Aging Mule is indeed a consolidation target, worth more in a strategic combination with a stronger player than on a standalone basis. Once that recognition is reached and pursuit of such a transaction is targeted, the evaluation focus shifts to examining the relationship between available price and underlying value.

If the business is viewed externally as highly distressed and likely to fail on its own, an interim restructuring and stabilization period may be necessary to persuade the market that there is a viable option to a forced sale – and thus a reason to increase the price. In other cases, if a convincing pro forma analysis can be prepared to demonstrate anticipated synergies from the combination, a prompt sale and quick exit can be achieved.

AUTHORS' CASEBOOK: Forest Products Business Sale

A Canadian forest-products operation producing plywood and lumber at four separate plants was being held for sale. The nature of this commodity business was a pattern of sharply fluctuating prices outside the control of management. Over time, asset values of timber rights had been liquidated to maintain continuous production and a significant ongoing corporate overhead structure. Sale of the business was complicated by a five-year history of operating losses and disputes with a local Indian tribe over timber-cutting rights. Working on behalf of the owners with a new interim management, a turnaround consulting team reviewed the company's operating losses in detail to understand reasons for lack of profitability and to develop a plan for maximizing value. Analysis was focused on plant-operating configurations and strategies that would ensure profitability at each plant under various market price scenarios.

   Critical Challenge: Resolve issues relating to control over timber, make plants more consistently profitable and reduce corporate overhead and administration costs that were greater than profit contribution from the plants.

   By taking a more conciliatory approach to outstanding timber-cutting rights issues, a settlement was negotiated with the Canadian government and local Indian tribes. This made the plants attractive to strategic buyers, which could eliminate the excessive corporate administrative structure that was a major reason for operating losses. Two strategic buyers were found, and each purchased two plants at an attractive price for the sellers, while adding significant plant profit contribution for each buyer.

Management Changes

A detailed review of our experience with the management of Aging Mules demonstrates again a trend that defies conventional wisdom. The following table shows a summary of project results compared with CEO changes.

EXHIBIT 18-2

CEO CHANGES AT AGING MULES

Project Results	No. of Co's.	CEO Changes	Percent
Turnarounds	6	1	17%
Restructurings	6	1	17%
Sales	7	4	57%
Liquidations	9	7	78%
Total	28	13	46%

These were all financially troubled companies at which conventional wisdom says the management that presided during the decline should be replaced. However, in 10 of the 12 cases where turnarounds or restructurings were accomplished, they were achieved with existing management. In both cases where a change in management was made, the previous incumbent in the position could not face the reality that growth had failed and a strategy of downsizing provided the path to profitability.

More logically, in the case of sales and liquidations, only about one-third were accomplished with existing management. This of course raises the conundrum of which came first, bad management or bad business.

Our general observation is that management of the businesses that were liquidated had generally persisted in a state of denial or complacency about the deteriorating competitive state of the business for so long that they had destroyed the companies' sale value. Their positions were so rigid that new management, generally represented by a turnaround consulting firm, were required to manage the liquidation. In these cases, managers lacked the flexibility to understand the brutal facts of the situation, yet the key problems of the business were external, not internal management ineptness. Better management would have produced better long-term recoveries, but not a turnaround.

Where existing managers stayed to complete a business sale, they generally did so to support reasonable transactions and bring resolution to long-term problems, not because there was a continuing role for them personally. Where managers were removed while a sale was pursued, it was generally because of their continued resistance to the sale process.

Bankruptcy Filings

Of the 12 Aging Mule projects resulting in turnarounds or restructurings only three required a bankruptcy filing, in each case to accomplish specific objectives:

- A parent company with only unsecured debt filed for bankruptcy protection while leaving its profitable subsidiaries operating independent of the bankruptcy process. All liabilities were paid in full.
- A retailer filed Chapter 11 to reject a large number of unprofitable store leases.
- The bankruptcy court process was used to obtain legal approval for a consensual foreclosure by creditors on a significant portion of a company's operating assets in exchange for debt forgiveness.

Eight of the nine liquidation projects involved a bankruptcy filing. The one exception was an estate-owned troubled business with operating losses but no debt.

Chapter Summary

The problems of Aging Mules are overwhelmingly related to the external competitive environment. Although management *might* have addressed these changes more effectively, it was relatively rare in our experience that inept management caused the decline of a mature and inherently sound business.

Once a business combines financial stress with declining operating trends, it becomes nearly impossible to attempt a growth strategy as a turnaround plan.

Except where deterioration has been prolonged over an extended period of time, there are generally valuable components imbedded within Aging Mules' operations. When dealing with an Aging Mule, the typical course of action is to identify and operationally restructure around its profitable core. Once that profitable core structure has been identified, a determination can be made as to whether to restructure as a standalone or seek a sale of the business.

Whether headed toward turnaround, debt restructuring or sale, every Aging Mule with which we dealt required operational restructuring and downsizing, cost reductions and asset redeployment in order to maximize the value of its core operations. The difference between a turnaround and a restructuring is typically dependent upon the size and value of the profitable core that can be identified.

Of the turnarounds and restructurings, 85% were accomplished with existing management. However, when exit by sale or liquidation was required, in more than 60% of the situations it was effected by new interim management, generally a consultant on troubled businesses.

Typically in businesses being liquidated, management had persisted in a state of denial and/or complacency about the deteriorating competitive environment for so long that they destroyed the company's sale value.

RECOMMENDED READING

Who Says Elephants Can't Dance?: Inside IBM's Historic Turnaround (Harper Business, 2002) by Louis V. Gerstner, Jr..

This readable best-seller covers the turnaround of IBM by the CEO who accomplished it. In our categorization of businesses, IBM was an Aging Mule rather then an Overburdened Workhorse when Gerstner arrived in 1993. It was financially troubled not as a result of financial leverage, but because industry technology and market changes were rapidly leaving the company behind. IBM's market leadership and high prices in mainframe computers had historically generated the gross margin to support a huge overhead structure. However, between 1992 and 1994, major hardware price reductions and volume losses to competitors took away the cash flow needed to fund this overhead. Despite highly capable people and technology leadership, inflexible, bureaucratic business processes rendered the company incapable of responding to its rapidly changing competitive environment.

Gerstner's book is the story of how IBM overcame the organizational problems and excessive costs that might well have become terminal or, at the least, resulted in a split-up of the company. Details of how the turnaround was achieved are largely covered in Part I, "Grabbing Hold," and Part III, "Culture." Part II , "Strategy," provides insight into the redirection of IBM toward new patterns of growth.

The Six-Month Fix: Adventures in Rescuing Failing Companies (John Wiley & Sons, 2002) by Gary Sutton.

This practical and opinionated book covers the nuts-and-bolts of the turnaround process through the eyes of someone who has been in the trenches as a CEO at several turnarounds. Sutton believes that you should "think of turnarounds as blacksmith work, throwing off sparks, energy surrounded by clanging noises while the turnaround manager flails away reshaping some stressed iron."

He places heavy emphasis on the need to bring in new management who will act quickly to determine where a company is making and losing money by "finding the margin" and cutting costs. If an Aging Mule can be saved, then quickly turned over to a new permanent CEO, Sutton makes an excellent case that he would be the guy to do it, and he explains exactly how he would go about getting the required results.

The Innovator's Dilemma: When New Technologies Cause Great Firms to Fail (Harvard Business School Press, 1997) by Clayton M. Christensen.

This book reviews histories of businesses and industries that lost position to lower-cost "disruptive technologies." Christiansen explains how, under certain circumstances, "the mechanism of profit-maximizing resource allocation causes well-run companies to get killed." He analyzes in detail the reasons why not responding to lower-cost competition may be a logical business decision for a long period of time as industry leaders give up the low-margin, low-quality products that are being increasingly supplied using lower-cost disruptive technologies.

As outlined by Christensen in his steel industry example, what was good management for each of the individual integrated steel companies businesses was ultimately unsuccessful. This concept has great force in understanding the limited options for turnaround of Aging Mule businesses, particularly when financial resources are not available to attempt a major technology improvement.

Part VI

CONCLUSIONS AND ADVICE

Knowledge, understanding, insight and leadership: we believe these are the fundamental components of effective management and constitute the core of our recommended approach to dealing with business challenges. Certainly, many people have been successful by following their intuition and aggressively, sometimes even impulsively, seizing opportunities as they present themselves. But when operations and performance begin to falter, we believe that disciplined, fact-based analysis and evaluation provide the framework with which to reassess strategy and direction, combat denial and understand the risks and rewards of available alternative courses of action.

Whether as a business manager, entrepreneur, investor, consultant or lender, operating successfully in the world of troubled businesses requires an ability to recognize that change is inevitable – and the flexibility and willingness to adapt accordingly. It is all-too-easy to become fixated on a chosen perspective or view of the world and lose sight of changing forces and conditions. Although the issue of the fundamental viability of a business is sometimes difficult to contemplate, we strongly recommend that this be addressed as the critical first step in assessing every troubled company.

There is a popular perception that the "right management" can be successful with any business. This perception fuels the corresponding image of a turnaround manager as a save-the-day gun-for-hire whose job is to throw the bums out and put the business back on track. We do *not* believe this view is accurate or, if acted upon, productive. As Warren Buffett once said, "When a management team with a reputation for brilliance tackles a business with bad economics, it is the reputation of the business that remains intact." Not all businesses can be saved, and stubbornly seeking to resuscitate a non-viable business seldom accomplishes anything other than prolonging the continuing deterioration in value.

The first and most important challenge in addressing any troubled situation is to accurately diagnose the problems, evaluate the alternatives and establish realistic objectives. Only after that has been completed and achievable new goals have been established can reliable decisions be made about matching management strengths with corporate objectives. Our experience, which runs contrary to popular opinion, is that most real operational turnarounds are accomplished by maintaining management continuity and using internal resources to pursue the new plan.

Success in navigating the hazards of a changing environment requires identifying, understanding and addressing the fundamental issues underlying business challenges, not just the symptoms. A clear and accurate diagnosis and an understanding of a company's problems provide the keys both to identifying appropriate remedial responses and to accurately evaluating associated risks and rewards. These risks and rewards and the likelihood of success vary greatly with the nature of the challenge. Internal problems of process execution and strategy are generally readily fixable, if addressed in a timely and efficient manner. External challenges, competitive incursions, technological changes and fundamental market shifts can be daunting and difficult to control, particularly in a company that has become financially distressed and has limited resources with which to respond.

The heart of our consulting services is providing assistance with business diagnoses and viability assessments to assist companies in reassessing strategy, direction and priorities. The highest value-added component that we bring to these situations is not our great intellect, or even our extensive background of hands-on project experience – though we do not underestimate the value inherent in either – but the *disciplined analytical process* that we've outlined in this book. Although it may sound like heresy to some of our consulting compatriots, crafting solutions for troubled businesses is neither rocket science nor a mystical art that can only be practiced by a few uniquely talented individuals. Rather, it is a problem-solving challenge that we believe is best accomplished by actively involving management and staff in a cooperative and inclusive process of disciplined and objective analysis and review. Despite the frequency with which group denial occurs in troubled companies, there are always individuals who have a clear idea of what is wrong, and they often have a realistic plan for fixing it. It is important to find them and encourage them to become part of the problem-solving process.

The results of the disciplined analytical process then provide the basis for the second major value that we bring to the process – helping management overcome denial and complacency in order to move forward. If moving forward means an exit by sale or liquidation of the business, the sooner the process is started the better.

Looking back at our accumulated project experience, we have identified clear and recurring troubled company characteristics that we find provide reliable and predictable insight and guidance to both useful responses and likely outcomes. We have identified three categories of troubled companies:

Undisciplined Racehorses: dynamic, growing businesses that usually have stumbled with internal, self-inflicted wounds, either isolated strategic missteps or administrative weaknesses of execution. These are the prime turnaround candidates. The correction of specific errors or addition of certain clearly defined resources and disciplines can lead to renewed strength and continued growth.

Overburdened Workhorses: fundamentally stable, historically cash-positive businesses that are dragged down and hobbled by unachievable debt-service burdens caused either by unrealistic profit-growth expectations or cyclical profit declines. These are the restructuring candidates, where a combination of incremental operational improvements and debt forbearance or restructuring can generally return the business to financial stability.

Aging Mules: businesses that have passed their prime, becoming subject to stagnation and decline. Typically facing external competitive incursions or market changes, these businesses have often been stubbornly locked into failing strategies and are difficult to turn around. However, they may prove attractive candidates for strategic sale in their maturing markets; the alternative is generally to downsize the business to a more viable remaining core and generate a cash return on a declining value base.

Identifying and addressing the nature of underlying problems and thinking conceptually about how an individual situation fits in the continuum of these categories can provide a useful framework for evaluating responses and assessing risks and rewards.

In preceding chapters, we've set forth at some length our guidance on how to diagnose and address the issues and challenges faced by distressed businesses:

Exercising caution with regard to specific insolvency issues, legal and operational pitfalls that arise as a company operates near the zone of insolvency;

Controlling and managing cash by implementation of cash-driven working capital control practices, rolling weekly cash-flow forecasts and top management focus on cash rather than reported profitability;

Identifying conflicting agendas and objectives among the various, often adversarial parties of interest;

Conducting management interviews to obtain detailed insight into the organization and operations of the business;

Assembling and documenting a factual understanding of key issues, which will help define the situation, capabilities and opportunities of the business and identify improvement potential consistent with the competitive environment and management and organization structure.

All of these tasks are aimed at obtaining the factual knowledge, understanding and insight required to identify and develop the most promising alternative courses of action to maximize the value of the business. Only then can productive negotiations among the various parties commence to confirm the course of action. Decisions about the ideal management characteristics and leadership qualities most suitable to ensure success should, when possible, be deferred until after the desirable course of action has become clear.

As noted throughout the book, our perspective is primarily focused on operational viability and potential and our recommended business diagnosis process. Thus our advice and observations have been primarily aligned and organized toward management and the board of directors, addressing how to identify and seek the path to maximum business value. But we believe that much of what we describe offers benefit to other constituencies as well.

Lenders

Our experience over the years has been predominantly filled with situations in which management has resisted taking action to correct problems until forced to do so by creditors, typically senior secured lenders. This results from either repeated breaching of loan covenants or a true liquidity crisis. Our typical lament has been, "We wish we could have gotten here sooner when there was more to work with," because opportunities for a true operational turnaround are greater the earlier that the crisis occurs. The crisis forces denial and complacency to be discarded in favor of action.

We generally advocate that lenders take action to force this crisis upon troubled companies and require a disciplined reassessment of the situation earlier than is the normal practice. On the other side of the coin, we also recommend that, in conjunction with acting sooner, lenders show a greater willingness to be flexible. In some respects, we are recommending that the term "workout" be added back to the lenders' vocabulary. In recent years, as new sources of funding have become active in the lending markets and credit controls have loosened, the benefits of pressing companies to move promptly to address performance declines seem to have diminished. Lenders have found it easier either to trade out of declining situations or to press the company to refinance them out.   The art of the long-term workout seems to have been in decline. But lending patterns are cyclical and easy credit won't last forever. When the credit markets tighten and it becomes more painful to trade out, both lenders and borrowers will wish that they had moved more quickly to confront their problems.

Investors

Investors, voluntary or involuntary, in troubled companies can use the conceptual thinking involved in our business categories as a guide to understanding the prospects for success. While detailed development and analysis of actionable alternatives requires an expansive diagnosis process, it is often possible to reliably hypothesize the broad category within which a company falls, using very basic information about the company's operations and challenges.

Among our categories, the highest investment potential is among the Undisciplined Racehorses with internal problems that are not overleveraged. These are more likely to be correctable, although there is no assurance in any specific case that a turnaround will actually happen. This is the area where the knowledgeable, patient investor with the interest and motivation to understand the problems and the likelihood of a fix should do well. The competition for high returns in this area will likely be impatient speculators who don't take the time or have the inclination to understand which problems are easily fixable and which are not.

A second category of high potential returns to investors is the Overburdened Workhorses in cyclical markets. Understanding the cycle and having the patience to wait for it to improve is the key. New investors must buy when the industry is out of favor, and the wait for the upturn can be a long one, as with the steel industry. Conversely, involuntary investors should be thoughtful and cautious about forcing a sale at the bottom of a market – particularly if the alternative of a conversion to equity and/or an extended forbearance agreement can leave the company with sufficient stability to wait out the cycle. Whether evaluating a new investment opportunity or a forbearance or workout, careful attention should be addressed to understanding the debt structure of these businesses. Understand whether debt service problems are due to operating losses during the low part of the cycle or to high debt levels compared with assets of the business. If debt is excessive compared with tangible assets employed in the business, be very careful about making equity investments.

Aging Mules may offer short-term, speculative trading opportunities as the cycle of hope triumphing over experience ebbs and flows. But this is not typically the place to expect the greatest operational turnaround opportunities or the best long-term results. Occasionally, these businesses can make attractive investment targets based upon a breakup strategy, particularly if control of the process can be acquired at the time of the investment.

The issue of control is, of course, one of the primary challenges of operating in the distressed business market, regardless of which category of troubled business is under examination. It raises the corollary question of where in the capital structure to initiate investments. Acquiring the existing equity may nominally provide immediate control, but, by definition, the equity in an overleveraged company is at risk of being out of the money, and even majority shareholders can quickly find themselves pushed out of control if a company is teetering on the edge of insolvency.

In recent years, the most common form for making a major investment in troubled situations has been through the discounted purchase of debt. When debt is acquired at a discount from face value, if it manages to pull through and perform, its effective return on investment can be quite impressive. Obviously, the deeper the discount, the more impressive the return. A fairly active distressed-debt trading market has developed, with investors seeking higher effective yields from the volatile pricing variations of debt issued by out of favor, less-than-investment-grade companies.

More-aggressive investors in this arena acquire debt at deep discounts with the clear understanding that they may become subject to restructuring negotiations prior to maturity. Occasionally, they do so with the express intention of forcing such a negotiation on an accelerated basis. Still others engage in "loan to own" strategies, aggressively acquiring deeply discounted debt with the confident intention of seeking a conversion and control if, or when, the debt defaults.

However, acquiring distressed debt without control is a risky process and not for the squeamish, particularly if the debt is in the form of high-yield subordinated or unsecured notes. If either operations or negotiations stray seriously from expectations, holders of unsecured or under-secured debt can find themselves watching from the sidelines, unable to effectively influence the direction of the business while values plummet.

Business Owners

Owners, for the purposes of this discussion, are defined as shareholders in the financially troubled, privately held business. Such owners may be founder-entrepreneurs, families holding control in long-established businesses or private equity firms. In any event, there is full, readily identifiable shareholder control over the board of directors and company management.

Businesses owned by these groups may or may not be financially troubled as a result of over-leverage. From the standpoint of the owners, this really doesn't make any difference, if the businesses are underperforming. If returns are not actually negative, they are below what could be earned from alternative investments. Often the returns are much more negative than perceived by owners, because dividends are continued at historical rates while operating losses or under-investment in capital expenditures continues for extended periods.

For such owners, our message is: don't wait, don't quietly accept management excuses – but don't reflexively change management. Demand and obtain an independent, objective diagnosis of problems of the type outlined in this book. Then confront the reality of its conclusions, whatever they may be. After a careful evaluation of risks, establish a plan to take action and make those changes necessary to protect and enhance the long-term value of the business, however unpalatable and uncomfortable taking such actions may be. Finally, put in place appropriate leadership to execute the plan that is developed. This leadership may be present management, it may be another insider, it may be an interim CEO from a turn-around firm or it may be an executive recruit from outside sources. What is essential is that the plan be realistic and that whichever leaders are selected be absolutely and totally dedicated to execution of the agreed-upon strategy while having the flexibility to adjust to ever-changing circumstances.

Management

We believe that the most important management deficiencies are denial, arrogance, greed, complacency and lack of leadership. We also postulate that it is unlikely that the arrogant and greedy are reading this book, so our message is addressed to the others, be they CEO, CFO or other managers of underperforming businesses, financially troubled companies in crisis or not. And that message is: arm yourself with objective and disciplined factual analysis to protect against complacency and denial and ensure that you understand and face the realities of your situation. Once you understand those realities, be honest with yourself in assessing your willingness and ability to address them. If your interests or abilities are not in sync with the needs of the business, and you can't or don't want to provide the leadership to take the appropriate corrective action, don't set yourself up for angst and failure by trying to force-fit an inappropriate solution.

In most cases, we advocate that the diagnosis of problems be facilitated by an experienced third-party professional who can provide distance and objectivity and a focus to the process that is difficult to maintain by someone fighting the alligators in the swamp. Such an individual or firm can also act as a navigator around the obstacles, leading the business toward a solution acceptable to its various parties with different agendas and risk/reward profiles.

While our observations and experience have been developed in work with predominantly troubled companies, we believe the concept and process of KUIL management are readily transferable to problem-solving and strategic challenges faced by management everywhere.

Although the challenges of financial distress and crisis certainly provide added impetus for the process we recommend, it is sound business and investment management practice to step back periodically and reexamine the landscape, reassessing changing circumstances and reestablishing goals, targets and expectations. Who knows what you will find?

APPENDIX A

Better Management Through Control of Cash
By Stephen J. Hopkins

Growth projections and operating results as reported under Generally Accepted Accounting Principles (GAAP) may drive a company's stock price and market value, but cash is king when it comes to creating long-term underlying value and surviving periods of trouble.

Having been involved in turnaround management and troubled-company consulting for more than 25 years, we have worked with many companies that must manage for positive cash flow to survive, and we have developed a system to control cash and working capital. In addition to helping financially troubled, overleveraged businesses, our system is needed by undercapitalized startup firms, those facing earnings declines and those in situations where asset-based financing is involved. The system can also be useful to mature, profitable businesses as a way to control spending, focus management attention on key disbursement trade-offs and enhance return on investment.

Many troubled companies, even those with good management and control procedures related to cash collections and disbursements, have extremely poor cash-flow forecasting for periods beyond a few days. To some extent, this seems to be a symptom of management's desire not to face bad news ("If we don't know how bad things really are, we won't have to think about a solution"). In such cases, companies may have become "insolvent" in the sense of being unable to pay obligations as they become due, without recognizing it.

Frequently, turnaround consultants arrive on the scene in the midst of a cash-flow crisis that requires immediate short-term action in order to avoid a bankruptcy filing. In these situations, the key to survival is cash-flow control and the top planning priority of both consultant and company becomes a short-term (six-to-eight-week) cash-flow forecast done on a brutally realistic basis. The key objectives of this process are to identify the scope of the immediate problem, define timing of expected periods of negative cash availability and develop alternatives for effecting improvement.

Accounting systems used in all sizable companies provide information on an accrual accounting basis. The key to good management control is getting back to the tried-and-true, easily understandable, cash-is-king method of looking at things. Operations can be better managed by removing the excess accounting underbrush of accruals and cost allocations and focusing on the responsibility for managing cash receipts and disbursements to keep cash flow positive.

Our approach to cash-flow control in many ways resembles the simplified production-control systems many manufacturers have installed in recent years. Among others, Womack and Jones summarize these processes in their milestone book *Lean Thinking*.[15] One underlying principle is that control is best achieved by making key information readily and regularly available to all employees who can impact the improvement process.

Our system is targeted specifically to cash-flow control. It is not driven from a multipurpose accounting system, which is typically ineffective for real control of cash-flow because of accounting complexity and a lack of focus on the sources and uses of cash occurring as specific receipts and disbursements. The objectives of the cash-flow reporting system that we recommend and use regularly in our consulting practice include:

- Providing an early warning of potential cash problems while helping CFOs report on cash flow in a systematic manner that identifies responsibility for fixing looming problems. Too often responsibility, after the fact, is pinned on the CFO as the bearer of bad news that he had no ability to impact.

- Forcing management, particularly the CEO and CFO, to fully understand the cash flow of the business and to focus quickly on the trade-offs and follow-up actions required to keep cash flow positive. This is vital in companies with declining operating trends, where business plans are often just wishful thinking that things will get better as a result of external market forces. In the meantime, management may be searching for accounting changes to help improve reported earnings in order to camouflage the problem while waiting for these external changes to occur.

- Requiring all levels of management and other employees who have control over receipts and disbursements to become involved in the process,

---

[15] James P. Womack and Daniel T. Jones, *Lean Thinking: Banish Waste and Create Wealth in Your Corporation* (New York: Simon & Schuster, 1996).

be measured on their ability to forecast and face peer-group scrutiny of expenditure levels.

- Improving dramatically the visibility of significant cash outflows that may be concealed by internal accrual and expense allocation procedures.
- Establishing and communicating reasonable expectations regarding the cash situation both within the company and with lenders. Without good information and understanding, the situation is often allowed to worsen.

Business turnarounds are never simple, and they require many vigorous management actions. A cash-flow control system that focuses attention on key problems and measures remedial progress can often be the key to remarkable improvements. For example, our recommended system was installed in a consumer products company with annual sales of approximately $100 million. On Jan. 15, cash in the bank was $50,000 with more than $1 million in checks outstanding as float. At the same time, accounts payable totaled more than $8 million, with approximately 60% past due more than 30 days. By Sept. 1, cash in the bank had increased to more than $3 million with accounts payable reduced by $3 million and all amounts essentially current. Reported operating profits of the business obviously improved significantly during this period. But the improvements were driven primarily by the cash management and control process rather than the reverse of improved cash flow being a function of higher reported profits.

There is extensive literature on cash management, including regularly published articles in the journal of the Treasury Management Association and a number of books. However, the focus is almost always on management of cash as a business asset, including receipts and disbursements management, forecasting cash available for investment, movement and availability of funds, and the development of banking relationships. The assumption is typically that cash is available for a treasury function to manage and that this should be done as efficiently as possible. There is also a considerable body of literature related to asset management, inventory forecasting and control, credit and collection activities for controlling receivables, and extensive mathematical models for evaluating fixed-asset investments.

Although the above all provide highly useful information, the situations we normally face represent far more basic problems. The environment is often one in which there are key questions, such as "Will this Friday's payroll checks bounce if we distribute them?" or "How do we deal with the $10 million reduction in our working capital line that the bank has just unilaterally imposed?" or "What C.O.D. payments for production materials can we afford?"

In other situations, the company's position may be less dire. However, managers of a strong viable business with negative cash flow often lose control over working capital asset balances, leading to missed forecasts of borrowing requirements, loss of credibility with lenders and higher interest expenses than a similar business with better controls.

In these situations, particularly if there are loan defaults, bleeding caused by negative cash flow must be stopped. The first step is understanding the details of the company's expected near-term receipts and disbursements, and the condition and position of its major controllable working-capital assets and liabilities, normally receivables, inventories, and accounts payable.

Public reporting requires that companies prepare consolidated cash flow reports that start with net income and reflect balance sheet changes. This format is useful for after-the-fact analysis of trends but almost useless as a management-control tool. Control requires detailed, hands-on receipts-and-disbursements management. Quickly putting this type of forecasting in place is the first step in getting operational control over a business with negative cash flow.

Periods covered by the initial receipts-and-disbursements forecast will vary with the circumstances. However, the first pass should usually be weekly for the first six weeks. This is startup mode, with the objective of quickly moving to weekly preparation of a rolling 13-week forecast. The format to be used would be somewhat as shown on Exhibit A-1, depending on specifics of the business.

EXAMPLE

EXHIBIT A-1

XYZ CORPORATION

WEEKLY CASHFLOW DETAIL REPORT
(Dollars in thousands)

	Week 1	Week 2	Week 3	...(Weeks 4-13) –a)	13 Wks. Total	Average
Cash Receipts						
Accounts receivable	$ 1,381	$ 1,277	$ 1,424	$12,802	$ 16,884	$ 1,299
Other	0	0	0	0	0	0
Total receipts	1,381	1,277	1,424	12,802	16,884	1,299
Cash Disbursements						
Payroll and related	158	561	123	3,058	3,900	300
Purchases/Material	607	670	500	3,947	5,724	440
Rents and leases	1	23	0	86	110	8
Telephone/Utilities	29	89	1	245	364	28
Professional services	51	416	80	1,558	2,105	162
Insurance	0	53	0	107	160	12
Other (detail as useful)	844	448	224	4,290	5,806	447
Total operating disb.	1,690	2,260	928	13,291	18,169	1,398
Operating Cash flow	(309)	(983)	496	(489)	(1,285)	(99)
Non-recurring costs:						
Capital expenditures	8	8	8	80	104	8
Debt service	4	3	0	1,123	1,130	87
Non-operating disb.	12	11	8	1,203	1,234	95
Net Cash flow	(321)	(994)	488	(1,692)	(2,519)	(194)

(a – To be forecast and reported by week

Note that expenditures in Exhibit A-1 relating to operating cash flow are segregated from those related to non-recurring costs, capital expenditures and debt service. Line-item details of the forecast must be oriented toward key control centers of the business. For effective use of the forecast as a management tool, it is essential that the parties who control receipts and disbursements – not financial employees without direct operating responsibilities – supply the forecast data. The forecasts should ignore expense allocations among business centers and functions and should assign forecasting responsibility to employees with disbursement approval authority. Provide enough detail in the forecast to be clear without becoming immersed in non-essential detail. In a business with a relatively small group of customers, forecast receivable collections by customer to cover 60 to 80% of the total receipts anticipated. Project payroll by a few natural, easily controllable categories. Intra-division transfers of products or services cleared through intra-company accounts should be shown separately with concurrence among divisions regarding transfers to be forecast.

Integrate the forecast of receipts and disbursements into a cash reconciliation that reports both book and bank cash balances in a format similar to that shown in Exhibit A-2. Bank-ledger cash balances are the focus because it is third-party data. Book cash is subject to numerous internal influences, including the timing of transactions. Forcing a bank to book reconciliation requires analysis and understanding of check float, and that should help eliminate the big surprise of an overdrawn bank account.

EXAMPLE

EXHIBIT A-2

XYZ CORPORATION

WEEKLY CASH BALANCE AND FLOAT FORECAST
(Dollars in thousands)

	Week 1	Week 2	Week 3	Week 4	...(weeks 5-13 by week)
Cash Reconciliation					
Beginning bank cash	$131	$750	$750	$750	
Net cash flow	(321)	(994)	488	(584)	
Change in float	(116)	125	(711)	149	
Revolver borrowings	1,056	869	223	435	
Ending bank cash	750	750	750	750	
Less: outstanding checks	950	1,205	1,350	889	
Ending book cash	(200)	(455)	(600)	(139)	
Revolver availability	0	0	0	0	
Ending cash and availability	(200)	(455)	(600)	(139)	

A company operating with negative book balances as shown above is running a heavy risk, but this frequently happens for extended periods in troubled companies. Of course, this may be a regular practice for divisions or subsidiaries where a parent company funds disbursement accounts as checks clear. The control issue is to understand clearly what the numbers mean and risks that may be involved.

Deciding what disbursement categories are to be forecast and who is going to be responsible for the forecast is one major key to cash management. Upon careful examination, most receipts and disbursements of a business tend to be relatively predictable over the course of a monthly cycle, but they are highly variable from week to week. The key to good forecasting is helping employees responsible for the forecast identify these patterns and establish the procedures for mechanically incorporating them in the forecast. With rare exceptions, payroll and benefits disbursements are highly predictable but amounts will vary greatly from week to week depending on pay periods and timing of benefits payments. However, there are always a few items, both recurring and non-recurring, that are of major significance but do not follow patterns of receipts or disbursement easily predictable by a finance employee not directly responsible for the functions. Examples are capital expenditures, advertising programs and receipts from projects involving partial billings for work completed.

In establishing a good cash-management system, it is critical to get the company's information technology personnel involved as early as possible. Key areas to be addressed must include:

- Categorizing vendors and customers by payment and receipts patterns;
- Integrating the cash disbursements forecast with the accounts payable system;
- Forecasting the pattern of receipts based on known billing terms for repetitive shipments to major customers;
- Identifying poor business processes, such as improper and delayed recording of transactions that impair system visibility.

In truly troubled situations, we often find a company's financial management controlling cash by preparing checks as scheduled but releasing them only as receipts become available. This is generally an excellent route to loss of management control. A $600 million retailer we encountered was holding more than $10 million in signed disbursement checks, with two full-time people using specially designed personal computer spreadsheet programs to account for checks not released. The first concrete result of an appropriate receipts-and-disbursements forecast system should be to eliminate all held checks. Otherwise, the ability to control vendor relationships often becomes unmanageable and has a major negative impact on management and financial function workload requirements.

Other "worst case" examples of situations where cash was totally out of control include:

- A $1.5 billion conglomerate with 14 subsidiaries in diverse businesses was requiring that checks over $1,500 be sent to corporate headquarters for a third signature. The company was holding thousands of checks at headquarters for signature and release, while subsidiary management lost control over their businesses as vendor relationships deteriorated.

- A metal-products manufacturer with less than $100 million in sales had more than $10 million in held checks, some more than a year old. Bank account reconciliation was impossible, and the company was regularly issuing duplicate payments.
- A health-care company that rolled up a series of 35 Physician Practice Management acquisitions did not control disbursements or checks in float. Each PPM was allowed to write checks against the company's corporate disbursements account with only monthly reporting and regular delays in making local deposits of receipts.

When beginning near-term cash-receipts-and-disbursements forecasts, it is important to put two other measurement procedures in place for distribution of information with the Weekly Cash-flow Forecast Report:

1. Detailed weekly trend analyses of receivables, inventories and accounts payable. If significant to the business, add trends for other working-capital accounts such as customer prepayments or major accrued liabilities.
2. Regular actual disbursements-to-forecast comparisons for selected periods covered by the cash-flow forecast.

Among the reasons that the managers responsible for receipts and disbursements should prepare the trend analysis are:

- Making those individuals responsible for managing working capital assets and liabilities regularly measure and report to management on their performance in controlling these investments. We firmly believe in the old truism that you can't manage what you don't measure.
- Providing both top management and the manager's peers with an objective, widely distributed measurement of forecasting performance.
- Improving the accuracy of forecasts by assigning responsibility to the individual with the greatest knowledge of the situation.
- Determining a baseline for measuring future improvement actions without a lot of debate over whether the past trend numbers are accurate. The first line of defense of the manager not properly managing a situation often is, "Finance's numbers are wrong."

Ultimately this trend analysis of historical working capital account balances should cover at least a full year; showing account balance details by week for the preceding three months and by month for at least the prior nine months. Format (using an abbreviated time frame) for the receivables balance trend should be as shown in Exhibit A-3. Trend formats for inventory and accounts payables would be similar.

EXAMPLE
EXHIBIT A-3
XYZ CORPORATION

ACCOUNTS RECEIVABLE TREND
(Dollars in thousands)

| | | Past Due | | | | | |
Month-End	Current	1-30	31-60	Over 60	TOTAL	Total A/R	% Past Due
July	$5,772	$4,010	$614	$295	$4,919	$10,691	46%
August	5,677	3,566	564	426	4,556	10,233	45%
September	5,329	2,783	513	202	3,498	8,827	40%
October	4,942	2,989	286	272	3,547	8,489	42%
November	6,328	2,402	357	373	3,132	9,460	33%
December	4,321	2,949	130	442	3,521	7,842	45%
Week Ended:							
7-Jan	4,921	1,737	159	403	2,299	7,220	43%
14-Jan	4,913	1,609	220	284	2,113	7,026	41%
21-Jan	5,203	1,575	185	357	2,117	7,320	39%
28-Jan	5,097	1,296	269	303	1,868	6,965	37%
5-Feb	5,584	1,509	321	235	2,065	7,649	35%
12-Feb	5,100	1,559	124	189	1,872	6,972	33%

Actual-versus-forecast comparisons are essential for improving forecasting accuracy by:

- Highlighting overly-optimistic sales volume and receivable collection forecasts;
- Identifying areas where disbursements are not under control, as indicated by significant forecast variances;
- Focusing attention on the individuals and/or operating functions not devoting significant attention to providing accurate forecasts.

The first concrete results in gaining better control over cash will typically come two to three weeks after starting the forecasting process, when large unfavorable variances from initial forecasts are reported. The cause will almost always be (1) overly-optimistic collection forecasts and/or (2) major expenditure commitments that represent an outflow of cash and that were not included in original forecasts due to lack of communication. Such expenditure items are often those considered as untouchable or uncontrollable because they are driven by the CEO, the founder or a powerful functional manager.

Among the types of disbursements that we have seen that were not on the radar screen of financial employees developing the forecasting model are major capital expenditures, large legal bills from longstanding litigation, advance payments for new advertising programs and C.O.D. payments required on raw material imports. Once the extent and specific timing of projected negative cash flows are determined and documented, major planned disbursements will have to be eliminated or postponed and, to the extent practicable, receipts of cash accelerated.

As the weekly cash-flow reporting system becomes fully implemented, actual-versus-forecast comparisons should be made as follows: most recent week, current month (four or five weeks) and current quarter (13 weeks). Although this may appear to require excessive clerical work, when properly formatted on a personal computer spreadsheet, these comparisons are relatively easy and are absolutely vital to the control process. Comparisons focus the attention of financial management (who should drive the process), top management, and functional management and employees preparing the forecasts on both significant flaws in the forecasting process and opportunities to improve cash flow.

The format used for this comparison is shown in Exhibit A-4 on the following page (using four-week and 13-week examples). Note that the degree of accuracy shown would be highly unlikely.

EXAMPLE
EXHIBIT A-4
XYZ CORPORATION

CASH FLOW VARIANCE ANALYSIS
(Dollars in thousands)

	Four Weeks Ending 7/4			Thirteen Weeks Ending 9/5		
	Forecast	Actual	B/(W)*	Forecast	Actual	B/(W)*
Cash Receipts						
Accounts Receivable	$5,327	$5,250	$(77)	$16,884	$16,825	$(59)
Other	0	0	0	0	0	0
Total receipts	5,327	5,250	(77)	16,884	16,825	(59)
Cash Disbursements						
Payroll and related	1,225	1,201	24	3,900	3,915	(15)
Cost of materials	2,300	2,337	(37)	5,724	5,754	(30)
Rents and leases	24	24	0	110	110	0
Telephone/Utilities	119	101	18	364	334	30
Professional Services	547	585	(38)	2,105	2,098	7
Insurance	53	55	(2)	160	161	(1)
Other (Detail as useful)	2,012	2,056	(44)	5,806	5,836	(30)
Tot. operating disb.	6,280	6,359	(79)	18,169	18,208	(39)
Operating Cash Flow	(953)	(1,109)	(156)	(1,285)	(1,383)	(98)
Non-recurring disbursements:						
- Capital expenditures	32	32	0	104	104	0
- Debt service	375	375	0	1,130	1,130	0
Total	407	407	0	1,234	1,234	0
Net Cash Flow	(1,360)	(1,516)	(156)	(2,519)	(2,617)	(98)

*Better/Worse

Two key assumptions are inherent in this discussion:

1. Actual cash disbursement information (checks written and released) is available in the same categories used in preparing the forecast.
2. Employees doing disbursement forecasting know plans for releasing payments.

In most companies, it is unlikely that either of these assumptions is entirely correct. Therefore, as part of the forecasting startup, it is necessary to install procedures to (a) list actual disbursements in the same categories as planned for forecasts and (b) consolidate disbursements already captured in the accounts payable system both with invoices not yet approved for payment and with planned future expenditures. Installing these procedures is usually relatively straightforward with a properly motivated accounting staff but can often take the greatest amount of time in getting the weekly cash-flow reporting system operating effectively.

A key issue, and a point of major resistance, with CFOs asked to install our cash-flow control system is the time, effort and talent required for installation, regular maintenance and reporting. With proper management support, most companies can install the system quickly using existing employees. In the $100 million consumer products manufacturer mentioned earlier, we had the advantage of the "management incentives" of an impending cash crisis, loan defaults and a highly motivated and competent new CEO. We also found an existing accounting system that, surprisingly, was designed to capture actual cash disbursements by category. With these advantages, the weekly cash-flow reporting system was operational on a reasonably accurate basis within three weeks. An aggressive young clerical employee with only a high school education but good computer skills handled consolidation and follow-up. She prepared first-pass forecasts for CEO and CFO review and action on the important trade-offs required to ensure a positive ongoing cash flow.

At the other extreme is the $600 million retailer noted above, where two people controlled held checks. Because of the complexity of the payables system and a lack of top-management support, it took three months to get accurate, timely reports of actual expenditures in the right disbursement forecasting categories.

A caution to CEOs and CFOs who decide to install the type of cash-flow controls we recommend: Do not spend time and effort on detailed reconciliation of forecasts and summaries of actual expenditures to sources and uses of funds for financial reporting purposes. This is both difficult and an unproductive use of resources. Accuracy and control come from the regular weekly actual-versus-forecast comparisons and visibility of data provided by the process.

The objective when the full cash-flow reporting system is installed is a weekly 15-to-30-minute discussion of the latest draft report, either directly between the CFO and CEO or as a presentation by the CFO at a regular staff meeting. Either way, the report provides a quick management overview of the situation, focuses on key unfavorable receivable and inventory trends, allows resolution of accounts payable and/or vendor payment issues if the company is in a cash crisis and draws attention to newly forecast cash disbursements that appear to be of marginal value. This allows management review and debate of disbursement trade-off issues that need to be addressed and highlights other control actions that the CEO needs to take.

Specific actions of the CEO and/or CFO as a result of these discussions will depend largely on the CEO's management style. However, this regular review and appropriate reporting to both the board of directors and the company's lenders make it more difficult for management to continue in a state of denial that ignores critical problems.

As a minimum, a top-line summary of the forecast should become part of monthly data reported to the board of directors. Details of the forecast, including actual-versus-forecast variances, should be circulated to all employees responsible for forecast input.

Although we believe that the reporting process outlined here is more complete and systematic than those typically used by others, cash receipts-and-disbursements forecasting is an essential tool of all knowledgeable turnaround consulting firms. The unfortunate fact is that it is often only partially implemented and then usually only by firms in crisis when forced by lenders. In our experience, such a system is effective in a wide range of businesses. At a minimum, we believe that the board of directors should insist that management install regular weekly or biweekly cash-flow reporting and control procedures in businesses with any of these characteristics:

- Businesses with asset-based financing outstanding;
- Highly leveraged businesses with increasing debt despite good reported earnings;
- Mature companies reporting earnings declines. Although perhaps only a cyclical downturn, this is often a precursor of major problems. If increases in negative cash flow begin to exceed reported earning declines, appropriate controls need to be installed in advance to understand quickly what is happening.
- Businesses with entrepreneurial CEOs who do not understand finance or do not look upon the CFO, if they have one, as a key partner in running the enterprise.

Even in profitable, mature businesses generating excess cash, the system can provide a simple control device to focus divisions and subsidiaries on the need to manage cash flow and to provide corporate management with timely advance warning of potential significant cash needs not disclosed by other financial forecasts. Specific examples of where we believe this to be the case include:

- Rapidly growing subsidiaries or divisions, as a basis for (a) forcing discipline in the use of cash as a scarce resource and (b) separating investment spending from operating cash flow.
- Businesses with declining sales volume caused by either cyclical market conditions or long-term loss of market share. In either case, management should focus on preserving operating cash flow earlier rather than later.

In each of these situations, data should be refined further, of course, to determine the extent to which operating cash flow is being preserved and/or enhanced by liquidation of working capital. Liquidation of working capital is the first line of defense against insolvency but a poor response to deteriorating business conditions.

The type of cash-flow control system described here can prove very useful at private equity funds or other investment-holding companies that manage a diverse portfolio of businesses as independent standalone entities. These businesses are often highly leveraged and thus need a heavy emphasis on cash control by both owners and management. As with companies facing demands of asset-based or other secured lenders, there is often some type of receipts-and-disbursements forecasting in place. However, it is frequently viewed and managed as a financial exercise with limited operating management input or commitment. Unfavorable variances may generate a lot of internal finger-pointing but little change in management effectiveness other than to ensure that the CFO insists on more conservative forecasts.

Appendix Summary

The system of responsibilities and measurements outlined above encourages better management of the business due to:

- Assignment of cash-flow forecasting responsibility to employees with ability to control results;
- Visibility of both forecasts and actual results across the entire enterprise;.
- Inclusion of trend analysis of key working capital assets in the reporting process.

In installing the cash-flow control system, two key issues to be addressed are the responsibility level at which to install the system and the amount of backup detail needed.

We believe that:

- Cash-flow forecasting should be summarized and controlled at the business unit level where profit-and-loss reporting responsibility resides. If there is no profit-and-loss reporting responsibility, there cannot be a total business cash-flow reporting responsibility. Such control may reside at the corporate level where the CEO has responsibility for a functional organization or at the business-unit level in a decentralized company.

- The extent to which detailed supporting forecasts should be provided to the financial employee managing and coordinating preparation of the forecast will vary widely based on specific circumstance. It is desirable to forecast receivable collections individually for major customers. Forecast disbursements individually for key vendors, significant professional services (like legal and advertising) and capital expenditures. This data should then be available as supporting detail for the CEO and CFO during the regular weekly or biweekly forecast review.

- In general, the material circulated weekly or biweekly within the company should be a report of 8 to 10 pages with weekly updates and key information highlighted. Data should be limited to exhibits discussed specifically above. (Use separate pages to report trends for each key working capital account.) Finance should provide the CFO with more extensive details of problem areas which require follow-up. These would normally include:

  - Details by week in the standard reporting format of the latest 13 week actual receipts and disbursements with weekly averages that can be bridged to the current forecast.
  - Summary by week of top-level adjustments to the forecast (there should not be many) made to reflect management (CEO and/or CFO) revisions to data submitted by responsible employees. An example of such changes would be adjustments in the timing of disbursements to reflect borrowing availability.
  - Roll-forward details of projected changes in receivable, inventory and payable balances by week.
  - Loan balances and borrowing availability together with the related effect of debt service payments.

- Details of receivable balances due from key customers.
- Details of payable balances outstanding with major and/or critical vendors.

Two additional recommendations are based on our personal experience:

1. Personally signing all significant checks is one of the best devices for the CEO or CFO to maintain good knowledge of and control over disbursements.
2. Intra-company clearing accounts to settle balances between subsidiaries and divisions are frequently a bad idea. In theory, cash management of float and bank balances is more efficient with intra-company clearing accounts. In reality this advantage is often more than offset by the costs of reconciliation of transactions involved and the loss of visibility and accountability for receivables, payables, and accruals balances. When assuming interim management of troubled multidivision companies, a key first action while installing this cash-control system is often to begin settling all intra-company balances by check, including corporate overhead allocations where applicable.

We believe that this cash-flow management system has applicability across a wide spectrum of business situations, can be implemented at minimal cost, and will have the following key benefits:

1. Installs the type of cash-flow controls required for credibility with lenders, boards of directors of undercapitalized companies and others monitoring troubled situations.
2. Provides an easy focus of attention for management control of the business and communication with appropriate employees.
3. Helps management that does not have a strong financial background understand and control cash, the key driver of business success.

Cash-flow control is only one management control tool among many, and it requires time and regular attention. But if this control cannot be installed and managed capably by a company, it is highly unlikely that other aspects of the business are being well managed.

APPENDIX B

LIST OF EXHIBITS

Number	Title	Page
1-1	Authors' 100 Project Sample	9
3-1	Organizational Lifecycles	31
3-2	Authors' Categorization of Troubled Businesses	34
3-3	Type of Problems by Lifecycle Category	35
6-1	Liquidity and Financing Risk Assessment	83
8-1	Management Interview Guide	114
9-1	Apparel Manufacturer – Comparative Financial Data	124
9-2	Equipment Manufacturer – Profit Contribution by Product Line	128
9-3	Food Products Manufacturer – Profit Contribution by Product Line	130
9-4	Home Products Retailer – EBITDA to Cashflow Reconciliation	132
9-5	Operations Risk Assessment	136
10-1	Competitive Environment Risk Assessment	153
11-1	Organization and Business Processes Risk Assessment	168
12-1	Expected Actions Required for Turnaround	178
12-2	Bankruptcy Filings Compared with Project Results	186
14-1	Likely Alternative Scenarios and Associated Management Characteristics	201
14-2	Likely Actions / Management Changes Needed for Turnaround	204
15-1	Hypothetical Deal Structure	223

16-1   Undisciplined Racehorse Businesses
        – Project Results   228
16-2   CEO Changes at Undisciplined Racehorses   237
17-1   Overburdened Workhorse Businesses
        – Project Results   241
17-2   CEO Changes at Overburdened Workhorses   248
18-1   Aging Mule Businesses
        – Project Results   253
18-2   CEO Changes at Aging Mules   258

BIBLIOGRAPHY

Adizes, Ichak. *Corporate Lifecycles: How and Why Corporations Grow and Die and What to Do About It*. Englewood Cliffs, N.J.: Prentice-Hall, 1988.

Altman, Edward I. *Corporate Financial Distress: A Complete Guide to Predicting, Avoiding and Dealing With Bankruptcy*. 2nd ed. New York: John Wiley & Sons, 1993.

Bethune, Gordon with Scott Huler. *From Worst to First: Behind the Scenes of Continental's Remarkable Comeback*. New York: John Wiley & Sons, 1998.

Bibeault, Donald B. *Corporate Turnaround: How Managers Turn Losers Into Winners*. New York: McGraw-Hill, 1982.

Bossidy, Larry and Ram Charan. *Execution: The Discipline of Getting Things Done*. New York: Crown Business, 2002.

Bossidy, Larry and Ram Charan with Charles Burck. *Confronting Reality: Doing What Matters to Get Things Right*. New York: Crown Business, 2004.

Buffett, Mary and David Clark. *Buffettology*. New York: Simon & Schuster, 1997.

Buffett, Warren. *The Essays of Warren Buffett: Lessons for Corporate America*. 1st rev. ed. Selected, arranged and introduced by Lawrence A. Cunningham. Durham, N.C.: Carolina Academic Press, 2001.

Christensen, Clayton M. *The Innovator's Dilemma: When New Technologies Cause Great Firms to Fail*. Boston: Harvard Business School Press, 1997.

—— and Michael E. Raynor. *The Innovator's Solution: Creating and Sustaining Successful Growth*. Boston: Harvard Business School Press, 2003.

Collins, Jim. *Good to Great: Why Some Companies Make the Leap...and Others Don't*. New York: HarperCollins, 2001.

Deal, Terrence E. and Allan A. Kennedy. *Corporate Cultures: The Rites and Rituals of Corporate Life*. Boston: Addison-Wesley, 1982.

Dell, Michael with Catherine Fredman. *Direct From Dell: Strategies That Revolutionized an Industry*. New York: HarperCollins, 1999.

Drucker, Peter F. *The Practice of Management*. New York: Harper & Brothers, 1954.

——. *Management: Tasks, Responsibilities, Practices*. New York: Harper & Row, 1973.

——. *Managing for Results: Economic Tasks and Risk-Taking Decisions*. New York: Harper & Row, 1964.

Gerstner, Louis V. Jr. *Who Says Elephants Can't Dance?: Inside IBM's Historic Turnaround*. New York: HarperCollins, 2002.

George, Bill. *Authentic Leadership: Rediscovering the Secrets to Creating Lasting Value.*   Hoboken, N.J.: Jossey-Bass, 2003.

Goldratt, Eliyahu M. *Theory of Constraints: What Is This Thing Called and How Should It Be Implemented?* Croton-on-Hudson, N.Y.: North River Press, 1990.

Grove, Andrew S. *Only the Paranoid Survive: How to Exploit the Crisis Points That Challenge Every Company and Career.* New York: Currency-Doubleday, 1996.

Hamel, Gary and C.K. Prahalad. *Competing for the Future.*   Boston: Harvard Business School Press, 1994.

Harvard Business Review on Change.   Boston: Harvard Business School Press, 1998

Henderson, Bruce D. "Cash Traps."   In *Perspectives on Strategy.* Ed. Carl W. Stern and George Stalk Jr. New York: John Wiley & Sons,1998.

Kets de Vries, Manfred F.R. and Danny Miller. *Unstable at the Top: Inside the Troubled Organization.* New York: New American Library, 1998.

Koch, Richard. *The 80/20 Principle: The Secret to Success by Achieving More With Less.* New York: Currency-Doubleday, 1998.

Lewis, Michael. *Moneyball: The Art of Winning an Unfair Game.* New York: W. W. Norton & Company, 2003.

Lowenstein, Roger. Buffett: The Making of an American Capitalist. *New York: Random House, 1995.*

Miller, Danny. *The Icarus Paradox: How Exceptional Companies Bring About Their Own Downfall.* New York: Harper Business, 1990.

Miller, Lawrence M. *Barbarians to Bureaucrats: Corporate Life Cycle Strategies.* New York: Fawcett Columbine, 1989.

Owsley, Henry F. and Peter S. Kaufman. *Distressed Investment Banking: To the Abyss and Back.* New York: Beard Books, 2005.

Pate, Carter and Harlan D. Platt. *The Phoenix Effect: Nine Revitalizing Strategies No Business Can Do Without.* New York: John Wiley & Sons, 2002.

Peters, Thomas J. and Robert H. Waterman Jr. *In Search of Excellence: Lessons From America's Best-Run Companies.* New York: Harper & Row, 1982.

Platt, Harlan D. *Why Companies Fail: Strategies for Detecting, Avoiding and Profiting From Bankruptcy.* New York: Beard Books, 1999.

Porter, Michael E. *Competitive Advantage: Creating and Sustaining Superior Performance.* New York: Simon & Schuster, 1998.

Rome, Donald Lee, ed. *The Business Workouts Manual – The Practitioner's Guide.* 2nd ed. Boston: Warren, Gorham & Lamont, 1992.

Rouse, William B. *Don't Jump to Solutions: 13 Delusions That Undermine Strategic Thinking.* Hoboken, N.J.: Jossey-Bass Publishers, 1998.

Slywotzky, Adrian J. and David J. Morrison. *The Profit Zone: How Strategic Business Design Will Lead You to Tomorrow's Profits.* New York: Times Business, 1997.

——, David J. Morrison, Ted Moser, Kevin A. Mundt and James A. Quella. *Profit Patterns: 30 Ways to Anticipate and Profit From Strategic Forces Reshaping Your Business.* New York: Times Books, 1999.

Suters, Everett T. *The Unnatural Act of Management: When the Great Leader's Work Is Done, the People Say, "We Did It Ourselves."* New York: Harper Business, 1992.

Sutton, Gary. *The Six-Month Fix: Adventures in Rescuing Failing Companies.* New York: John Wiley & Sons, 2002

Taleb, Nassim Nicholas. *Fooled by Randomness: The Hidden Role of Chance in Life and in the Markets.* 2d ed. New York: Thomson/Texere, 2004.

Tichy, Noel M. and Stratford Sherman. *Control Your Destiny or Someone Else Will: How Jack Welch Is Making General Electric the World's Most Competitive Corporation.* New York: Currency-Doubleday, 1993.

Topchik, Gary S. "Attacking the Negativity Virus." Management Review. *87(8). September 1998. 61-64.*

Treacy, Michael and Fred Wiersema. *The Discipline of Market Leaders.* Boston: Addison-Wesley, 1995.

Tregoe, Benjamin B. and John W. Zimmerman. *Top Management Strategy: What It Is and How to Make It Work.* New York: Simon & Schuster, 1980.

Welch, Jack with Suzy Welch. *Winning.* New York: HarperCollins, 2005.

Whitney, John O. *Taking Charge: A Management Guide to Troubled Companies and Turnarounds.* New York: Beard Books, 1999.

Womack, James P. and Daniel T. Jones. *Lean Thinking: Banish Waste and Create Wealth in Your Corporation.* New York: Simon & Schuster, 1996.

INDEX

A

Accounting, 21–22, 51, 53, 74, 77, 98, 108, 120, 125–127, 160
    fraud, 49
    manipulation, 208–210
    principles (*see* GAAP [Generally Accepted Accounting Principles])
    systems, 128
    write-offs, 314
Accounting manipulations, 159
Accounts receivable, 29, 275, 279, 281
Accruals, 74, 222, 272, 286
    as a source of financing, 222
Acquiring distressed debt, 268
Acquiring existing equity, 268
Acquisition plan, 9, 232, 234, 244
Acquisition plan shortfalls, 9, 232, 234, 244
Acquisitions, 8–10, 16, 18, 23, 28, 32–33, 49, 51, 77, 97, 118–120, 127, 136, 148, 158, 160, 164, 178–179, 190, 192, 198, 205, 209, 214, 218, 220, 223, 228, 230, 232–234, 238, 240–244, 248–249, 278
    integrating, 16, 18, 223
Acquisitions made outside of company's core, 310
Action plans, 139, 171, 204
Assessing, 235–237
    developing, 226–249
    for various categories of troubled companies, 24, 263, 203
    short term, 345, 346
Adequate protection, 257
Adizes, Ichak, 31, 162, 169, 202
Administrative controls, lack of, 28, 32, 76, 167
Adolescence, 46, 47

Advertising, 77, 111, 123, 127, 130, 141–142, 148, 159, 214, 229, 256, 277, 280, 285
Advisors, *see* Consultants
Aerospace industry, 216
After-market sales, 183
Aging Mules, 12, 33, 38, 52, 176, 180, 201, 206, 225, 241, 251–260, 267
    actions required to turnaround, 267
    bankruptcy filings, 331
    core competencies of, 322
    decline of competitive position, 322–324
    dilemma of, 322
    downsizing, 330
    external problems, 321, 323–324, 331
    forecasting long-term prospects of, 328–329
    internal problems of, 323
    key assumptions of, 265
    liquidation, 328
    management, 330
    management change at, 267, 267, 269, 274–275, 329, 329
    obtaining going concern value of, 328
    operational turnaround opportunities, 341
    recommended management characteristics of, 265
    restructuring, 326, 332
    threats to, 267
    turnaround plan for, 234–235, 238
    turnarounds, 327–328, 332
Agreement, reaching, 254, *see also* negotiation
Agricultural products company, 182
Allen, Woody, 45
Allocation, 74, 120–121, 126–128, 194, 262, 272–273, 275, 286
Allowed claims, 63–69, 87–88, 90, 185–187, 219, 222, 255

Alternative scenarios, 35, 81, 166, 174–175, 181–183, 185, **187**–189, 194, **201**, 206

Alternatives, 26, 37
  assessing, 235–237
  comparable forecasts, 244
  Developing, 226–249

American Management Association, 209

Analyzing profitability by product line, 130

Analyzing trends,
      working capital, 162

Apparel manufacturer, 124

Arrogance, 44, 49–50, 56, 94, 157, 204–205, 232, 237

Asian companies, 221

Asian currency crisis, 20

Asset management literature, 273

Asset sales, 76, 82, 171, 180, 193, **214**, 215, 243

Auction, 164, 285, 294

Authors' Casebook, 16–23, 29–30, 35–36, 46, 64–65, 70, 75–77, 89, 95, 97, 111, 121, 124, 127, 130–131, 142, 144, 148–150, 186, 205, 209, 215–216, 218, 229–230, 232, 235–236, 243, 246–247, 254, 256, 258
  bankruptcy filings in, 242–243
  overview of, 16–22, **19**–21, 50
  companies with external problems, 17–**19**
  companies with internal problems, 18–20

Auto parts manufacturer, 29

Auto parts supplier, 253

Automotive manufacturing, 94, 164

B

Bad management, **1**, 39–40, 43–47, 55–56, 87, 92, 110, 129, 155–156, 259

Bank of America, 223

Bank-legder cash balances, 276, 351

Bankruptcy, 49–50, 53, 62–64, 72–73, 75, 83, 93, 98
  alternatives to, 187–188
  benefits of, 240–241
  Chapter 11, 30, 36, 66 ,86 ,90 ,98
  Chapter 7, 83, 84
  forced, 241–243
  in case studies, 242, 243

Bankruptcy Act of 2005, 207

Bankruptcy law, 62, 66, 185, 197

Barbarians to Bureaucrats, 213

Base period, 119

Berkshire-Hathaway Inc., 141, 190

Bet-the-business risks, 232

Bethune, Gordon, 250

Bibeault, Donald B., 213

Big Box, 21–22, 131, 141, 150, 164

Blame, 1,13,39,92,105,109,113,208

Board of directors, 41, 43, 51, **54**, 65, 70, 77, 91, 99, 111, 113, 155, 164, 166, 188, 203, 212, 240, 266, 268, 283

Bondholders, 86

Borrowing, excessive, 28, 72–73, 75, 77

Borrowing capacity, 77, 244

Borrowing-base availability, **78**, 82, 90

Bossidy, Larry, 154

Boston Consulting Group, 21, 147

Brand name value, 20, 217–218, 247

Branded consumer products manufacturer, 257

Breakup value, **175**

Bridge analysis, 132, 134–135, 215

"Brutal facts," 6, 22, 44, 47–48, 87, 120, 133–134

Buffalo Evening News, 142

Buffett, Warren, 142, 147

Built to Last, 250

Burck, Charles, 154

Business cycles, *see also* Cyclical downturn issues, 33, **37**, 244–245

Business lifecycles, *see also* Aging Mules; Overburdened Workhorses; Undisciplined Racehorses,163
  Aging, Early bureaucracy, 32
  Growth
      Adolescence, 31–32, 163
      Go-Go, 31–32, 163
  Maturity
      Aristocracy, 31–32
      Prime, 31–32
      Stable, 31–32

Business owners, 93, **268**
  advice to, 341–342

Business processes, *see* operations

Business viability, *see* Viability, business

Buyers, 10, 24, 214–215, 220–224, 258
    financial, 150, **218**

C

C.O.D.,
Capital Cities Communications, 142
Capital expenditures, 16, 71, 75, 132, 138,
    141, 148, 159, 179, 214, 241, 242,
    269, 275, 277, 280, 281, 285
Capital structure, 66, 84, 85, 146, 180, 192,
    197, 232, 240, 268
Case studies, *see* Authors' Casebook
Cash, controlling and managing, 3–4, 14–15,
    17–19, 21–22, 24, 27, 29–30, 32–33,
    36, 42, 46–47, 59, 65, 67, 71–82
Cash balance and float forecast example, 276
Cash flow, 3, 14–15, 17–22, 24, 27, 33, 36, 42,
    46–48, 59, 71–77, 79, 82–83, 85, 89,
    93, 110, 119, 131–132, 134, 148–149,
    159, 175, 180, 187, 189, 195, 198,
    200, 214–217, 219–220, 222,
    240–241, 249, 254–255, 257, 271–272
    crisis, 175
    discounted, 27,187, 189, 200, 214
    forecasting, 74, 89,271, 284-285
    measurement procedures, 278
Cash-flow forecasting system, 74
    Actual-versus-forecast comparison, 280
    backup details, 285
    benefits of, 361–364
    businesses needing, 360, 361
    check float, 276
    checks, 276
    implementation time, 359–360
    issues and resistance regarding, 359
    objectives of, 346–347
    period base, 348
    resistance toward, 359
    sample report, **350**
    variance analysis example, **281**
Cash reconciliation, **276**
Cash trap, 21
Cash trap industries, leverage options for, 147,
    219

CEO (chief executive officer), 18–19, 21, 23,
    29, 32, 36, 44–45, 49–50, 52–53, 67,
    70, 73, 76, 91–92, 100, 103, 105, 110,
    113, 155, 164–166, 178, 190, 198,
    201, 203–210, 212, 236–239, 243,
    248, 250, 258, 261, 269, 272, 280, 282
CFO (chief financial officer), 18, 53, 73, 103,
    110, 141, 155, 163, 166
Chapter 11, *see* Bankruptcy, Chapter 11
Chapter 7, 62–63
Charan, Ram, 154
Check float, 276, *see also* cash-flow forecasting
    systems
Checks, 71, 276–278, 282, 286, *see also*
    cash-flow forecasting system
Chemical and pharmaceutical manufacturer,
    257
Chicago, 141
Christensen, Clayton M., 150, 162, 261–262
Claims, *see* Allowed claims
Classifying organizations, 46
Coca-Cola, 142
Collateral, 7, 36, 74, 79–81, 85–90, 193
Collins, Jim, 6, 250–251
Columbia Business School, 154
Commodities, 50
    price, 50, 78, 140–142, 153, 183, 244
    pricing, 189
Communication, 17, 22, 207
Comparable forecasting, *see* Forecasting
Compensation liabilities, 219
Competitive environment, 11, 15, 19–20, 30,
    32, 46
    Aging Mules in, 322–324
    evaluating the, 36, 42
    importance of positioning in, 33–34
Complacency, 47, 52–53, 56, 157, 259–260,
    264, 266, 269
Computer products company, 15
Computer repair services company, 258
Conflicts of interest and agenda, *see* Stakehold-
    ers, conflicting agendas and interests of
Consolidation, 13, 37, 99, 130, 198, 206
Consumer products company, 19, 93,
    111–112, 273

Continental Airlines, 250

Contracts, 91

Control Your Destiny or Someone Else Will, 250

Controls, Administrative, 8, 28, 32, 49, 76,
113, 157–158, 162–163, 167, 179, 205

Core competencies, 161, 167

Corporate culture, 156–157, 167

Corporate Lifecycles, 45, *see also* Business
lifecycles, 31, 169, 213

Corporate Turnaround, 213

Covenants, 46, 77, 83, 85, 87, 90, 130, 160,
197, 266

Credibility, 3–4, 17, 26, 36, 51, 71

Credit, 1, 3, 30, 39, 76, 87, 97, 193, 198, 235,
242, 267, 273

Credit issues, 310, 348

Crisis management, 4–5, 97, 148, 150, 154,
213

CRO (chief restructuring officer), 166, 201,
213, 235

Customers, 14–15, 19, 32, 36, 52, 65, 71, 76,
86, **95–96**, 100, 107, 114–115, 118,
122, 125, 129, 149–150, 159, 167,
183, 204, 210, 212, 216, 230–231,
251, 254, 275, 277, 285–286

Cycles, business, 53

Cyclical downturn issues, 17
Overburdened Workhorses and, 33, 176,
179

Cyclicality, 17, 115, 144

D

Data General, 15

Debt, *see also* Loans; Overleverage
compared with tangible assets, 341
differing levels of, 120
discounted, 341
excess, 28, 42, 310 (*see also* Overleverage)
mezzanine level, 120–121
reduction of, 33
restructuring, 12, 304, 311
secured, 28, 87, 121, 259, 311, 342
service capacity, 310, 341
subordinated, 342
swapping for equity, 22, 39, 121, 341
unsecured, 342

Debt restructuring, 10, 17, 81, 99, 131, 143,
167, 180, 189, 193, 202, 205–206,
232, 235, 242, 249, 260

Debtor-in-possession financing, 72, 80

Declining markets, 14

Declining unit sales, 251

Default, 3, 17

Delays, 43, 278
acquisition/project integration, 18, 214

Dell, Michael, 239

Denial, 13, 42, 44, 47–**49**, 54, 56, 78, 87–88,
92, 108–109, 121, 154, 157, 160, 165,
174, 179

Deteriorating operational trends, 134

Diagnosing turnaround potential, 4, 33

Diagnostic process, *see also* Management,
interviews, 135, 171
benefits of, 252–253
objective of, 37, 101

DIP financing, 65

Direct From Dell, 239

Disbursement, 65, 67, 72–75, 82

Disbursement categories, forecasting, 276

Discounted liquidation values, 81

Discounted purchase of debt, 268

Disruptive technology, 69, 107, 122, 138, 142,
153, 162, 254

Distressed-debt trade, 342

Divestiture, 142, *see also* Asset divestiture

Documentation, 62, 76–77, 90, 113, 150, 197,
222

Doskocil, Inc., 243, 248

Dotcoms, 192, 193, 293

Downsizing, 110, 237–238, 259–260

Drucker, Peter, 14, 40, 162, 240
Managing for Results, 33, 120, 126–127,169

Dunlap, Al "Chainsaw," 51

E

Ease of entry, 145–146, 152

Ebbers, Bernard, 49

EBITDA, 21, 27, 128, 131–132, 148, 241

Ego, 13

80/20 principle, 117, 126, 129, 137

Electronics businesses, 86, 268, 304

Employee development, **160**

Engineering consulting company, 298
Enron, **50**, 160, 234
Entrepreneurs, 7,162,268
Environment, 119, 284, 285, 287, 315, 325
Environmental claims, 219
Equitable subordination, **66**
Equity, 3
    acquiring existing, 342
    owners, 107, 114, 120, 121
    value, 106, 124, 298
    warning against making investment in, 341
Equity owners, 80, 85–86, 90–**91**
    advice to, 342
    inability to maintain debt, 258
Equity value, preserving, 22, 80, 93, 192, 232
Establishing a selling price, 220
Establishing realistic objectives, 263
European companies, 19, 21, 221
Evans Products, 254
Excessive debt, 11, 16, 119, 201, 218, 242,
    247, 250
Exclusive agreements, 129, 287
Exercising caution, 265
Exit barriers, **219**
Exit strategy, developing an, 10, 19, 24, 29, 48,
    93, 139, 141, 152, 166, 174, 181, 187,
    193
External problems, 8, 29
    business cycle issues, 37
    for Aging Mules, 33
    permanent market shift, 166
    weak competitive position, **19**

F
Factory management issues, 18
Fad and fashion product businesses, 15
Fairfield Communities, 144, 248
Faulty information, 43
Finance company, 235
Financial modeling, 187–189
Financial restructuring, *see* Restructuring,
    financial
Financing, accruals as a source of, 288–289
First impaired party, motivations and leverage
    of, **196**, 198

Fixed costs, 122, 126, 128, 130, 134, 143, 236,
    246
    converting to variable costs, 315
Flexibility, 81, 94, 167, 245, 259, 263, 269
Fooled By Randomness, 57
Forbearance, 81, 89–90, 121, 179, 191,
    196–198, 231, 234, 243, 265, 267
    price of, 255, 341
Forecasting, 21, 65
    comparable, 244
    long-term, 328–329
Four-wall contribution, 131
Fraud, **234–235**, 237–238
Fraudulent conveyance, 67, 185
From Worst to First, 250
FUD Factor (Fear, Uncertainty, Doubt), 220

G
GAAP (Generally Accepted Accounting
    Principles), Growth projections under,
    271
General Electric, 21, 41, 140
General Motors, 46, 52, 254
Geographic issue, 45
Geographic issues, 171, 191, 199, 205, 317
Gerstner, Louis V. Jr., 261
Gillette, 142
Globalization, 20–21, 46, 142, **147**, 152, 183,
    221
Go-go, 31–**32**, 163
Going-concern value, 257
    obtaining, 29
    Aging Mules, **180**
Good to Great, 6, 250–251
Greece, 235
Greed, 235
Grossman's Inc., 254–255
Grove, Andrew S., 48, 239
Growth, 16, 18–19, 21, 28–29, **32–33**, 45, 47,
    49, 51, 72, 76–77, 84, 92, 94, 108,
    117–119, 136, 138–144, 150, 153,
    158, 160, 163, 176–177, 180, 189,
    198, 202, 205, 208, 218, 227, 229,
    231, 242, 252

long-term, 189, 212, 240, 283
management, 19, 293, 296
projections, 345
rapid, 64, 96, 183, 295, 305, 312, 313
unrealistic expectations of, 16, 45, 118–119,
    134, 151, 155, 201

H

Hamel, Gary, 161
Harm, avoiding, 45, **61-71**
Harvard Business Review on Change, 57
Health-care company, 232
HealthSouth, 162
Hedge funds, 90
High-speed wireless communications network,
    228
Hiring practices, 43, 113, 155, 158
Home Depot, 15, 22
Home nutritional services company, 77
"Home run" potential, 27, 61, 93, 197
Home products retail chain, 256
Hopkins, Douglas, 20, 30, 121, 235
Hopkins, Stephen, 271
Huler, Scott, 250

I

IBM, 261
Illinois Tool, 223
Implementation failures, 230–232, 234, 244
Inertia, 42, 121, 204
Information systems, 77, 163, 253
Information technology, 163–164, 198, 209,
    277
Information technology personnel, 277
Innovator's Dilemma, The, 150, 252, 261
Insolvency, 61–62
Intangible benefits, **93**
    representing, 93
Intangible problems, 30
Integration, 18, 21, 23, 33, 64, 145, 156, 162,
    166, 178, 181, 198, 201–202, 207,
    215–217, 223–224, 233–234, 243, 248
Integration assistance, **223–224**
Interest rate, 78–79, 88–90, 196
Internal problems, 8, 9, 11, 28

acquisition plan shortfalls, 9, **232–236**, 244
Aging Mules, 33, 38, 52, 176, 180, 201,
    206, 225, 241, **251–260**, 265, 267
    correcting, 78, 106, 108, 155, 236
    project or growth management issues, 18,
        115, 167
    unqualified/ inattentive management, 9, 244
Interviews, *see* Management interviews
intra-company balances, 286
Inventory, 72
    distressed, 29
    forecasting and control, 21, 76
    POS, 30
Investment banker's perspective, 190
Investments, initiating, 144
Investors, advice to, 267–268
Involuntary investors, 267

J

Jobs, 37, 51, 88, 95, 105, 129, 160, 169, 193,
    202, 217, 224, 263
    preserving, 95
Joint venture, 89, 217, 246
Jones, Daniel T., 74, 137

K

Kaufman, Peter S., 190
Kitchen products company, 218
Koch, Richard, 126, 137
Kotter, John P., 57
Kroc, Ray, 213
KUIL (Knowledge, Understanding, Insight,
    Leadership), 40–42, 182, 269

L

Labor, 17–18, 69, 95, 122–123, 127–128, 140
    relations, 18
Landlords, 99, 196
LBO (Leveraged Buyout), 247
    firm, 247
Leadership, 22, 28, **39–56**, 94, 112, 140, 148,
    157, 161, 201, 213, 250, 261, 263,
    266, 269
    lack of, 47, 53, 56, 157, 269
Lean Thinking, 74, 137, 162, 272

Leases, 22, 30, 87, 99, 131, 150, 180, 185, 219, 222, 256, 259, 275, 281

Legal bills, 280

Leverage, 4, 6, 10, 15, 23, 30, 46, 62-64, 75, 90–91, 118–119, 123, 131, 138, 141, 146, 148, 150–151, 153, 171, 188, 219, 234, 261, 268, 283–284

Lewis, Michael, 57

Liabilities, 22–23, 61, 64, 70, 73–74, 89, 119, 130, 144, 186, 196, 199, 218–224, 243, 246–248, 255, 259, 274, 278

effect on value, 22, 64, 223

new, 61

tax, 22–23

working capital, 223, 274, 278

Lifecycles, organizational, 30–31

Liquidating assets, 6, 62

Liquidation, 4, 6, 16–18, 23, 28, 36, 48, 59, 71–82, 124, 131, 159, 175, 195, 198, 200, 203, 230, 241–242, 245–249, 266

Aging Mules, 52, 141, 253

as baseline alternative, 195, 216

Liquidation analysis, 80, 175, 195, 216

Liquidity, 3, 4, 6, 16–18, 21, 23, 28, 36, 48, 59, **71–83**, 124, 131, 147, 164, 175, 195, 198, 200, 203–204, 230, 241–242, 244–245, 249, 266

Liquidity crisis, 17–18

Litigation, 61, 63

outstanding, 67, 70, 73, 96, 185, 280

Loan agreement covenant waivers, 87

Loan defaults, 235, 274, 282

Loan to value ratio, 78–79, 81, 88, 100, 180, 194–195, 197

Loan-to-own strategies, 268

Local and regional markets, 146

Long-term effectiveness, 40

Long-term growth, 51, 139, 144, 161, 184, 218

Long-term profitability, 138, 142

Long-term profitability trends, keys to, 138, 142–144, 152

Long-term viability, 17, 24, 171

Losers, 20, 75, 94, 108, 126, 141, 149, 178–179, 189, 201, 204–206, 213, 223

Low-ball bidders, 220

Lowenstein, Roger, 141

Loyalty, 96

Lucent, 162

Luck, 28, 39, 43–45, 49, 61

M

MAI, 27, 15

Management

advice to, 49, 61, 66, 149, 251

Aging Mules, 204, 206, 210, 253–254, 258–259

bad (*see* Bad management)

bonuses, 207, 210, 271

challenges facing, 1, 205, 209

challenges of, 1, 205, 209

change of, 203–204, 207–208

compensation, 210

deficiencies, 18, 47–**53**

evaluation of, 55–56, 59, 68, **110–111**

in denial, (*see* denial)

incentives for, 196, 209, 223, 282

inept, 241, 244, 249, **253–254**

interviews, 94, **103–113**, 265

key organizational functions of, 202

matching needs with objectives, 40, 46, 203

middle, 93–95, 108, 168, 205, 234

preparing trend analysis, 278

recommended characteristics of, 201

reporting systems, 68–69, 108, 209

retaining, 66, 90, **206**

selecting, 200–211

structured interview process, 103, 113

tactical, 110, 165, 220

temporary retention agreements, 207

top, 5, 44, 47, 52, 86, **91–92**, 209, 265, 278, 280, 282

trend analysis by, 278

Managing expectations, 45

Manufacturing, 36

Manufacturing business, **35**, 122, 247

Market leadership, 261

Market maturity, 138–140, 152

Mathematical models for evaluating fixed asset investments, 273

Mature businesses, turnaround strategy for, 94
McDonald's, 213
Measuring enterprise value, methods for, 27
Meat products manufacturer, 243
Meat-packing business, 122
Meltdown, 35, 61, 186
Mercer Management Consulting, 154
Mergers and acquisitions (M&A), 190
Metal container manufacturer, 75
Metricom, 228
Mezzanine debt, 90, 223
Milking the business, 10, 140
Milking the equity, 159
Miller, Danny, 162, 169
Miller, Lawrence M., 213
Moneyball, 57
Morrison Knudsen, 53
Morrison, David J., 154, 184
Motivations of negotiating parties, 85–86
Mutual fund investment results, 44

N

Nature of business problems, 26–37
Near-term cash flow forecasts, 72, 175
Near-term crisis, 75
Near-term receipts and disbursements, 274
Negative cash flow, 15, 72, 74, 82
    stopping, 48, 93, 254, 274
Negativity, dealing with, 209
Negotiation, **79–80**
New money, 4, 6, 27, 80–82, 191, 196
Non-recurring costs and events, 275
Nortel, 162
Nucor, 95

O

Oakland Athletics, 57
Oceangoing fleet operator, 235
Offshore capacity, 153
Only the Paranoid Survive, 48, 239
Operational turnaround, 6, 8, 14
    Aging Mules, 33, 38, 52, 176, 180, 201,
        206, 225, 241, **251–260**, 265, 267

Operations
    analyzing and evaluating, 125–130, 157
    costs and contribution margins of, 117–132
    risk assessment, 136
Options available for dealing with a troubled
        company, 6, 26–27, 31
Organizational evaluation, 165
Overburdened Workhorses, 12, 33
    actions required for turnaround at, 178
    bankruptcy filings, 248
    change of management, 206
    debt restructuring, 176, 179, 201, 246, 265
    external problems, 206, 243
    in cyclical markets, 267
    internal problems, 244
    key assumptions of, 201
    liquidation of, 246, 249
    management change at, 248
    operational characteristics of stable, 241
    recommended management characteristics
        for, 201
    threats to, 204
    turnaround plan for, 242, 249
    working capital control for, 246
Overhead costs, 130, 135
Overleverage, 3–4
Overleveraged businesses, compared to
        troubled businesses, 271
Owners, 10, 13, 20, 23, 36, 75, 80, 84–86, 91,
        99, 155, 167, 181, 198, 208, 219, 230,
        233, 253, 268–269, *see also* Business
        owners
Owsley, Henry F., 190

P

Pareto, Vilfredo, *see* 80/20 principle
Partial billings, 277
Partnership, 96
Payroll, 3, 57
Pension liabilities, 219
Pensions, 219, 255
Permanent market change, **20–21**, 33,
        228–229, 238, 241, 243–244, 253
Perspectives of stakeholders in liquidity crisis,
        84

Ponas, Jerry, 250
Prahalad, C.K., 161
Preferred warrants, 16
Prepackaged plans, 40, 185–186
Pricing power, 139, 142
Priority of interests, 197
Pro-forma projections, 215
Product liability claims, 219
Profit Zone, The, 154, 184
Publicity, 88, 230

Q

Quality, 18, 20, 30, 39, 43, 55, 69, 75, 95,
    111–113, 128, 134, 148–149, 158,
    168, 171, 244, 246, 262

R

Rapid growth, 16, 33, 45, 139, 150, 157, 198,
    203, 229–230, 238
Ratio analysis, 122
Real estate, 30, 75, 82, 86, 99, **144**, 180,
    216–217, 219, 246–247, 253, 255–256
Receipts and disbursements, variability of,
    74–75, 272–276, 278, 283–285
Receivables, 19, 23–24, 28–29, 36, 48, 67, 72,
    76–78, 81–82
Receivables management, 76–77, 82
Recession, 17, 37, 143
Redesign options, strategic, **184**
Relationships, 7, 10, 16, 47, 51–52, 61, 68, 80,
    83, 88, 92, 95, 100, 112, 115, 136,
    151–152, 157, 164–165, 167–168,
    201, 203–204, 208, 218, 231, 233,
    273, 277–278
Renegotiation of loan terms, 78
Responsibility for Diagnosis, **36**
Restructuring, 6, 10–11, 14, 17, 19, 22, 24–
    25, 47, 51, 64, 80–82, 90–92, 99, 119,
    130–132, 143, 160, 174, 179–180,
    182, 186, 189, 193–199, 202–203,
    215, 221, 228, 234, 237, 242,
    246–249, 255, 257, 259, 265
  debt, 208
  financial, 6, 8, 11, 14, 17, 19, 24, 47, 51, 64,
    80–82, 90, 93, 119, 130, 134, 141,
    169, 185, 190, 203, 246–247, 250

  success, 193–194
  through bankruptcy, 237
Retail, **30**
Retail automotive services chain, 209
Return of investment, 76, 136, 153, 214, 249,
    267–269
Revolver borrowings, 276
Rights of lenders and creditors, 80, 88
Risk, assessing, 1, 7–8, 11, 14–16, 26–27,
    32–33, 41, 45–46, 50–51, 57, 65, 67,
    69, 80, 83, 85, 89–90, 93, 100, 121,
    136, 140, 143, 150, 153, 158, 168,
    182, 199, 200, 205–206, 265
Risk/ reward, 14, 26, 85, 173, 269
Rogers, Kenny, 19
Rollups, industry, **23**, **233**
Rome, Donald Lee, 73
Rouse, William B., 190

S

Salomon Brothers, 57
Sarbanes-Oxley Act, 48–49, 67, 160
Seasonality issues, 146
Secured creditors, 17, 22–23, 30, 47, 66, 85,
    87, **89**, 91
Securities and Exchange Commission (SEC),
    49, 51, 163
Segregating asset values, **216**
Self-inflicted wounds, 28
  legal, 61–68
  operational, 34, 61–62, 68–69, 227, 230,
    265
  political, 61–62, 69
Selling the business, 6
  demonstrating anticipated synergies,
    214–215, 232, 242–243, 258
  essential steps, 220–221
  making the business or product lines
    attractive, 215
  presenting detailed assumptions to buyers,
    215
Selling, General and Administrative expenses
    (SG&A), **123**
Shareholders, 4, 7, 14, 61, 65, 77, 84, 144,
    165, 182, 185, 192, 212, 239–240, 268
Sherman, Stratford, 250

Slywotzky, Adrian J., 154, 184
Southwest, 95
Spin, 160
Stakeholders, competing interests and agendas
    of, 84
Standalone survivors, 10
Status quo, 52, 68, 94, 176, 256
Steel business, 20, 94, 122, 127, 139, 150,
    215, 262
Strategic buyers, 10, 24, 221, 258
    value of troubled company to, 215
Strategic redesign, 184
Subordinated debt, 243
Subordinated lenders, 16, 90, 196
Successful businesses, 233, 245
Super-priority liens, 80
Suppliers, 16, 29, 69, 76, 86, 95–97, 100, 112,
    121, 150, 151, 196, 218, 230, 244, 253
    relationships, 69, 95, 97–98, **151–152**
Suppliers of forecast data, 275
Suters, Everett T., 239
Sutton, Gary, 261
SWOP (Strengths, Weaknesses,
    Opportunities, Problems), 107–108,
    151
Synergy, 215, 233

T
Taleb, Nassim Nicholas, 57
Tangible assets, compared with debt, 90, 216
Target, 13, 37, 150, 154, 221, 256–257, 267,
    270
Taxes, 128
Technical compliance, 160,
Technical support, 143
Technology, disruptive, 69, 107, 122, 138, 142,
    153, 162, 254
Technology laggards, 15, 22
Texas Instruments, 169
The Business Workouts Manual, 73
The Six-Month Fix, 261
The Unnatural Act of Management, 239
Theory of the business, 14–15
Third parties 48, 62, 65, 92, 160, 188, 208,
    212, *see also* Consultants

Tichy, Noel M., 250
Time, 3–4, 20, 24, 35, 39–40, 44, 49, 53, 64,
    91, 97–98, 104, 106–107, 123, 126,
    132, 139, 141, 146, 163, 166, 183,
    189, 193, 202–203, 209, 217, 232,
    243, 247
Timing, 11, 35, 257, 271, 276, 280
Topchik, Gary S., 209
Trade creditors, 65, 86, 149, 187, 219
Trade payables, as a source of financing, 222
Treasury Management Association, 273
Trend analysis, 126, 278
    example report, 278
    historical working capital account balances,
        279–280
    initial conclusions of, 132–134
    working capital, 279–280, 284
Troubled companies
    Categories, 33–35, 204, 265
    defined, 11
Turnaround
    action plans, 81, 236
    Undisciplined Racehorses, 205
    defined, 236
    operational, 6, 14, 24, 27, 48, 97, 133, 137,
        149, 156, 166, 176, 186, 196, 218,
        227, 236, 256, 264, 266
    process, common errors in, 5
    process outline, 5–7
    tasks, fundamental, 26

U
Undisciplined Racehorses, **33, 176, 179, 203**
    acquisition problems encountered by,
        232–235
    actions required for turnaround of, 235–237
    bankruptcy of, 237–238
    external problems, 228–230
    internal problems, 230
    project and growth management, 231–232
    management change at, 236–237
    recommended management characteristics
        for, 237
    threats to, 234–235
    turnaround, 205

Unit sales, **251**

United Auto Workers, 254

Unpredictable items, 280

Unrealistic expectations for profit growth, **16**

Unsecured creditors, 63, 86

Unsecured debt, 90

V

Value

assessing (*see* measuring enterprise value)

creating maximum, 6, 38, 89, 215–217

Value added, 10, 55, 122

Value Line, 138

Venture capital, 15, 80, 196, 218, 242

Viability, 14–24, 36, 47, 55, 73, 81, 94, 144, 148–149, 176, 181, 195, 232, 243, 263, 266

defined, 14–15

evaluating, 14–15, 148

long-term, 55, 149, 180

Non-viable businesses, 19–20

Non-viable plans, 272

threshold questions of, 14

unviable business types, 19–20

Volume, 10, 20, 28, 37, 51, 59, 96, 105, **121**–124, 127, 129–131, 135, 139–140, 144, 146–148, 151, 153, 158, 179–180, 182, 194, 205, 238, 242, 244–245, 256, 261, 279, 284

W

Wal-Mart, 15, 22, 30, 149–150, 156–157

Wall Street Journal, 44

Wang, 15

Warrants, 16, 193

Welch, Jack, 21, 140, 213, 250, 255

Welch, Suzy, 213

Who Says Elephants Can't Dance?, 261

Wilson Foods, 243

Winning, 57, 213

Wire and tube manufacturer, 215

Womack, James P., 74, 137, 272

Working capital, 6, 14–16, 22, 28, 30, 32, 36, 64–65, 72, 75–76, 79, 82, 85, 92, 115, **123**–124, 132, 135, 160, 179–180, 198, 214, 217, 222, 232, 246, 249, 265, 271, 273–274, 279, 284–285

liquidation of, 6, 284

Workout groups, 88

goals of, 195

restrictions to, 193

World Series, 57

WorldCom, **49**, 159–160, 234

Worlds of Wonder, 29

Printed in the United States
91380LV00002B/109-132/A